CLASHES *of*
CAVALRY

CLASHES *of* CAVALRY

The Civil War Careers of
GEORGE ARMSTRONG CUSTER
and JEB STUART

by

THOM HATCH

TURNER PUBLISHING COMPANY

For my wife, Lynn, and daughter, Cimarron,
who make each day truly joyous

Turner Publishing Company
Nashville, Tennessee
www.turnerpublishing.com

Cover design: Bruce Gore
Book design: Tim Holtz

Library of Congress Cataloging-in-Publication Data

Names: Hatch, Thom, 1946- author.
Identifiers: LCCN 2019047996
(print)
LC record available at https://lccn.loc.gov/2019047996

9781684424566 paperback
9781684424573 hardcover
9781684424580 ebook

Printed in the United States of America
17 18 19 20 10 9 8 7 6 5 4 3 2 1

Table of Contents

If you want to have a good time, jine the cavalry
Jine the cavalry! Jine the cavalry!
If you want to catch the Devil, if you want to have fun,
If you want to smell Hell, jine the cavalry!

Introduction

THE QUESTION MAY BE ASKED: Why a dual Civil War biography of George Armstrong Custer and James Ewell Brown Stuart? The answer is quite simple: Two famous, flamboyant, swashbuckling cavaliers in one book means twice the fun—and twice the understanding of the mindset and strategies from both sides of the conflict. Most importantly, Custer and Stuart were destined to meet on the field in a series of significant battles, a couple of which had a huge impact on the war and on their lives.

Jeb Stuart had been a thorn in the side of the North throughout the first two years of the war. As commander of the Army of Northern Virginia's elite cavalry, he had redefined the role of horsemen as an independent arm capable of wreaking havoc upon his enemy and had not come close to being challenged by the outclassed Yankee cavalry.

Stuart's bold raids into enemy territory had disrupted communication and supply lines, gathered vital intelligence, and destroyed millions of dollars' worth of property—in addition to bloodying his enemy at will. His spectacular ride around McClellan's army had embarrassed the North and instilled confidence in the South's belief that it could prevail in this bitter conflict.

Stuart had been elevated to a lofty position in the hearts of his Southern admirers which rivaled that of a knight of King Arthur's court, and had gained at least grudging respect from his Northern opponents. Now he had been called upon to play a significant role in the Gettysburg battle.

The historic image and reputation of George Armstrong Custer has been unfairly established from the events of one day in his life—the day he died. Every other aspect of his career has been overshadowed by that lone Indian fight on the frontier. In his time, however, Custer was not a symbol of defeat but a national hero on a grand scale for his heroic achievements in the Civil War.

Just three days out of West Point, Custer had been cited for bravery for his actions during the Union retreat from Bull Run. His career as a cavalry officer was temporarily interrupted when he was assigned as an aide-de-camp to a succession of generals, including George B. McClellan, commander of the Army of the Potomac. But even in this noncombatant role, Custer could not be deterred from upon occasion joining the fray on the battlefield and distinguishing himself.

His propensity for a more active role eventually earned him the cavalry command that he so craved. He would time and again prove his leadership ability, personally leading electrifying cavalry charges in key Union victories, which would result in his accepting the Confederate white flag of surrender at Appomattox.

And much of Custer's glory would come at the expense of Jeb Stuart—beginning with the bloody skirmish east of Gettysburg that would have a consequential impact on the course of that battle, if not history. Gettysburg was, however, only the first in a series of engagements between these two remarkable cavalry generals who shared numerous similar personal traits and whose Civil War legacies were destined to be intertwined.

The early chapters of this book will familiarize the reader with the backgrounds and accomplishments of both Custer and Stuart through the first two years of the war, leading up to the largest cavalry engagement of the century at Brandy Station.

Then, the stage has been set to mount up and ride alongside the blue and gray horsemen into the sanguinary fields of saber strokes and pistol fire, witnessing events through the eyes and actions of Jeb Stuart and Armstrong Custer as they engage each other in clashes of cavalry.

CHAPTER ONE

BEAUTY

THE SOUTH'S MOST CELEBRATED CAVALRYMAN, James Ewell Brown Stuart, was born at eleven thirty on the morning of February 6, 1833, at Laurel Hill, the family farm located in southwestern Patrick County, Virginia, on the fringes of the Blue Ridge Mountains. James, who was named after a paternal uncle, was the seventh child and youngest son born to Archibald and Elizabeth Stuart in a family that would eventually include ten children—four boys and six girls.

His father, Archibald, was of Scotch-Presbyterian heritage whose ancestors had departed Londonderry, Ireland, in 1726 to escape religious persecution. Archibald had served as an officer in the War of 1812 and was a lawyer who had embraced the political arena. He had been a delegate to the Virginia Constitutional Convention of 1829–30, would be elected by the Whig Party to a term in the United States House of Representatives (1837–39), and would later serve in the Virginia Senate (1852–54). Archibald, for whatever the reasons and in spite of his connections and reputation for possessing more than his share of wit and good humor, which made him the center of attention at social gatherings, would never prosper materially.

In June 1817, Archibald married Elizabeth Letcher Pannill, whose Welsh ancestors had immigrated to Virginia from Ireland some time before the Revolutionary War. The growing family would be raised on the fertile soil of the Laurel Hill plantation that Elizabeth had inherited from her grandfather. Archibald often traveled, and the responsibility of managing the place fell upon the shoulders of Elizabeth, which perhaps contributed to her being somewhat ill-tempered and judgmental from a Biblical standpoint. Elizabeth taught the children basic school subjects at home, with special emphasis on religious virtues. She made all her sons promise to never touch a drop of liquor, a pledge to which James remained faithful throughout his life.

1

Patrick County was an isolated rural community where the farmers grew tobacco and corn, and raised livestock, but many, including the Stuarts, also provided for themselves by subsistence farming with as many as twenty-eight slaves. James and his siblings were assigned chores around the farm but were also afforded ample time for play.

James spent many days in the saddle and considered his relationship with horses to be equal with that of friends or relatives. He enjoyed roaming the rolling hills that surrounded Laurel Hill and, perhaps through his love and appreciation of the outdoors, developed a sensitive side to the extent that he wrote poetry about nature. That trait, which included a love of flowers, was rarely displayed around his siblings or other boys for fear of appearing unmanly. Make no mistake about it, however, James was a rough-and-tumble youngster who would upon occasion demonstrate his youthful pluck.

His older brother, William Alexander, told the story about an encounter that he and nine-year-old James had with a hornet's nest. The boys had happened upon the nest one summer day and decided to dislodge it. The nest was located too high in the tree for sticks to reach it, so they climbed up the branches with intentions of knocking it free. The hornets, however, instinctively protected their nest and attacked in force. William prudently leaped from the tree to escape the stinging insects. James, on the other hand, endured the pain of numerous stings until he had managed to remove the nest. This physical courage impressed William Alexander enough to speculate that James just might make a good soldier someday.

For all intents and purposes, childhood ended for James at the age of twelve. In order to continue his education, he was sent to boarding school in Wytheville, Virginia, in 1845. He lived with relatives or family friends and would return home over the ensuing years only for brief visits. From all indications, James resigned himself to this independence, reveling in his self-reliance, and quickly asserted himself in the pecking order of his peers. He proudly boasted to an older cousin that he had not had a single fight since leaving home, and added, perhaps conscious of suspicions about his tender side, that the reason was not related to cowardice.

But he was, after all, just a boy, and would complain about the lack of news from home. At one point, in an effort to solicit a letter, he humorously pled for his parents to "have mercy upon a poor, little, insignificant whelp away from his mammy."

In 1848, James volunteered for service in the Mexican War, but was rejected due to his youth. He then ventured into the realm of higher learning by enrolling at Emory & Henry College, which was affiliated with the Methodist Church. He immersed himself in his studies, favoring classical literature to the extent that he joined a literary and debating society—and once became so absorbed while making a speech that he fell off the stage.

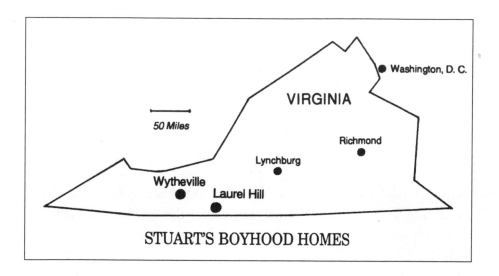

STUART'S BOYHOOD HOMES

James Stuart also at this time abandoned his Episcopalian roots to embrace the Methodist religion. His letters indicated that he had undergone a conversion that today could be termed a "born again" experience. This personal relationship with God and Jesus Christ that he developed at an early age was often reflected in his character throughout life, and it set the tone of his future correspondence, in which he would frequently mention his prayers or invoke some element of spirituality.

James understood that he would not inherit property or wealth from his family and therefore would be required to make his own way in the world. Disdaining what he called "hireling professions," such as law, medicine, or engineering, he set his sights on furthering his education with an appointment to the United States Military Academy at West Point.

Two years earlier, his father had been defeated in a bid for Congress, but the first official act by the gracious winner of that election, Democrat Thomas Hamlet Averett, was to appoint young James to West Point.

James departed Wytheville for West Point in late May 1850. On his way north, James visited Thomas Jefferson's Monticello—where he appropriated two roses from the yard—and spent a day touring Washington, DC. He paid his respects to his benefactor, Congressman Averett, visited the Senate and House chambers, and observed President Zachary Taylor while walking around the city streets.

He described Taylor as "a plain looking old fellow with a slight squat as he walks," and called Daniel Webster "the finest looking man in the Senate." Henry Clay was "very nervous" but displayed "an air of dignity and command," and Sam Houston "appears better with his mouth shut than open." But, he added, "of all the pleasant speakers give me Jeff Davis of Mississippi."

On July 1, 1850, James Ewell Brown Stuart joined 101 other cadets at West Point to comprise the class of 1854. As was the custom, the cadet corps spent the summer months at Camp Gaines, a tent complex in the nearby woods. First-year students, or plebes, were drilled by cadet officers three times a day in infantry tactics and once a day on the use of artillery. Within a month, Stuart had adjusted quite well to the military routine and social aspects of life at West Point and was particularly impressed with the ceremonies and parades. Before summer camp ended, he wrote to a cousin: "So far as I know of no profession more desirable than that of the soldier."

On the first day of September, the cadets moved into sparsely furnished barracks rooms to begin their first year of classes. James shared his room with Judson D. Bigham from Indiana and fellow Virginian George G. Rogers. He was impressed with his roommates, whom he called "very studious and clever fellows."

At this point in his life, the blue-eyed, brown-haired James stood about five feet, ten inches tall with a stocky build. He was rather plain looking with a high forehead, prominent nose, weak chin, and blunt features. Detracting from his appearance were occasional black eyes or cuts and bruises owing to his propensity to engage in fistfights—no matter the odds against him.

In the judgment of some classmates, James was not considered a particularly handsome young man. This characteristic was quickly exploited—for the most part good-naturedly—and he acquired a lasting nickname. According to his friend and future Confederate comrade in arms Fitzhugh Lee, Stuart was called "Beauty" to describe his "personal comeliness in inverse ratio to the term employed."

At the end of his uneventful first year at West Point, Beauty Stuart ranked eighth in mathematics, fifteenth in French, twelfth in English, and eighth overall in a class that now numbered seventy-two. He had joined a debating club called the Dialectic Society but otherwise endured a mundane existence that he described as the "dull career of a student" and the "monstrous routine of military and college life."

At the beginning of his second year, James distinguished himself by being appointed corporal of the corps, the third-highest rank in his class. He once again studied mathematics and French, and added a course in drawing, which was designed to familiarize the future officers with the representation of features on a map. Riding exercises and drills were included in this year's curriculum, and James established himself as the best horseman in his class. He also had a romantic fling with the sister of a classmate, but by spring the relationship had become just a fond memory. The school year concluded with Stuart standing seventh overall in his class.

The end of classes brought a welcome respite from two years of rigorous studies. For the first time since entering West Point, cadets were awarded a furlough and could enjoy the summer at their leisure. James whiled away his ten-week vacation by visiting relatives, which oddly enough included only a ten-day stay at Laurel Hill. But, in his defense, there was a significant reason why he spent most of his time at a plantation near Martinsville, Virginia, called Beaver Creek. Sixteen-year-old Bettie Hairston, a distant cousin on his mother's side of the family, lived at Beaver Creek, and James had become infatuated with her.

James courted Bettie throughout the summer, taking long walks with her, sharing his love of flowers and the garden, and relating his aspirations for the future. Although any seriousness to the relationship was likely more one-sided than mutual, the two would correspond for years after his return to West

Point—his letters more frequent that those from her. She had presented him with a gourd as a going-away present, which later compelled him to write a poem, "To Bettie," about the gift that would hang in his room until graduation:

> That gourd I'll bear where're I go
> That name will be a charm
> To nerve my arm 'gainst ev'ry foe
> And ev'ry foe disarm.
> 'Mong those whom I can ne'er forget
> (Let none their worth gainsay)
> I'll prize thee dearest-fondest yet
> My Bettie—far away.

In September 1852, Colonel Robert E. Lee was appointed the new superintendent of West Point. James was already good friends with Lee's son, Custis, and soon became a favorite of the Lee family and would often visit their home. He enjoyed the company of Lee's daughter, Mary, to whom he was somewhat attracted, and developed a special fondness for Mrs. Lee. Another member of the family, Lee's impetuous nephew, the aforementioned Fitzhugh, entered the academy that fall and became a lasting friend to Stuart.

James Ewell Brown Stuart, c. 1854 (The Museum of the Confederacy)

In between his studies, which included courses in philosophy and chemistry, James became quite social during the school year. He attended gatherings at the superintendent's home and escorted various young ladies to cotillion parties. He developed a discriminating taste, once confiding that the more he saw of Northern girls, the more he was "convinced of their inferiority in every aspect to our Virginia girls, in beauty especially."

James continued his active social life during the summer encampment of 1853, where he was named cadet captain and was selected by the Dialectic Society to read the Declaration of Independence at the annual Fourth of July observance.

Beauty Stuart was honored at the beginning of his fourth and final year at West Point with an appointment as second captain and one of eight cadets awarded the title of "cavalry officer" due to superior horsemanship. His courses this year included international law, mineralogy and geology, ethics, and civil engineering. He admitted that he found his engineering class quite interesting but fared poorly due to his lack of drawing skills. James did, however, excel in infantry, artillery, and cavalry tactics. He graduated in July 1854, ranked thirteenth in a class reduced to 46 from the original 102 that had entered four years earlier.

While awaiting orders for assignment, Stuart spent the summer visiting family and friends. According to family tradition, Stuart at this time proposed marriage to Bettie Hairston, but for unknown reasons, she either turned him down or put him off for the time being. Finally, he received a commission as a second lieutenant in the Mounted Riflemen and was ordered to report to Fort McIntosh in Western Texas by October 15.

After outfitting himself in New York for the trip west, he arrived in Washington to learn that due to a yellow fever epidemic in New Orleans his leave had been extended. He waited until November 29, when he booked passage on a steamer out of New Orleans.

After a bout of sea sickness when a storm swept through the Gulf of Mexico, Stuart reached Corpus Christi, where he stayed until December 29 before joining a wagon train headed for Laredo, 450 miles away. Upon arrival in Laredo, he learned that his company was on an expedition toward Fort Davis, located in the heart of western Texas between the Pecos and Rio Grande rivers. At Fort Davis on January 29, Stuart was told that his company was fifty miles farther west. Finally, two months after leaving St. Louis, he joined his unit, commanded by Major John S. Simonson, which was out hunting renegade Mescalero Apache and Comanche Indians.

Stuart quickly discovered that the rugged terrain in West Texas could be quite challenging. In many instances, the troopers were obliged to lead their horses. "I wore out a pair of very thick shoes," he wrote to Bettie Hairston, "and would have been barefooted but for a pair of embroidered slippers." The slippers had been a gift from a girlfriend, and he commented that she probably had no inkling that they would eventually walk "Comanche trails." Adding to the frustration was the army's inability to locate the enemy. "We have threaded every trail, clambered every precipice and penetrated every ravine for hundreds of miles around," and "we have not been able to find Mr. Comanche."

Despite the hardships, Stuart the nature lover became a student of the unusual scenery and wildlife. He called the blue quail "the prettiest bird I ever saw," and spent hours observing prairie dogs, which he judged one of the most remarkable animals he had ever seen. Wolves howled every night, but he thought the "most mournful cry" was that of the mountain lion, which he and a companion hunted without success.

On a patrol toward the Guadalupe Mountains near the New Mexico border, Stuart was placed in command of the unit's only piece of artillery. At one point, a series of switchbacks through a narrow mountain pass that rose 1,500 feet from the plain below thwarted his movements with the gun. Stuart refused to forsake the cannon and faced the predicament head-on. He ordered twenty-five of his men to embark on the arduous task of lowering the piece down the mountainside with ropes. Major Simonson, who had for all intents and purposes written off the gun, was pleased, if not amazed by Stuart's determination and ingenuity.

Two days later, the soldiers happened upon an infantry unit from El Paso that was also out hunting Indians, and both outfits traveled together in a futile search for the enemy. That evening the combined columns set up camp "in a deep and narrow valley or *arroyo*, clothed in luxuriant grass." The men turned out their horses to graze and lit their cooking fires. Without warning, a gust of wind swept down the valley and "scattered our fire over the grass like a tornado, setting the whole prairie in a blaze." Within a matter of moments, the fire had swept through the entire camp, burning bridles, saddles, blankets, caps, coats, and anything else that stood in its way—including many of the horses, which were badly singed.

Stuart patrolled West Texas for three more months, once having his horse stolen from outside his tent during the night, but never caught sight of his elusive prey. At that time, he grew a reddish-brown beard and mustache, which he would wear for the rest of his life.

During the spring of 1855, Secretary of War Jefferson Davis recognized the need to contend with the problem of renegade Plains Indians with a "big, swift-striking force able to find the enemy in his own country and endure long campaigns." To that end, he established two elite cavalry regiments, the 1st and 2nd United States Cavalry, to which only the most capable officers would be selected. Stuart was delighted when he received a permanent appointment as a second lieutenant in the 1st Cavalry regiment stationed at Fort Leavenworth, Kansas. He reported in July 1855 and was assigned duty as quartermaster and assistant commissary officer.

During that summer of 1855, Stuart was reviewing troops when he noticed a petite young lady handling a large and skittish horse like an expert. He fantasized that her mount would bolt, and he could gallop to her rescue, but that seemed unlikely given her riding prowess. At that moment, however, he decided that he would become acquainted with this lady.

The horsewoman who had impressed him was twenty-year-old Flora Cooke, the daughter of Lieutenant Colonel Philip St. George Cooke, who commanded the 2nd Regiment of Dragoons. Flora had recently completed finishing school and had rebuffed her parents' wishes that she make her social debut in Philadelphia society. She had chosen instead to spend the summer visiting them at Fort Leavenworth.

Never one to be bashful around the ladies, Stuart asked Flora Cooke to go riding with him, and she agreed. Before long, the couple could be seen riding together almost every evening engaged in conversation. James learned that Flora was not only an excellent horsewoman but could also shoot, sing, and play the guitar, and she shared other interests with him as well. In addition, she came from an established Virginia family, and her father had attained high rank in the army.

This spirited, blue-eyed young woman who was blessed with those special qualities certainly appealed to the incurable romantic in James Ewell Brown Stuart. In September—after courting Flora for less than two months—James proposed marriage. She readily accepted. The whirlwind courtship was summarized by Stuart with a variation of a famous Latin quote: "I came, I saw, I was conquered."

The couple received the blessing of their respective fathers and planned an elaborate wedding in November at Fort Riley, where Colonel Cooke had been recently named commandant. Lieutenant Stuart would first be required to accompany his unit on an 800-900-mile patrol along the Oregon Trail, which he did while attending to the details of the wedding by mail.

Upon returning from the patrol, James learned that Archibald Stuart had passed away on September 20. Stuart was predictably saddened by the loss of his father, although the two had not shared a close relationship. He nonetheless resumed his marriage plans, which due to the circumstances would be scaled down.

On November 14, a simple ceremony witnessed by a limited number of guests was performed to unite James Ewell Brown Stuart and Flora Cooke, who wore her white graduation dress, in holy matrimony.

The couple set up housekeeping at Fort Leavenworth in two rooms and a kitchen that Stuart jokingly called his "ranch." They remained there only long enough for Stuart to obtain a furlough. The bride and groom honeymooned in Virginia, where Flora met her new relatives and graciously refused the offer of a female slave as a wedding gift from Elizabeth Stuart. While Flora stayed in the East with plans to return in the spring, Stuart arrived back in Kansas to learn that he had been promoted to first lieutenant on December 20. The promotion was quite an honor when taking into consideration that such a rapid rise up the ranks was rare in peacetime.

During the following year, Stuart's unit was not only charged with keeping marauding Indians in check but confronted with the violent reaction resulting from the issue of whether Kansas should be a free or slave state. Pro-slavery bands from Missouri had been invading Kansas and attacking anti-slavery settlers, which had produced a small-scale civil war known by the term Bleeding Kansas.

On a peacekeeping mission in June 1856, Stuart became acquainted with the abolitionist John Brown, who had participated in several recent bloody skirmishes with pro-slavery Missouri militiamen. The army detachment, commanded by Colonel Edwin Sumner, entered Brown's camp to secure the release of a deputy United States marshal who had been taken prisoner. Brown grudgingly released the man, but the incident served to reinforce his belief that the United States government was in collusion with the pro-slavery factions. This would not be the last time that Stuart would encounter John Brown, and his role the next instance would decidedly be more active.

Army life chasing Indians on the Great Plains would not be complete without at least one tale of great bravery and a harrowing escape, and Jeb Stuart's personal experience assuredly qualifies in every aspect.

Cheyenne renegades had been killing and terrorizing settlers on raids in western Kansas, and the 1st Cavalry was ordered to participate in a campaign intended to punish the perpetrators. The column, which would eventually consist of six cavalry companies, three infantry companies, and a battery of artillery, rode out of Fort Leavenworth on May 20, 1857. First Lieutenant Stuart, after a dispute with Colonel Sumner, was relieved of his quartermaster duties and assigned leadership of G Company, his first command.

On July 29, the cavalry happened upon about 300 Cheyenne warriors on Solomon's Fork of the Smoky Hill River in northwest Kansas. Sumner dispatched two companies to attack the enemy flank and ordered the remainder of his troops forward in a battle line. When the cavalrymen came within carbine range, Sumner ordered the charge. Yelling wildly, their sabers drawn, the horsemen raced toward the massed Cheyenne. The Indians were shocked by the sight of those gleaming blades and wisely fled in the face of this overwhelming force. The troops pursued their fleeing enemy, which had separated into small groups.

Stuart continued the chase until coming upon several troopers battling with a dismounted Cheyenne, who had leveled his revolver and was about to shoot one of the men. Stuart instinctively drew his saber and charged to protect his comrade. Stuart swung his blade, feeling the steel strike its target, but simultaneously, the Indian discharged his weapon from a distance of about one foot. The bullet struck Stuart squarely in the chest. He toppled from his mount to the ground but never lost consciousness.

Stuart was carried three miles to the doctor, who announced that the bullet had bounced off a bone and lodged in fatty tissue without causing serious damage to any vital organ. Barring complications from infection, he would likely make a full recovery within several weeks.

Two days later, Colonel Sumner resumed his pursuit of the Cheyenne with the main part of his force. Stuart, with five other wounded soldiers and one Cheyenne prisoner, escorted by an infantry company, would head for Fort Kearny, 120 miles away, in several days. By the time they marched on August 8, Stuart had recovered enough to ride.

No one had a compass, which meant that the detachment would have to depend on Pawnee Indian guides who had been provided by Colonel Sumner. On the sixth day of their journey, however, they awoke in the midst of a thick fog to discover that their guides had vanished. They were lost, food rations were low, and some of the infantrymen had worn through their shoes and were walking barefoot.

Without anyone who could provide reliable directions and with food running out, the situation grew more desperate with each passing day. Stuart finally decided to assert his leadership skills and volunteered to lead a scouting party to search for Fort Kearny. He and two other men prepared to leave on the morning of August 15, but a dense fog forced them to wait until noon when an impatient Stuart decided to go in spite of the lack of visibility. A late afternoon rainstorm forced them to take refuge before continuing until dark when they made camp. They awoke in the middle of the wet, miserable night to find that the grassy ravine where they had tied their horses had virtually turned into a river. The rushing water had already risen halfway up the bodies of the horses. They quickly led their mounts to higher ground.

The following morning, the soaked, cold, and hungry men resumed their search for Fort Kearny. Clouds concealed the sun, which made it impossible to determine in what direction they were traveling. At one point, the sun briefly broke through, which enabled Stuart to realize that they had been marching in the wrong direction. He corrected their course, but they soon came upon a stream that was too swollen to cross.

Stuart led the group upstream in hopes of finding a ford but instead happened upon a trail. Although they did not know who might appear on this trail, they blindly followed it until dark. The sky cleared during the night. Stuart was able to observe the stars and determine that they were finally headed in the right direction.

The night passed slowly. At first light, Stuart insisted that they swim across the stream, a task that was completed with some difficulty. On the other side, they came upon a wagon road indented with recent wheel and hoof tracks. Stuart recognized that the road connected Fort Leavenworth and Fort Kearny. Later that afternoon, the three weary men arrived at Fort Kearny. A detachment was quickly dispatched to rescue the soldiers that had been left behind.

Within a three-week period, First Lieutenant Stuart had engaged in his first hostile encounter with Indians, suffered a bullet wound, and braved the cruel elements on the Plains to save his comrades from certain death. If he had any doubts about his capacity for leadership or ability to persevere when faced with great odds, they were certainly dispelled during that summer of 1857.

During the first week of September, Flora gave birth to their first child, a girl. Stuart insisted that his daughter be named Flora after her mother and proclaimed that he had "the prettiest and smartest baby in North America."

The 1st Cavalry was transferred farther west to Fort Riley in the fall of 1857. For the next year and a half, Stuart settled into routine duty at the post, which afforded him ample opportunity to enjoy his new family. He also began tinkering with several inventions, one of which was an attachment for cavalry sabers that permitted a trooper to easily remove his saber from his belt and quickly attach it to his saddle.

The War Department was duly impressed with Stuart's idea and granted him a six-month furlough in late 1859 to visit Washington and present his invention. He successfully patented his "saber hook" and peddled the rights to the government for $5,000 and a one-dollar royalty on each one sold.

On October 17, Stuart was at the War Department waiting for an appointment with Secretary of War John B. Floyd when rumors began to circulate that a slave revolt by a mob that some estimated as high as 3,000 in number was taking place at Harpers Ferry. Floyd decided to summon

Colonel Robert E. Lee, who was on leave from his post in Texas and presently across the Potomac at his father-in-law's estate in Arlington. Stuart, who had been a visitor at Arlington on many occasions, volunteered to take the message to Lee.

Colonel Lee, accompanied by Stuart, went immediately to the White House and met with President James Buchanan. The president placed Lee in charge of an operation to put down this uprising with whatever force was deemed necessary. Stuart volunteered his services to Lee as an aide, and the colonel accepted. The two men boarded a special locomotive and roared off to rendezvous with a detachment of ninety United States Marines, which was already on its way to Harpers Ferry.

Shortly after their arrival about a mile outside Harpers Ferry at 10:00 p.m., Lee learned that the rumored 3,000 insurgents actually amounted to less than twenty, who were led by a man known only as "Mr. Smith." They had sought refuge inside a fire engine house on the armory grounds and had taken a few of the town's prominent citizens as hostages.

Lee ordered the Marines, who were commanded by Lieutenant Israel Green, to march onto the armory grounds, and then deployed Virginia and Maryland militia units to surround the armory as a show of force. Lee worked on a message addressed to "the persons in the armory building," demanding their surrender and warning that if they chose to fight, he could not "answer for their safety."

At daylight, the militia units remained in place while Lieutenant Green and twelve hand-picked Marines—wielding only bayonets to avoid harming the hostages—prepared for an assault on the engine house. Lieutenant Jeb Stuart, under a white flag of truce, would deliver Lee's message. If unable to persuade the insurgents inside to surrender, Stuart would step away from the door and wave his hat as a signal for the Marines to storm the building.

Stuart walked toward the engine house door waving his white flag. The door opened about four inches to reveal the barrel of a cocked cavalry carbine pointing at Stuart. The man holding the weapon, who had called himself Mr. Smith, was immediately recognized by Stuart as none other than John Brown, the abolitionist whom Stuart had met three years earlier in Kansas. Brown wanted to negotiate, but Stuart refused his outrageous terms.

Finally, convinced that no amount of discussion would resolve the situation, Stuart stepped away from the door and waved his hat.

The Marines moved forward and rammed the engine house door with a wooden ladder to gain entry. Lieutenant Green cornered John Brown in the rear of the building and knocked the insurgent leader senseless with several strokes of his saber. Within three minutes, the Marines had secured the area without harming any hostages.

Later that morning, Stuart and a group of Marines visited Brown's farmhouse in Maryland and confiscated a large cache of weapons, including over 1,500 pikes—poles with metal points—as well as numerous incriminating letters and documents.

John Brown was tried and found guilty of treason, conspiring to incite a slave rebellion, and murder. He was hanged on December 2, 1859.

Soon after the incident at Harpers Ferry, Stuart returned to Kansas and the command of Company G, 1st Cavalry. On May 15, 1860, he rode out of Fort Riley with his company on a campaign against hostile Kiowa and Comanche Indians. The only significant action was a minor engagement on July 11 at Blackwater Springs near Bent's Fort on the Arkansas River that resulted in the capture of fifteen Kiowa women and children and twenty or thirty horses. The soldiers, two units that had combined during the chase, lost three men wounded in the skirmish.

That evening, Stuart rode to Fort Larned where he learned that Flora had given birth to a "fine son" on June 26. The boy was named Philip St. George Cooke Stuart in honor of Flora's father.

In September, Stuart left Flora and the children at Fort Riley with his in-laws and accompanied four cavalry companies and two infantry divisions on a march of 387 miles. The column traversed the rugged Plains to the Arkansas River just east of Bent's Fort, where they established Fort Wise. The duty was at such an isolated location that a week after Abraham Lincoln had won the presidential election, Stuart and his troops still had not heard the news.

Lincoln's election had triggered a fiery response from the Southern states. On December 20, the first state to secede from the Union was South Carolina. At that time, Stuart wrote, "I believe the north will yield what the south demands thereby avert disunion." If not, he pledged to "go with Virginia . . . I for one would," he wrote, "throw <u>my sabre</u> in the scale consecrated by principles and blood of our forefathers—our constitutional rights without which the Union is a mere mockery."

Stuart's prediction of preserving the Union proved wrong. South Carolina was followed by six other Southern states, and on February 8, 1861, the Confederate States of America was formed.

Stuart had requested leave on March 4 but was delayed and did not reach Fort Riley until early April. On April 14, Confederate forces fired on Fort Sumter in Charleston harbor. Three days later, Virginia seceded from the Union. Stuart immediately packed up his family and left for St. Louis, where they boarded a steamboat for Memphis. His letter of resignation from the United States Army was mailed from Cairo, Illinois, on May 3, and a letter was written to the new Confederate Army, requesting an appropriate rank and command. Ironically, his mail was being held in Cairo, and he found a letter waiting from the United States War Department that informed him that he had been promoted to the rank of captain, effective April 22.

The Stuart family arrived in Wytheville, Virginia, on May 7. Three days later, Captain Stuart became Lieutenant Colonel Stuart of the Confederate Army and prepared to fight against the army in which he had served since entering West Point almost eleven years earlier.

CHAPTER TWO

FANNY

ON DECEMBER 5, 1839, in the back room on the first floor of a house in New Rumley, Harrison County, Ohio, a yellow-haired, blue-eyed baby was born to Emanuel Henry and Maria Ward Kirkpatrick Custer. He was formally named George Armstrong, but the family would call him Armstrong. As the child learned to talk, however, he became known as Autie, his childlike way of pronouncing his own name.

Emanuel Custer was of German descent, whose original family name, Kuster or Kuester, was changed to Custer by the time his ancestors had settled in Maryland in the 1750s. Emanuel's grandfather had fought as a sergeant in the militia during the Revolutionary War, and the family maintained that George Washington was a distant relative. In 1824 at age eighteen, Emanuel had journeyed to Rumley Town in southeastern Ohio to learn blacksmithing, the family trade, from his uncle, Jacob Custer. In 1828, he married Matilda Viers, who bore him three children before passing away in 1835. Seven months later, he married a widow from Burgettstown, Pennsylvania, named Maria Ward Kirkpatrick, who brought three children of her own to the union.

Within five months of his marriage to Maria in February 1836, Emanuel's three-year-old son, John, died. Two other children born to Emanuel and Maria died in infancy before five healthy children, beginning with George Armstrong, survived. Three boys followed: Nevin Johnson, Thomas Ward, and Boston; and later a daughter, Margaret Emma (Maggie).

Emanuel, the village blacksmith, was a respected member of the community and for twelve years served as New Rumley's justice of the peace. He had helped found the New Rumley Methodist Church and was a prominent member of the New Rumley Invincibles, the local militia. He did not drink or play cards and regarded his fidelity to the Democratic party to be as sacred as his church membership.

The family was not by any means well-to-do but had enough to be inde-pendent and self-sufficient. Emanuel and Maria compensated for the lack of material possessions by creating a home full of love and family unity. Years later, Maria wrote: "I was not fortunate enough to have wealth to make home beautiful, always my desire. So I tried to fill the empty spaces with little acts of kindness."

The siblings from the three families bonded together with loyalty and affection. The Custer household was said to be always in a happy uproar, and what discipline and responsibility that existed was taught with assigned chores and regular church attendance. From all accounts this rather unre-strained atmosphere was engendered by Emanuel, who acted like a big kid when he was around his children. He would romp, wrestle, and play aggres-sively, making them the target of his practical jokes, which became a lifelong practice between them, and dodging their mischief in return.

Autie enjoyed hanging around the blacksmith shop listening to gossip and watching his father work. The boy would ride the newly shod horses, and he quickly developed an early skill in horsemanship and an acceptance of hard work. When the Invincibles would hold musters or parades, young Autie would attend—appropriately attired in a little boy's militia uniform made especially for him and carrying a toy musket or wooden sword. He could perfectly execute the manual of arms, and the militiamen called him a "born soldier."

Custer later wrote to his father: "I never wanted for anything necessary. You and Mother instilled into me principles of industry, self-reliance, hon-esty. You taught me the value of temperate habits, the difference between right and wrong. I look back on the days spent under the home-roof as a period of pure happiness, and I feel thankful for such noble parents."

Maria was often referred to as being in ill health or an invalid for much of her life. It is probable that Armstrong, who was an only child for his first three years, was her favorite. Custer adored his mother throughout his life and never quite severed that invisible umbilical cord that bonded them together.

Custer's wife, Libbie, once wrote: "The hardest trial of my husband's life was parting with his mother. Such partings were the only occasions when I

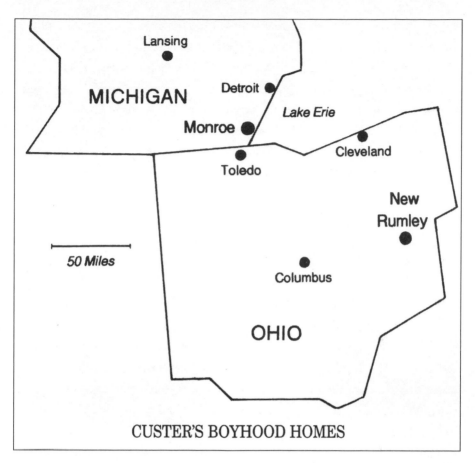

CUSTER'S BOYHOOD HOMES

ever saw him lose entire control of himself ... She had been an invalid for so many years that each parting seemed to her the final one ... (He) would rush out of the house, sobbing like a child, and then throw himself into the carriage beside me, completely unnerved."

The children attended school in New Rumley where Autie was known, in the words of a schoolmate, as "a wide awake boy full of all kinds of pranks and willing to take all kinds of chances." The teacher's son added that Autie "was a rather bad boy in school, but one thing would be said of him, he *always* had his lessons, yet he was not considered an unusually bright lad."

In 1849, Emanuel sold his shop in town, and the family moved to an eighty-acre farm on the outskirts of New Rumley, where Armstrong began attending Creal School. But due to either his lack of interest in education or the cost of sending so many children to a subscription school, Armstrong was apprenticed to a furniture maker in Cadiz. This arrangement soon failed, and the unhappy boy was sent to live with his half-sister, Lydia Ann Reed, who had married David Reed, a drayman, and moved to Monroe, Michigan. Ann, as she was called, would become a surrogate mother and trusted confidant to the youngster and later the adult George Armstrong Custer.

Autie would be enrolled first in New Dublin School then at Alfred Stebbins's Young Man's Academy. Custer's desk mate at the academy enjoyed telling about Armstrong's habit of sneaking adventure novels into class and reading them instead of textbooks. His favorite titles included *Tom Burke of Ours*, *Jack Hinton*, and *Charles O'Malley, the Irish Dragoon*, the latter also being a favorite of future 7th Cavalry comrade Captain Myles Keogh across the ocean in Ireland. Young Armstrong was hardly a bookworm, however, but a spirited and aggressive youngster who was a natural-born leader. The minister of the Methodist Church in Monroe remembered the irrepressible boy as the instigator of mischief and minor disruptions during services.

Custer returned to New Rumley at age sixteen to attend McNeely Normal School in Hopedale, where he was "quite a favorite" with the young ladies. One student remembered that "Custer was what he appeared. There was nothing hidden in his nature. He was kind and generous to his friends; bitter and implacable towards his enemies." In 1856, he interrupted his own education to teach at the Beech Point School in Athens Township for $28 a month. The young teacher was known as a "big-hearted, whole-souled fellow," whose fun-loving disposition made him extremely popular.

At that time, Armstrong arrived at the conclusion that he would require some sort of assistance in order to further his education at an institution of higher learning. To that end, he wrote to the district's Republican representative, John A. Bingham, and requested an appointment to the US Military Academy at West Point. This audacious act demonstrates the undaunting determination that would be Custer's lifelong hallmark. The odds that a son of an outspoken Democrat could gain political patronage from a Republican were astronomical. And Armstrong did not particularly help his cause when he participated in a rally for Democratic presidential hopeful James Buchanan, and later protested an appearance by Republican John C. Fremont in Cadiz.

Differing stories have been written about why Armstrong Custer was even considered for such a prestigious appointment from a man whose politics were contrary to those of the staunchly Democratic Custer family. Bingham later related—after Custer had become famous—that the "honesty" of the young man's letter "captivated" him. Others have speculated that the father of a girl with whom Custer was romantically involved pulled strings with the congressman in order to remove Custer from his daughter's life.

While teaching in Cadiz Township, Armstrong had boarded with a farm family and fallen madly in love with the farmer's daughter, Mary Jane "Mollie" Holland. The attraction was apparently mutual, and the two began spending much time together. Custer was so enamored with the girl that he penned his youthful passions on paper in a poem titled "To Mary."

> I've seen and kissed that crimson lip
> With honied smiles o'erflowing.
> Enchanted watched the opening rose,
> Upon thy soft cheek flowing.
> Dear Mary, thy eyes may prove less blue,
> Thy beauty fade tomorrow,
> But oh, my heart can ne'er forget
> Thy parting look of sorrow.

The two lovers exchanged photographs—Custer's depicting himself admiring her photo. Mary's father, Alexander Holland, did not consider the young man with the Democratic father a proper suitor for his daughter. He was aware that West Point cadets were forbidden to marry and interceded on Custer's behalf with his old friend Congressman Bingham, who was in the process of filling appointments to the military academy.

In January 1857, seventeen-year-old George Armstrong Custer received notification—bearing the signature of Secretary of War Jefferson Davis—that he had been awarded an appointment to West Point that would take effect in June. The decision to enter the academy became a matter of family discussion, with Custer's mother at first voicing her opposition. Maria preferred that her son become a minister and fretted about the ominous threat of an impending war. But she was outvoted by the other family members and finally acquiesced. Emanuel sold his farm and received a $200 down payment to pay for his son's expenses and admission fee.

On July 1, 1857, Armstrong Custer and sixty-seven other plebes reported for duty as the Class of 1862 at the US Military Academy at West Point, New York.

Custer's record at West Point can be summed up in a statement he later wrote: "My career as a cadet had but little to commend it to the study of those who came after me, unless as an example to be carefully avoided. The requirements of the academic regulations, a copy of which was placed in my hand the morning of my arrival at West Point, were not observed by me in such a manner at all times as to commend me to the approval and good opinions of my instructors and superior officers. My offences against law and order were not great in enormity, but what they lacked in magnitude they made up in number."

That inherent urge by Custer to be the fun-loving prankster was at odds with the strict Academy code of conduct, which was calculated by a system of demerits. This subject was not mentioned when chronicling the West Point career of James Ewell Brown Stuart, for he was never in danger of receiving enough demerits to affect his class standing. George Armstrong Custer, on the other hand, would test the limits of this code of conduct before his tour at West Point had been completed.

Demerits or black marks—called "skins" by the cadets—were awarded for various offenses, including tardiness, absence, talking after taps, an unshaven face or untrimmed hair, inattention, unkempt quarters, untidy uniform, dirty equipment, failure to salute an officer, altercations or fights with fellow cadets, and many other instances of unacceptable military behavior. One hundred skins in a six-month period would be grounds for dismissal from the academy.

The blue-eyed Armstrong Custer stood nearly six feet tall, weighed about 170 pounds, and was called "Fanny" by his classmates due to his wavy blond hair and fair complexion. Fanny Custer quickly learned that infractions such as being late for parade, not keeping his eyes to the front, throwing stones on post, or not properly carrying his musket during drill would cost him both demerits and extra duty. He had accumulated seventeen demerits by the time his class broke summer camp at Camp Gaines and moved into the barracks.

George Armstrong Custer, West Point Cadet, 1861 (Little Bighorn Battlefield Monument)

Custer was prudent and disciplined enough when his total of demerits would reach levels of dismissal, however, to behave for long periods of time or choose to work off minor infractions by walking extra guard duty. "If my memory serves me," he wrote, "I devoted sixty-six Saturdays to this method of vindicating outraged military law during my cadetship of four years."

Students were organized into sections according to their academic abilities, and Armstrong found himself for the most part among the Southerners and Westerners, who were generally inferior to the New Englanders. The rigorous curriculum, which had been expanded to five years, emphasized military courses, such as infantry, artillery, and cavalry tactics, but did not lack for challenging traditional subjects. Among the courses Custer would be required to study were algebra, geometry, trigonometry, spherical astronomy, English, French, Spanish, chemistry, drawing, electrics, civil engineering, philosophy, geology, mineralogy, history, and ethics.

At the end of his first year, Fanny Custer ranked fifty-second in mathematics, and fifty-seventh in English—in a class of sixty-two. His placement was due in part to the fact that he had accumulated 151 demerits, the highest number in his class. Despite this dismal showing, Custer was not discouraged, and wrote to David and Ann Reed on June 30 saying that "I would not leave this place for any amount of money because I would rather have a good education and no money, than to have a fortune and be ignorant."

His less-than-glowing academic record was not the result of a lack of intelligence on his part, but rather his propensity for pranks and devil-may-care attitude. "It was all right with him," a classmate recalled, "whether he knew his lesson or not: he did not allow it to trouble him." Another added: "Custer's course at West Point may be described in the remark that he merely scraped through." Fellow cadet Peter Michie wrote: "Custer was always in trouble with the authorities. He had more fun, gave his friends more anxiety, walked more tours of extra guard, and came nearer to being dismissed more often than any other cadet I have ever known." Roommate Tully McCrea reflected that "the great difficulty is that he (Custer) is too clever for his own good. He is always connected with all the mischief that is going on and never studies any more than he can possibly help."

Although his "boyish, but harmless frolics kept him in constant hot water," one area in which Custer excelled was popularity and leadership. Many a fellow cadet followed Custer into the "skin book" of demerits. One of his favorite haunts was Benny Havens' Tavern at Buttermilk Falls, an out-of-bounds establishment, where the adventurous Fanny Custer would lead late-night forays after taps.

"He was beyond a doubt," one cadet wrote, "the most popular man in his class." Another reported: "West Point has had many a character to deal with, but it may be a question whether it ever had a cadet so exuberant, one who cared so little for its serious attempts to elevate and burnish, or one on whom its tactical officers kept their eyes so constantly and unsympathetically searching as upon Custer. And yet how we all loved him."

Custer's closest friends were for the most part those with Southern roots—Kentuckians William Dunlop and George Watts, Mississippian John "Gimlet" Lea, Georgian Pierce M. B. Young, and Lafayette "Lafe" Lane, a Southern sympathizer and the son of the territorial delegate to Congress from Oregon. Kindred souls were John Pelham from Virginia, who would become Jeb Stuart's favorite artillery officer and was a year ahead, and North Carolinian Stephen D. Ramseur, who was a third classman. Custer's best friend was tall, swarthy Texan Thomas L. Rosser, who roomed next door and was full of humor. Other upperclassmen with whom Custer's future would be linked included Judson Kilpatrick, Wesley Merritt, and Alexander Pennington.

Armstrong Custer's second year was little improvement over the first. He had accumulated 192 demerits—only eight short of the 200 that would have resulted in his dismissal—for such offenses as having cooking utensils in the chimney and gazing about in ranks. His class standing was fifty-sixth out of sixty. He did, however, prove his skill as a horseman by, according to tradition, executing the highest jump of a hurdle ever at the academy while slashing at a dummy with his saber. That may be true but was not reflected in his grade in cavalry tactics, which was nowhere near the top of his class.

The end of this school year meant that Custer would receive his first furlough since entering the academy. He spent his two months alternating between his family home in New Rumley and the Reeds in Monroe, where he would for the first time see his new nephew, Harry—nicknamed Autie—who would perish with Custer at the Little Bighorn. Whether or not his romance with Mary Holland was resumed during this time would be a matter of speculation. The two had corresponded, but it appears that the flame flickered and finally was extinguished.

Custer's third year at West Point was another poor performance—he earned 191 demerits, one less than the preceding year, and ranked at the bottom of his class. His offenses this year ranged from making a boisterous noise in his sink and talking and laughing in drawing class to throwing snowballs outside and throwing bread in the mess hall. He had, however, proven that he could discipline himself, if necessary, by remaining demerit-free for a three-month period when threatened with dismissal. Also, to his credit, Armstrong was never assessed a skin for fighting or having an altercation with another cadet throughout his West Point career.

The 1860–61 academic year at the academy was anything but business as usual. Fanny Custer and his classmates received good news when Congress voted to reduce the school term from five to four years. The negative aspect of that decision was that the reason for this change was the threat of war between the North and the South, and new officers might be required to fight to preserve the Union. This possibility became more likely when Abraham Lincoln won the November election.

The Southern cadets vowed to resign from West Point when their states seceded. "You cannot imagine," Custer wrote to Ann Reed, "how sorry I will be to see this happen as the majority of my friends and all my roommates except one have been from the South."

Southern secession was initiated by South Carolina on December 20, 1860, and was soon followed by Georgia, Alabama, Mississippi, Louisiana, and Texas. Custer's friend John "Gimlet" Lea of Mississippi was one of the first to leave, but others who had resolved to join the Confederate forces were torn between loyalty to their states and the desire to remain at West Point long enough to earn their diplomas. Custer was walking one of his Saturday extra guard duty tours when two classmates from the South, John Kelly and Charles Ball, were carried toward the gate on the shoulders of friends. "Too far off to exchange verbal adieu," Custer wrote, "I responded by bringing my musket to a 'present.'"

The Confederate States of America was formed in February 1861 with Jefferson Davis as president, and it had a profound effect on the cadets. This separation of loyalties became evident at the academy with impromptu good-natured contests of regional pride. In one instance, to honor George Washington's birthday the band performed "The Star-Spangled Banner," which evoked wild cheering from those Yankee cadets who stood in their windows. The playing of "Dixie" followed, and the Rebels tried to outshine their comrades in volume.

Sadly enough, as winter turned into spring, these rivalries more often than not escalated into arguments that resulted in blows being exchanged. One can only imagine the emotions passing from room to room as these young men struggled to come to terms with the notion that today's friend and comrade in arms would likely be tomorrow's enemy on the field of battle.

Custer wrote to Ann Reed on April 10 and predicted that he expected the outbreak of war within a week. "In case of war," he pledged, "I shall serve my country according to the oath I took here." In spite of his friendship with Southern classmates, he would honor the oath of allegiance to which he had sworn upon entering West Point and offer his services to the governor of Ohio.

On April 12, the spark of rebellion ignited into full-fledged conflagration when Southern artillery opened up on Fort Sumter in Charleston harbor. The fort fell two days later, which compelled President Lincoln to call for 75,000 volunteers to preserve the Union. Southerners at West Point had no choice but to head for home, and thirty-seven cadets, including Custer's best friend, Texan Tom Rosser, departed the academy to offer their services to the Confederacy.

The Class of 1861 was graduated early on May 6, with Judson Kilpatrick delivering the valedictory address. Four days later, Kilpatrick would participate in the opening skirmish of the war and suffer a severe wound. Custer's class was subjected to an abbreviated curriculum that would supplant the final year of studies and was scheduled to graduate on June 24.

Perhaps amazingly to many instructors and fellow cadets, Fanny Custer satisfactorily completed his studies and was commissioned a second lieutenant. He had racked up an additional 192 demerits during the year, which included multiple occasions when he swung his arms while marching, threw snowballs, and showed up for inspections unshaven and with long hair. He had been in constant danger of dismissal throughout his years at West Point and had racked up an impressive four-year total of 726 demerits. Nevertheless, the class clown who excelled in horsemanship and athletic prowess but lagged behind in academics had overcome his own outrageous antics to qualify for graduation from West Point.

Custer wrote: "My class numbered upon entering the Academy about one hundred and twenty-five. Of this number only thirty-four graduated, and of these thirty-three graduated above me. The resignation and departure of the Southern cadets took away from the Academy a few individuals who, had they remained, would probably have contested with me the debatable honor of bringing up the rear of the class."

Perhaps predictably, Custer's military career was in trouble before he had even received orders assigning him to his first duty station. On June 29, he was officer of the guard when a fistfight broke out between two cadets— one of whom was William Ludlow, who would be chief engineer on Custer's Black Hills Expedition in 1874. Inexplicably, Custer disregarded his duty to break up the fight and instead told the assembled crowd to "stand back, boys; let's have a fair fight." The officer of the day, First Lieutenant William B. Hazen, a West Point instructor and future Custer critic, happened along to witness the event and placed Custer under arrest. While his classmates departed the academy and proceeded to Washington for further orders, Custer was detained to await a court-martial, which would convene on July 5.

George Armstrong Custer's military career was in jeopardy of ending before the ink on his diploma was even dry.

CHAPTER THREE

OPENING SALVOS
of the WAR

ON MAY 10, Lieutenant Colonel James Ewell Brown Stuart reported for duty in the Provisional Army of Virginia at Harpers Ferry as second in command to Colonel Thomas J. Jackson, the thirty-seven-year-old eccentric former professor. Stuart's commission was in infantry, but Jackson quickly recognized Stuart's cavalry experience and chose to consolidate his horsemen under the new lieutenant colonel as the 1st Virginia Cavalry.

The powerfully built Stuart dressed the part of a dashing cavalier. His double-breasted gray coat, which he buttoned to the chin, dazzled with gawdy buttons and gold braid, and the accompanying cape was lined with scarlet. He often displayed a rose in the buttonhole—a gift from some female admirer. His brown, soft felt hat, decorated with a black ostrich plume, was worn slightly atilt, the brim pinned to one side with a gold clasp. Around his waist was a yellow silk sash tied at the side with golden tassels. His buff gauntlets reached to the elbow; his cavalry boots rose above the knee; and his golden spurs were suitable for either battle or the ballroom. He was armed with a light, curved French saber and a pistol in a black holster. His complexion was ruddy, the features for the most part obscured by a thick, reddish-brown beard and curled mustache, and his penetrating blue eyes held the sparkle of a man always seeking a reason to laugh.

Two weeks after Stuart's arrival, General Joseph E. Johnston relieved Jackson of duty and assumed command of the army. Stuart was kept busy greeting new arrivals and drilling his troops at his camp—christened Camp Jeff Davis—at the crossroads village of Bunker Hill. The cavalry commander's training tactics were highly unorthodox and somewhat dangerous. His methods which personified his adventuresome character, was to make use of his enemy as a tool for schooling his troopers.

On one occasion Stuart led a green company behind enemy lines and deliberately permitted them to become surrounded by Union troops before finding a gap in the lines and racing away to safety. Another time Stuart had his men dismount and stand facing a detachment of advancing Union infantry. Only when the enemy was within 200 yards did Stuart allow his men to march backwards, firing as they moved, until reaching their horses. Instead of galloping away from his closing enemy, Stuart maintained their pace at a trot.

He counseled, "A gallop is a gait unbecoming a soldier, unless he is going toward the enemy. We gallop toward the enemy, and trot away, always." When artillery shrieked overhead, Stuart held his men in place and advised, "I wanted you to learn how shells sound." Frequent all-day forays behind enemy lines provided valuable lessons for the 1st Virginia, which now consisted of 21 officers and 313 enlisted men.

Both sides were anxious for hostilities to commence in earnest, but the outcry in the North was perhaps louder. The Northern public and press clamored for an immediate invasion to destroy the upstart Confederacy. President Lincoln, ignoring the pleas of his veteran officers who advised patience, bowed to this pressure for action.

To that end, on July 1, 18,000 Union troops under Major General Robert Patterson crossed the Potomac into the Shenandoah Valley with intentions of occupying the 12,000 Confederate troops commanded by General Johnston.

According to the plan, Patterson would keep Johnston busy while 35,000 troops led by Brigadier General Irvin McDowell would attack the 22,000 Confederate forces under General P. G. T. Beauregard, which were protecting the strategically vital railroad center at Manassas Junction. The Union could then waltz into Richmond and end the war. The Confederates, however, refused to cooperate with this strategy.

Stuart's outposts observed Patterson's crossing of the Potomac, and it was reported to General Johnston. Colonel Jackson commanding a brigade was dispatched to determine enemy strength and offer resistance if confronted by only a small force. The following day at Falling Waters, Jackson, with one regiment and Stuart's cavalry active on the flank, managed to check the advance of a Union division. Then, in compliance with orders, Jackson broke contact and retired beyond Martinsburg in the face of this superior number of troops.

During the encounter, Stuart had inadvertently placed himself in what could have developed into a dangerous situation if not for his courage and resourcefulness. He was riding alone through the woods and, upon emerging into open country, suddenly came upon a sizeable detachment of Union infantry. Rather than wheel about and make a run for it, Colonel Stuart brazenly ordered the men to tear down a fence.

The Yankee troops, mistaking Stuart for one of their own officers, complied. Within moments, Stuart issued his second order, directing the men to throw down their weapons and surrender. Stuart's cavalrymen arrived to assist, and forty-nine members of Company I, 15th Pennsylvania Cavalry, were taken prisoner. Stuart was singled out for praise when Jackson reported to Johnston.

The uncertain status of Second Lieutenant George Armstrong Custer was settled on July 5 when his court-martial was convened at West Point. Nine officers listened to evidence pertaining to charges of neglect of duty and "conduct to the prejudice of good order and military discipline" for Custer's failure to "suppress a quarrel between two cadets." Custer prepared a four-page statement and was aided by Lieutenant Hazen, who acted as a character witness, and by the two combatants, who testified that the fight was simply a "scuffle" of little consequence.

The court was not particularly impressed by Custer's defense and found him guilty on both counts. His punishment, however, was the ruling that he only be "reprimanded in orders" on account of his general good conduct as testified to by Hazen. Under normal circumstances, Custer likely would have been dismissed from the service.

"Custer's Luck," which was the term Custer and others would employ to characterize the favorable events that occurred to him throughout his life, had saved his military career. He was now free to apply the lessons that he had learned at the academy on the battlefield.

While Custer was preparing to depart West Point, Colonel Stuart and his 1st Virginia Cavalry were busy screening the Southern army and apprising superiors about enemy movements. On July 15, Stuart detected a move by Patterson toward Bunker Hill. General Johnston swiftly marched to Darksville to parry this threat. Johnston would spend several days attempting to bait Patterson into attacking. Patterson, however, was content to simply occupy Johnston's force at that location while McDowell moved into position and declined the invitation to engage.

By this time, the Federal troops commanded by McDowell were amassing at Centreville, Virginia, a village about twenty-five miles southwest of Washington, northeast of a muddy waterway named Bull Run. Beauregard was entrenched on the southern bank of that stream but was greatly outnumbered. Patterson had declined to attack Johnston, and the Confederate War Office ordered Johnston to march to Piedmont Station where his infantry could be transported by rail to Manassas as reinforcements for Beauregard.

On July 18, Johnston commenced what he hoped would be a covert movement to reinforce Beauregard. Stuart and his band of horsemen were charged with the responsibility of screening Johnston's march to Piedmont. So effective was Stuart's ability to shield this movement and harass Patterson that the Federals would not learn of Johnston's departure until his arrival at Manassas two days later.

On that same day, July 18, Second Lieutenant George Armstrong Custer departed the US Military Academy at West Point destined for Washington. He spent several hours in New York City to visit the well-known military firm of Horstmann's to purchase a lieutenant's uniform, saber, sash, Colt revolver, spurs, and other accouterments, and to have his photo taken for his sister. He then boarded a train to complete his journey to the nation's capital where he would receive orders directing him to his first duty assignment.

That following morning, Jeb Stuart and his 300 horsemen pushed across the Blue Ridge in an effort to rendezvous with the troops gathering at Manassas. Due to the congestion caused by Johnston's men and artillery on the road leading to Piedmont Station, the cavalrymen were obliged to ride through open fields, traversing a difficult, uneven terrain rife with ditches and fences to cross. To add to the misery, the men were sleepy and hungry—the wagons containing rations had been delayed—and the fast pace of the march was taking its toll. The arduous ride improved to some degree when the cavalry finally passed Piedmont and were unimpeded by the infantrymen.

Armstrong Custer arrived in Washington on Saturday morning, July 20. His first stop was a hotel where he briefly visited with Jim Parker, his former roommate, who had accepted a commission in the Confederate army. Custer made a concerted effort to persuade his friend to reconsider on the grounds that he had sworn an oath of allegiance at West Point, but the argument fell on deaf ears. Parker would remain a Rebel.

That afternoon, Custer reported to the adjutant general's office at the War Department to learn that he had been assigned to Major Innes Palmer's Company G, 2nd United States Cavalry. His unit was presently part of Irvin McDowell's Union forces at Centreville, where the battle for possession of nearby Manassas Junction was presumed imminent.

The adjutant general was about to direct a subordinate to write out Custer's orders when he paused to ask if Custer would like to be presented to Lieutenant General Winfield Scott, the seventy-five-year-old hero of the Mexican War who was serving as President Lincoln's chief military advisor.

"Scott was looked up to as a leader whose military abilities were scarcely second to those of Napoleon," Custer wrote, "and whose patriotism rivalled that of Washington." Custer was doubtlessly taken aback to imagine that he would be deemed worthy of being introduced to the country's most celebrated soldier, but "joyfully assented" to the adjutant general's invitation.

Custer was ushered into Scott's office, which was occupied by other officers as well as members of Congress who were studying maps of the vicinity of Bull Run. A cordial General Scott asked Custer if he would prefer drilling volunteers, which had been one of the duties assigned to recent West Point graduates, or did he desire something more active.

"Although overwhelmed by such condescension upon the part of one so far superior in rank to any officer with whom I had been brought in immediate contact," Custer remembered, "I ventured to stammer out that I earnestly desired to be ordered to at once join my company as I was anxious to see active service." Scott was impressed with that answer and ordered Custer to find a horse and return that evening to carry dispatches to General McDowell in the field on his way to the 2nd Cavalry.

Custer spent several hours searching for an available mount without success until finally happening upon an enlisted man whom he recognized from the academy. The soldier was a member of Capt. Charles Griffin's battery and had been retrieving an extra horse that had been left behind when the battery had moved out. Custer managed to secure the mount, which, ironically, had been a favorite of his from West Point that he had named Wellington.

With the dispatches from Scott to McDowell in hand, Custer and his companion rode out of Washington at nightfall and arrived in Centreville at about 3 a.m. The subject of the dispatches was unknown to Custer—and to history—but there is a distinct possibility that he was carrying the orders that would commence the first battle of the Civil War.

After delivering the dispatches, Custer remounted and made his way alone through the darkness in search of his unit, eventually coming upon a line of mounted cavalry. He located Major Palmer and, after introductions, was directed to his platoon to await orders for the march.

George Armstrong Custer, three days removed from West Point, was about to participate in the first grand struggle of the Civil War.

By the time Custer had reported for duty, Jeb Stuart, after thirty-six grueling hours in the saddle, led his weary cavalry into Manassas to a scene of what adjutant William Blackford termed "martial preparation." Blackford remembered: "Troops were arriving by the cars and marching out to the lines along Bull Run, six miles away. Great trains of wagons were hauling supplies of food and ammunition. Great crowds of men stood around everywhere. The clouds of suffocating dust, the bustle, and the knowledge of what it was the preparation for, made all this an impressive scene to us, whose eyes were yet unaccustomed to such sights." Stuart's troops bivouacked nearby where the Warrenton Turnpike crossed Bull Run and were supplied forage and rations before settling in for a night of rest.

The following morning, Sunday, July 21, Stuart was startled awake to the sound of small arms fire on the Confederate left. "Hello! What is that?" he asked of no one in particular. The answer was that McDowell had attacked on the flank in an attempt to catch his enemy off guard and roll up the left. Union troops had struck Stone Bridge, while others crossed Bull Run farther upstream at Sudley Springs Ford. Beauregard, who had been readying his own assault, rushed reinforcements to man his exposed flank. The battle quickly escalated into a furious scene of charges and countercharges amidst the roar of angry rifle fire and bursting artillery shells. Stuart and his cavalry briefly scouted across Bull Run, then assumed a position in the rear and awaited orders.

Armstrong Custer and the 2nd Cavalry had been relegated to supporting artillery batteries throughout the early action. "I remember well the strange hissing and exceedingly vicious sound of the first cannon shot I heard," Custer wrote about the experience of protecting Captain Griffin's battery, which was under fire from enemy artillery. "Of course I had often heard the sound made by cannon balls while passing through the air during my artillery practice at West Point, but a man listens with changed interest when the direction of the balls is toward instead of away from him. They seem to utter a different language when fired in angry battle from that put forth in the tamer practice of drill."

By noon, the Union army had pressed its advantage, and victory appeared within its grasp. Colonel Jeb Stuart was growing more impatient with each passing hour as the battle raged on while he sat waiting for orders to move out. Fearing that he would not be called upon, he had dispatched messengers to the front and had even ridden up to personally speak with Colonel Jackson in an effort to receive an assignment.

Finally, at about 2 p.m., a staff officer emerged from the woods to approach the exasperated Stuart. "Colonel Stuart," he said, "General Beauregard directs that you bring your command into the action at once and that you attack where the firing is hottest."

The bugle sounded "boots and saddles," and Stuart led his men away in a column of fours to seek a likely place to assist his comrades. Along the way, the cavalrymen were brought face-to-face with the horrors of war when they passed a field hospital where surgeons cut and sawed on screaming patients near a pile of severed, mangled limbs. The scene proved too much for some of the men, who leaned over the pommels of their saddles to vomit.

Jeb Stuart emerged from the woods on the Confederate left to view dense clouds of white smoke and artillery flashes that lit up the battlefield where Jackson's infantry was engaged in a fierce struggle. One disorganized unit to his front caught Stuart's eye. They were dressed in Turkish attire—scarlet caps and trousers, blue jackets, and white gaiters—and Stuart thought them to be the Louisiana Zouave regiment. He shouted for them to maintain their positions and then recognized the stars and stripes on their battle flag. It was not their boys but the New York Fire Zouaves. Stuart immediately ordered his men to charge.

The Zouaves noticed the approach of Stuart's horsemen and knelt to open fire. According to Blackford, "a sheet of red flame gleamed, and we could see no more." Horses squealed, and nine Confederates were struck in the initial volley, but the cavalrymen closed with the Zouaves "cutting right and left with their sabers." The Zouaves countered with bayonet thrusts that toppled many of Stuart's men from their saddles to the ground.

The impetus of the charge sent Jeb Stuart's men hurtling through the line of scarlet into the woods, where they halted to regroup at the position where they had begun the charge. Some of the cavalrymen had lost their zeal for battle and had thundered away down the road toward Manassas. Adjutant Blackford was dispatched to gather those men, who meekly returned without being disciplined for their impulsive act.

In fact, Stuart laughed off the incident. "He (Stuart) was so brave a man himself," Blackford explained, "that he never seemed to attribute unworthy motives to his men, and this was one of the secrets of his great influence over them in action. They were ashamed to be anything but brave where he was."

Stuart later claimed that his charge had demoralized the Zouaves to the extent that the rest of the Federal infantry had taken notice and fled. Contrarily, the Zouaves believed that they had scattered the cavalry and chased them from the field. Perhaps both sides had exaggerated the importance of such a brief engagement.

Regardless of the impact of the charge, Jeb Stuart chose not to chase the dangerous Zouaves. Instead, he moved his men to the left flank in support of Lieutenant R. F. Beckham's battery of artillery, which he hid behind a stand of trees and personally directed fire from a nearby vantage point. Stuart's observation post afforded him an excellent view of deployments on the field, and he dispatched couriers to relay vital information to various commanders.

At one point during this vicious battle, Lieutenant George Armstrong Custer's regiment formed in column of companies and prepared to move to the crest of a hill where it was presumed the order would be given to charge. Lieutenant Leicester Walker, who had been appointed from civilian life and outranked Custer by a few days, called out from his position at the head of his platoon, "Custer, what weapon are you going to use in the charge?"

Custer, the West Pointer who was expected to know such things, promptly answered, "The saber," and drew his blade. Walker instantly imitated Custer and drew his own saber.

As the formation moved at a walk up the hill, Custer began arguing in his mind about the comparative merits of the saber as opposed to the six-shot revolver and came to the conclusion that the firearm would be best at close quarters. Without a word, he replaced his saber in its scabbard and drew his revolver. Walker noticed and copied Custer's actions.

Custer's mind resumed its debate—a revolver quickly emptied in the midst of the enemy would be less effective than a saber, he judged. With that realization, he holstered the revolver and drew his saber. Walker had observed the exchange, and again followed Custer's example.

The company arrived at the crest of the hill and, finding no enemy within sight, cancelled the charge and returned to a sheltered place to await further orders. The need for either saber or revolver had been for the time being postponed.

At about 4 p.m., Jeb Stuart watched from his vantage point and judged that the Federal flank was vulnerable. He dispatched a message to Colonel Jubal A. Early to inform him that if he hurried to that position the enemy line could certainly be broken. Early moved at once and, supported by Stuart's and Beckham's fire, routed the Union troopers into a retirement that quickly escalated into a panicked dash across Bull Run. Some accounts claim that many Union soldiers did not pause in their flight until they had reached Washington or even the streets of New York City.

Custer's company acted as rear guard during this unorganized, every-man-for-himself retreat, and was one of the last units to leave the field. He arrived at the Cub Run Bridge, the main route of retreat to Centreville, to find that an artillery shell had struck a wagon to block passage. To add to the confusion, a panicked mob of troops had jammed the bridge in their haste to cross. Custer immediately rode forward and took charge. He soon cleared the way for an orderly withdrawal. "Though famished, exhausted, spent, Custer never gave up, never slackened control," wrote Company G bugler Joseph Fought.

Jeb Stuart and his cavalry chased the retreating enemy for a distance of twelve miles, and soon had captured so many prisoners that required escorts to the rear that his force was reduced to one squad and he was compelled to abandon his efforts. He established his headquarters in a farmhouse near Sudley Church and relaxed with his men exchanging stories and celebrating this great Confederate victory.

Both armies had fought gamely, but the troopers were green and unaccustomed to military discipline. The Union had initially gained the upper hand when the undermanned Confederates wavered under a series of determined assaults. The Confederate soldiers, however, had been inspired by the courage of Thomas Jackson, who had held his position on Henry House Hill "like a stone wall," thus earning him the illustrious nickname Stonewall. A steady stream of Confederate reinforcements throughout the day eventually proved to be the difference when the exhausted Federal troops could no longer withstand the assailment.

The Union had lost 460 killed, 1,124 wounded, and 1,312 missing, compared to the Confederate loss of 387 killed, 1,584 wounded, and 13 missing—numbers that fail to provide a clear view of the engagement. The Battle of Bull Run, or First Manassas—as the North and South, respectively, called the battle—had in truth concluded with a tactical and moral victory for the Confederacy.

Jeb Stuart wrote to his wife: "I am your own Darling husband whose thoughts and affection are centered in his own Dear Flora—and even in the fiercest fire of the battle field I thought of her and how proud she would be to see the conduct of her husband." He added, "The papers have said very little about my Regt, but the Generals have said a great deal. You need not be surprised to see your hubbie a Brigadier. I have been in one real battle now and feel sure I can command better than many I saw." In his report, he would accentuate his daring charge into the blazing rifles of the

Zouaves rather than his actual contribution of guiding Early's brigade to the federal flank.

Second Lieutenant Custer's coolness under fire and ability to maintain orderliness among the troops during this hectic retreat was also viewed with great regard by his superiors and earned him a citation for bravery. His actions even came to the attention of Congressman John A. Bingham, the man who had nominated Custer to West Point. "I heard of him after the First Battle of Bull Run," Bingham wrote. "In the report of that miserable fiasco he was mentioned for bravery. A leader was needed to re-form the troops, and take them over a bridge. Like Napoleon at Lodi young Custer sprang to the front—and was a hero."

The outcome of the battle, however, was a bitter disappointment to Custer. "I little imagined," he wrote, "when making my night ride from Washington on July 20th, that the night following would find me returning with a defeated and demoralized army."

The disaster at Bull Run spelled doom for the command of General Irvin McDowell. The Lincoln administration lost confidence in McDowell, and he was promptly replaced by Major General George B. McClellan.

This thirty-four-year-old Ohioan and West Point graduate had served on General Scott's staff during the Mexican War and had quit the railroad industry to rejoin the army when Fort Sumter fell. McClellan, the inventor of the famous "McClellan saddle," which became standard equipment for mounted units, had been chosen by Lincoln to reorganize every element of the army in order to restore sagging morale and produce a cohesive fighting force.

In the creation of the Army of the Potomac, however, McClellan's knowledge of cavalry equipment apparently did not translate into tactical innovation. Brigadier General George Stoneman was named chief of cavalry but would serve in a purely administrative role. While Colonel J. E. B. Stuart would redefine the purpose of cavalry as an independent arm of the army, the mounted Union regiments were assigned to infantry generals who could find no better use for the horsemen than, in the words of one Pennsylvania cavalryman, "as escorts, strikers, dog-robbers and orderlies for all the generals and their numerous staff officers from the highest rank down to the second lieutenants."

Custer's 2nd Cavalry was renumbered the 5th Cavalry and attached to Brigadier General Philip Kearny's brigade, which was primarily detailed as part of the capitol defense force. Kearny, who had lost an arm in the Mexican War, was in need of staff officers. Custer, as the junior lieutenant in the 5th Cavalry, was assigned to Kearny's staff, and in a short time had risen from aide-de-camp to assistant adjutant general.

Colonel Jeb Stuart's admirable actions in the Valley and at Manassas had not by any means been overlooked by his superiors. On August 10, General Johnston wrote to President Jefferson Davis: "He (Stuart) is a rare man, wonderfully endowed by nature with the qualities necessary for an officer of light cavalry. Calm, firm, acute, active, and enterprising. I know of no one more competent than he to estimate the occurrences before him at their true value. If you add a real brigade of cavalry to this army, you can find no better brigadier-general to command it."

Stuart's cavalry diligently maintained surveillance of the enemy throughout the summer and fall. On September 11, his 300-man cavalry attacked a Union force of 1,800 at Lewinsville, Virginia, and escaped without suffering any casualties. Stuart's report of the minor skirmish was sent to his immediate superior, James Longstreet, who forwarded the report to Generals Johnston and Beauregard with his own endorsement of Stuart.

"Colonel Stuart," Longstreet wrote, "has been at Munson's Hill since its occupation by our troops. He has been most untiring in the discharge of his duties at that and other advanced positions. Colonel Stuart has, I think, fairly won his claim to brigadier, and I hope the commanding generals will unite with me in recommending him for that promotion."

The two other generals heartily agreed with Longstreet's assessment, and added their endorsement: "His (Stuart's) calm and daring courage, sagacity, zeal, and activity qualify him admirably for the command of our three regiments of cavalry, by which the outpost duty of the Army is performed. The Government would gain greatly by promoting him."

Jeb Stuart's cousin-in-law, John Esten Cooke, a novelist by trade, also helped the cause by acting as the colonel's unofficial publicity agent. Cooke, in his role for the *Charleston Daily Courier* as "Our Virginia Correspondent," compared Stuart to the Italian hero Garibaldi and wrote that "probably no man in the South is more hated and feared by the Yankees." Cooke predicted that Stuart would "find a niche in two places—first with his trusty sabre upon some flying Yankee's caput [head], and second with his proud untainted name in the temple of Southern freedom."

On September 24, the Confederacy officially recognized James Ewell Brown Stuart's worthiness, as well as its own need of experienced officers, and he was commissioned a brigadier general. Additionally, he was assigned the command of a reorganized cavalry comprised of six regiments, more than 1,500 horsemen.

The promotion was greeted with nearly unanimous approval by the cavalrymen who served under Stuart. The men demonstrated their pride by emulating their commander's style of dress as best they could, replacing Stuart's trademark ostrich plume in their hats with chicken feathers, if necessary. He was affectionately called "Jeb," eliding his initials "J. E. B.," a nickname that would endure through the ages.

In early October, Armstrong Custer was stricken with a mysterious illness and was granted a leave of absence. He returned home to the Reed household in Monroe and also visited his parents at their newly purchased eighty-acre farm in northeastern Ohio.

Custer at this time learned that his younger brother, Tom, had run away from home a month earlier at age sixteen to join the 21st Ohio Infantry. This impulsive act by the boy had greatly distressed his parents. Emanuel Custer had thwarted Tom's initial attempt to enlist in Monroe, but the determined youngster had slipped across the border to the state of his birth to accomplish the task.

Custer was greeted in Monroe as a local war hero and enthusiastically immersed himself in the social scene. He could be found on most nights romancing an adoring young lady or carousing with friends and other soldiers on furlough at any one of the establishments that served alcohol and the merriment of music.

General Jeb Stuart's nights were also filled with music, but his carousing was for the most part confined to the companionship of his fellow cavalrymen at his winter camp, which was located in a farmhouse halfway between Fairfax Court House and Centreville. Camp *Qui Vive*, which was French for

"Who goes there?" was a reflection of Stuart's love of song and laughter and certainly did not lack the uniqueness that personified its commander.

In front of the farmhouse door stood a Blakely cannon, which had been imported from England. Guarding the gun, in John Esten Cooke's words, was "nothing less than an enormous raccoon—black, wary, with snarling teeth, and eyes full of 'fight!'"

Days were occupied patrolling the immediate vicinity, but the nights were reserved for relaxation. Stuart surrounded himself with black minstrels and dancers, a ventriloquist, and fiddlers, and he scoured the ranks of his cavalry for other talented musicians, whom he would select as couriers. His favorite was a dark, handsome banjo player in his early thirties named Sam Sweeney. With Mulatto Bob on the bones, Sweeney would lead the campfire chorus in such Southern favorites as "Listen to the Mocking Bird," "Sweet Evalina," "Her Bright Smile Haunts Me Still," and Stuart's personal choice, "Jine the Cavalry."

Jeb Stuart's staff consisted of a variety of skilled soldiers that he had handpicked from other units for their compatibility in creating a cohesive and jolly atmosphere. He chose Colonel Fitzhugh Lee, nephew of the general and Stuart's West Point friend who was remembered for nearly being expelled due to excessive demerits. Lee's lifelong friend, Lunsford Lomax, had served with Stuart in the West. Two classmates and friends of George Armstrong Custer, John Pelham and Tom Rosser, came to Stuart's attention. The general selected Pelham over Rosser to command the Stuart Horse Artillery, a light three-gun battery.

Other staff members would include cousin-in-law John Esten Cooke; adjutant William Blackford; scout Redmond Burke, who always had "a wonderful set of yarns to tell"; Marylander Tiernan Brien; seventeen-year-old Chiswell Dabney, the "Adonis of the staff"; and Reverent Major Dabney Ball, the "Fighting Bishop." Perhaps his favorite staff member was a huge Prussian officer turned soldier-of-fortune named Heros Von Borcke, who stood six feet two and weighed 250 pounds—a large man for his times.

The decision of Stuart's father-in-law, General Phillip St. George Cooke, to remain with the Union was an act that, to say the least, had outraged Stuart. In his judgment, Cooke was a traitor who would "regret it but once, and that will be continually." Jeb and Flora had named their son in honor of General Cooke, and now Stuart insisted that they change the boy's name. Flora was reluctant but finally acquiesced. Phillip St. George Cooke Stuart was renamed James Ewell Brown Stuart, Jr., nicknamed Jimmy.

Family matters came to the forefront in Monroe, Michigan, as well when an episode occurred that would greatly affect the future of George Armstrong Custer—negatively in the short term but positively for the remainder of his life.

Custer had been frequenting the local taverns, and on one particular occasion had imbibed to excess. He and a male companion staggered through the streets of Monroe on their merry way to Armstrong's sister's house. The soldiers created quite a ruckus as they loudly laughed and sang without regard for the delicate ears of those within listening distance of the boisterous serenade. The two revilers happened to pass the Bacon residence where they were observed by Judge Daniel Bacon and his nineteen-year-old daughter, Libbie.

Custer was unaware of it at the time, but Libbie Bacon would later in the year become the object of his affections. Due to the improper behavior that the young man had displayed on that winter day, Judge Bacon would forbid any contact between his daughter and the raucous cavalry officer.

Additionally, Custer's sister, Ann, who was deeply religious, was appalled by her brother's condition. Once home, Ann—with her Bible in hand—took Autie into her bedroom, delivered a temperance lecture, and made him promise before God that he would never touch another drop of intoxicating beverage. Her efforts were successful. From that day forth, Custer never again touched alcohol, not even wine at formal dinner parties.

On December 20, Jeb Stuart was placed in command of about 1,600 infantrymen and 150 of his cavalry and charged with protecting a wagon train sent by General Johnston to collect fodder and forage from the countryside around Dranesville. Unknown to Stuart, the Union had at the same time dispatched General E. O. C. Ord, commanding three brigades of Pennsylvania infantry—4,000 strong—with orders to chase off Confederate pickets at Dranesville and gather the forage from the fertile farmland for themselves. Stuart had failed to scout the area in advance of his wagon train and happened upon a line of blue-clad riflemen running parallel to the Leesburg-Alexandria Turnpike.

Stuart and Ord were both concerned about the safety of their foragers. With that in mind, the opposing commanders did what came naturally— they attacked each other. Ord's artillery had been posted in a favorable posi- tion, and, as Stuart wrote in his report, "every shot of the enemy was dealing destruction on either man, limber, or horse."

Stuart's own artillery had been placed on the road where it not only was exposed to the enemy but could not fire with any effectiveness. To make matters worse, Stuart's infantrymen had charged into a thickly wooded area where two regiments began firing upon each other. After two hours of aim- less engagement, Stuart withdrew his force to a distance of about five miles from Dranesville.

Stuart exaggerated the size of the enemy force—three-to-one in his official report; four-to-one in a letter to Flora—but without question had been on the short end of the casualty count. Ord had lost 7 killed and 61 wounded compared to Stuart's 43 killed, 143 wounded, and 8 missing.

Despite the casualty numbers, Stuart's conduct in the eyes of his men had not diminished their confidence in his ability to command. Nor did the engagement put a damper on Christmas celebrations. Flora and the children visited Camp *Qui Vive*, and after the holidays the family moved into a house in nearby Warrenton. The days would settle into a routine of drill and patrolling and waiting for the roads to dry so major campaigning could resume.

Second Lieutenant Custer returned to Washington in early February 1862 with renewed ambition. Several members of his former West Point class, Tom Rosser, John Pelham, and Stephen Ramseur, who had joined the ranks of the Confederacy had already been promoted to captain, and it was rumored that Jim Parker had become a lieutenant colonel. It appeared that Custer once again lagged at the rear of his class.

The opportunity for possible glory presented itself on March 9 when Custer's unit was ordered into action. The Confederates under Johnston— with Stuart's cavalry—had abandoned their lines around Centreville, and McClellan dispatched the cavalry to trail this withdrawal in an effort to gather information. Custer was the only officer with the 5th Cavalry, and for the first time would command a troop.

The 5th Cavalry was in the advance when the column arrived at Catlett's Station, near Cedar Creek. Enemy pickets from Johnston's rear guard were spotted on a hill about a mile away. General Stoneman, who was in command, sent word that an officer from the 5th be selected to lead a detachment to drive away the pickets. Custer immediately volunteered for the assignment and was accorded permission.

Custer formed his fifty men and advanced to the base of a hill where the pickets were known to be posted. A few bullets were fired from the enemy position, which convinced Custer to order a charge. Custer led the assault with drawn saber, which coaxed the Rebels to flee before the advancing horsemen could overrun their position.

Custer pursued until encountering about 300 of his enemy who opened up with carbines. At that time, with at least one man wounded and one horse down, Custer, who stated that "the bullets rattled like hail," ordered his men to retire. The troop and its jubilant commander returned to camp, where Custer reported directly to General Stoneman. For the first time in his career, George Armstrong Custer had led a cavalry charge.

The exhilaration of his first command and first charge evidently bubbled over in admiration for the man who now called the shots for the Army of the Potomac. "I have more confidence in General McClellan than any man living," Custer wrote to his parents on March 17. "I would forsake everything and follow him to the ends of the earth. I would lay down my life for him. I would fight anyone who would say a word against him."

McClellan, however, had not been aggressive enough to suit President Lincoln. He finally responded to the president's demands by devising a plan to land at Fort Monroe and advance up the Virginia Peninsula between the York and James Rivers in an attempt to attack Richmond before the Confederates in that vicinity could be reinforced. This would require the shipment from Washington to the Peninsula of 121,500 men, 14,592 animals, 1,150 wagons, 44 batteries, 74 ambulances, and assorted other materials and equipment aboard approximately 319 steamers, schooners, and barges.

"The greatest expedition ever fitted out is going south under the greatest and best of men, Genl. McClellan," Custer wrote to his sister on March 26 as he prepared to board the *Adele Felicia* at Alexandria, Virginia.

This movement, however, was no secret to the Confederates. Jeb Stuart, whose cavalry had been kept busy scouting and skirmishing around Warrenton Junction, had correctly predicted McClellan's plans for taking Richmond, and the army prepared for the Union's arrival.

Twenty miles upriver from Fort Monroe, Confederate Major General John B. Magruder held Yorktown with less than 12,000 troops, which he moved from one point to another to create the impression of greater than actual troop strength. General Johnston, whose army with Jeb Stuart's cavalry attached was nearly fifty miles away, rushed through the sleet and snow to reinforce Magruder before McClellan could overpower the small force at Yorktown.

Magruder's strategy served its purpose. The ever-cautious George McClellan overestimated the Confederate strength at the works behind the Warwick River and declined to order an assault. Instead, he chose to initiate a siege intended to blast the enemy into submission with artillery before sending in troops.

Jeb Stuart and his cavalry, acting as Johnston's rear guard, had paraded through the streets of Richmond to the delight of the cheering residents before arriving in Yorktown on April 18. He held the opinion that Yorktown would escalate into a major battle, perhaps comparable to the siege of Sebastopol in the Crimean War, and may very well decide the outcome of the war. The surrounding terrain was heavily wooded with deep ravines, however, which Stuart noted would preclude his cavalry from an active role if such a battle commenced.

On the other side of the lines, Armstrong Custer's unit was deployed on reconnaissance missions during this siege and came under fire on two occasions. The second encounter, in which casualties were sustained, made a lasting impression on the young lieutenant. In a skirmish that lasted an hour, Custer and his men withstood a pitted battle against enemy sharpshooters. "Everyone got behind a tree and blazed away as hard as he could," he described in a letter to Ann Reed. "But the rebels made their bullets so thick it was all we could do to look out for ourselves."

Custer was deeply affected by the burial of those troopers who had been slain in the firefight. For the first time in his life, the happy-go-lucky young man had become intimately involved with the tragic consequences of war. "Some were quite young and boyish," he wrote, "and, looking at their faces I could not but think of my own younger brother." The sight of one trooper evoked Custer to emotionally write: "As he lay there I thought of the poem: 'Let me kiss him for his mother . . .' and wished his mother were there to smooth his hair."

His graphic description of this dangerous mission and its aftermath was received with predictable concern by his family. Emanuel Custer wrote that Maria, Custer's mother, "troubles hir self so much about you and Thomas and she doant like to here of you being so venturesom." Ann Reed responded with: "My dear brother I want you to be very careful of yourself. Don't expose yourself you know how much your parents depend on you and how much we all love you."

The siege of Yorktown was well underway when Custer was assigned to the staff of Brigadier General William F. "Baldy" Smith as an assistant to the Chief Engineer, Lieutenant Nicholas Bowen. In this capacity, Custer was volunteered as a military observer from a hot-air balloon. Custer approached this unusual duty with some apprehension—they had been using a general to go aloft, but when the wind blew him toward Confederate guns it was decided that they needed someone more dispensable. Soon, Custer overcame his fear and, after a number of ascents, became comfortable with the procedure. With field glass, compass, pencil, and notebook in hand, he would on a daily basis note enemy gun emplacements, count enemy campfires, and plot the number of white tents with sketches.

In the wee hours of May 4, the day that McClellan had chosen for his grand assault, Custer made his second ascension of the night and observed indications that the enemy had abandoned Yorktown. His suspicions were confirmed by dawn, and he hurried to report his findings to General Smith. McClellan was notified and ordered Smith to dispatch troops to investigate.

Custer and another officer volunteered to cross the river and discovered that the Confederates had indeed vacated the town. McClellan, who understood that he would be vilified by the president, the press, and the public for allowing the enemy to escape without inflicting any damage, ordered an immediate pursuit.

Confederate General Joseph Johnston had chosen to withdraw from Yorktown in order to seek a more favorable location with which to engage McClellan's huge army. The cavalry under Jeb Stuart once again acted superbly as rear guard and screened the departure of the Confederates, who slogged through muddy roads up the Peninsula. On the afternoon of May 4, Stuart's scouts informed him that the Yankees were in hot pursuit on the road behind them. Stuart left the road and traveled along the sandy shore of the James River to reach Williamsburg at about dark. Stuart attached his command to Major General James Longstreet, whose division was entrenched at Fort Magruder, a system of detached earthen breastworks about two miles from Williamsburg.

On the morning of May 5, Union troops under Brigadier General Joseph Hooker attacked Longstreet's position and were met with fierce opposition. Stuart's cavalry was initially held in reserve but responded admirably when called upon to check the enemy at various locations along the line. Stuart served as Longstreet's personal courier throughout the battle and found himself in the thick of the fighting during most of the day. The cavalry general also was afforded the opportunity to observe the first action by the Stuart Horse Artillery under John Pelham and was pleased by the gallantry displayed by its young commander.

Union Brigadier General Baldy Smith's division was positioned on Hooker's right, covering the Yorktown Road. Smith received word about a road through the woods that crossed a dam beyond the enemy's flank that was said to be unguarded. Second Lieutenant Custer was dispatched to investigate and returned to confirm the information. Smith obtained approval to advance across the dam and selected Brigadier General Winfield Scott Hancock's brigade for the movement. Custer, who always wanted to be in the thick of things, volunteered to accompany Hancock and was granted permission.

Custer, who had already made the initial reconnaissance, led the leading regiment, the 5th Wisconsin, across the dam, where it deployed and prepared for battle. General Hancock, with Custer at his side, readied his artillery on the crest of a hill and placed skirmishers on the right and left of the road, reinforcing the Wisconsin regiment with the 6th Maine. It was not long before their presence was contested.

"The Confederates," Custer wrote, "with courage which has never been surpassed by the troops upon either side, boldly advanced, delivering their fire as rapidly as possible, and never ceasing to utter their inspiring battle cry."

Before long, however, the ranks of the advancing Rebels were being decimated, and the charge began to waver. Hancock rode along the line exhorting his men to counterattack with a bayonet charge into the faltering enemy. The anxious Union troops hesitated—until Second Lieutenant Armstrong Custer spurred his mount and burst from their midst.

This bold act rallied the men, and, as Hancock wrote in his official report, with "Lieutenant Custer, Fifth Regular Cavalry, volunteering and leading the way on horseback," the Confederates broke into a retreat.

Custer wrote: "I captured a Captain and five men without any assistance, and a large rebel flag. It was afterwards sent up by McClellan to the President at Washington."

If this "large rebel flag" was indeed a battle flag, although none was reported missing by the Confederate regiments, it would have been one of the first, if not the first, enemy colors taken by the Army of the Potomac. That feat would have been quite an honor for Custer. Nineteenth-century combatants considered the capture of enemy battle colors to be the highest measure of glory that could be bestowed upon an individual. This resulted from the belief that the loss of their flag was a unit's greatest shame. Therefore, had Custer indeed successfully captured this flag, it would not have been surprising that none of the Confederate regiments would admit to the loss.

The fighting ended after dark when Johnston withdrew and resumed his escape up the Peninsula. The day's losses totaled about 2,200 for the Union army, and at least 1,700 Confederates had been lost.

One of the Confederate prisoners taken at Williamsburg was Armstrong Custer's former West Point classmate and friend Captain John "Gimlet" Lea, who had been badly wounded in the leg. Upon seeing Custer, Lea cried and hugged him. The two young men then exchanged information about classmates on both sides of the conflict. Custer received permission to remain with Lea for two days, and upon leaving gave Gimlet much-needed stockings and some money. Lea reciprocated by writing in Custer's notebook that, if captured, Armstrong should be given good treatment by the Southerners.

Custer rejoined his outfit for the march up the Peninsula, which reached the swollen Chickahominy River on May 20. The Rebels had burned the bridges, and engineering officers were detailed to locate potential crossing sites. Custer accompanied the army's chief engineer, Brigadier General John G. Barnard, and on a number of occasions waded into the water at various locations to test the depth, despite the danger of being exposed to enemy sharpshooters.

At one point, Custer and Lieutenant Nicholas Bowen happened upon an ideal place at a bend in the river that could support the crossing of a raiding party into enemy occupied territory. That information was passed on to headquarters. On May 24, an infantry and cavalry operation was mounted at that position seven miles below Mechanicsville at New Bridge. Custer and Bowen led two companies of the 4th Michigan to this newly found ford on the Chickahominy. One company crossed, while the other moved downstream to New Bridge where the remainder of the regiment was engaged with Confederates pickets.

The company that had crossed the stream struck the enemy on the flank, which forced the Confederates back and resulted in fifty captured. Custer advanced with a line of skirmishers and battled the Rebels for three hours before withdrawing. Bowen wrote in his official report that Custer "was the first to cross the stream, the first to open fire, and one of the last to leave the field."

General McClellan was informed of the raid and was impressed. He requested the presence of the heroic second lieutenant named Custer. The commanding general remembered seeing Custer for the first time: "He was then a slim, long-haired boy, carelessly dressed [his uniform was likely dripping water and covered with mud from the stream]. I thanked him for his gallantry, and asked him what I could do for him. He replied very modestly that he had nothing to ask, and evidently did not suppose that he had done anything to deserve extraordinary reward."

McClellan asked if Custer would be interested in serving as an aide-de-camp on his personal staff. "Upon this," McClellan wrote, "he brightened up, assured me that he would regard such service as the most gratifying he could perform; and I at once gave the necessary orders."

George Armstrong Custer, the former West Point class clown, had been chosen to assist the man whom he had previously sworn that he would "follow to the ends of the earth." That admiration and devotion would soon become mutual.

McClellan wrote: "In those days, Custer was simply a reckless, gallant boy, undeterred by fatigue, inconscious of fear. His head was always clear in danger and he always brought me clear and intelligible reports of what he saw under the heaviest fire. I became much attached to him."

The position as an aide-de-camp at army headquarters, which carried with it the brevet, or temporary, rank of captain, entailed great responsibility. Custer would report directly to General McClellan and take orders only from him. As the commander's representative, he was required to be knowledgeable about troop positions, movements, routes, and locations of the officers, and to possess the ability to modify orders on the battlefield if McClellan was unavailable. He would spend long hours in the saddle without food or sleep and, if necessary, ride into the thickest of the fighting to gather information or deliver the commander's orders.

The adventurous Custer was perfectly suited for this position, which would also serve as a valuable learning experience for him. He would in the future, however, discover that his relationship with McClellan would be a mixed blessing when the reality of politics reared its ugly head.

General James Ewell Brown Stuart, on the other hand, had learned and taught many lessons during his tenure as cavalry commander. He now desired to combine this knowledge with his inherent ambition and daring to further his career. And that opportunity was about to present itself beyond his wildest imagination.

CHAPTER FOUR

THE CAVALIER *and the* AIDE-DE-CAMP

BY THE END OF MAY, McClellan's army had approached to within six miles of Richmond, close enough to observe church spires rising above the city. McClellan placed two corps south and three north of the swollen Chickahominy near the crossroads of Seven Pines and Fair Oaks Station on the Richmond & York River Railroad. The Federal commander was confident that he could now administer "one desperate blow" to destroy the Confederacy.

It was Confederate General Joseph Johnston, however, who seized the initiative and attacked one of McClellan's isolated corps on May 31. Johnston's hastily devised plan was perhaps too complicated to be effectively executed, and the two-day battle of Seven Pines and Fair Oaks resulted in enormous casualties on both sides, including the wounding of Johnston, who was struck in the chest with a shell fragment. Jeb Stuart was unable to maneuver his horsemen due to the heavily wooded terrain, and once again acted as General Longstreet's aide.

On June 1, President Jefferson Davis replaced Johnston with Robert E. Lee, whose first order of business was to name his command the Army of Northern Virginia. He then withdrew the troops to the outskirts of Richmond to await McClellan's next move.

General Jeb Stuart believed that his relationship with the Lee family would assist in gaining the ear of his commander. He was predictably disappointed with his role thus far in the campaign and sought an opportunity to help his country and distinguish himself in the process. He boldly wrote a letter to Lee offering his ideas regarding strategy and suggesting an attack on the Federal right, south of the Chickahominy. Lee did not respond to Stuart's letter.

The opportunity that Stuart sought to play an active role, however, would soon present itself. In fact, he perhaps would have never dared imagine the extent of the accolades that would be showered upon him in the near future.

Stuart had dispatched scout John Singleton Mosby on a reconnaissance mission to determine whether McClellan had protected his army's supply line on the right flank. Mosby returned to report that the Union had only some cavalry outposts in that area, which rendered the supply line quite vulnerable. An elated Jeb Stuart immediately rode off to General Lee's headquarters at Dabbs Farm.

The commanding general was impressed with the information but required confirmation. Stuart would lead his cavalry—1,200 men—on a raiding expedition into the Union rear for the purpose of gaining intelligence, disrupting supply and communication lines, and destroying wagon trains.

At 2 a.m. on June 12, a cheerful Jeb Stuart awakened his staff and announced, "Gentlemen, in ten minutes every man must be in the saddle!" He told no one of their destination, and when asked how long they would be gone, replied, "It may be for years and it may be forever."

The morning was sweltering and muggy as Stuart and his cavalry rode steadily northward up the Brook Turnpike. Near Yellow Tavern the column left the turnpike and veered in several directions before crossing the Richmond, Fredericksburg and Potomac Railroad and heading east. By nightfall, the column had traveled twenty-two miles and halted to camp at Winston's Farm a few miles north of Ashland. Stuart, however, did not remain in camp that night but rather rode several miles with Rooney Lee to the Lee family home at Hickory Hill plantation to visit subordinate Colonel Williams C. Wickham, who was recuperating after having been wounded at Williamsburg.

Back at camp, before dawn on June 13, Stuart ordered the firing of flares to signal the beginning of the day's march for fear that the sound of bugles would attract too much attention. Soon after the march commenced, Stuart summoned John Mosby and sent him ahead of the main body to scout the vicinity of Hanover Court House.

Later that morning, Mosby returned to report the sighting of about 150 Union cavalrymen up ahead at Hanover Court House. Stuart dispatched Fitz Lee and the 1st Virginia to ride around the town without exposing themselves and establish a position where they could block the Union cavalry's retreat. The main column was then marched forward to confront the enemy. The Yankee horsemen chose to flee instead of fight and dashed away into a swamp in the direction of Mechanicsville before Lee's men could intercept them.

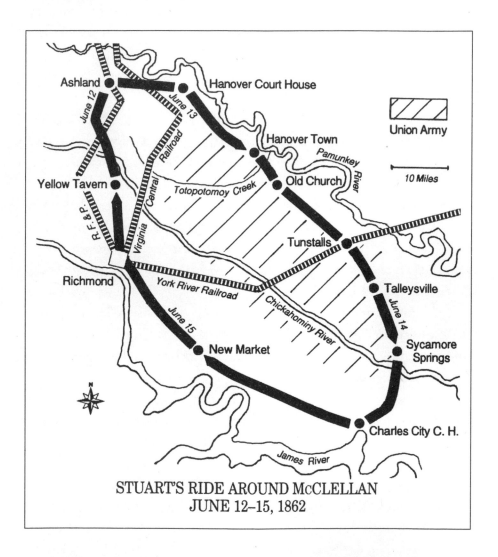

STUART'S RIDE AROUND McCLELLAN
JUNE 12–15, 1862

Stuart continued to move cautiously forward parallel with the Pamunkey River. He had entered enemy territory and understood that an attack in force by Union troops would delay his march and possibly jeopardize his mission. Stuart also was aware that his father-in-law, Brigadier General Philip St. George Cooke, was operating in the vicinity.

Rooney Lee and the 9th Virginia led the way and brushed aside small enemy outposts until reaching a bridge over Totopotomoy Creek. The Confederates crossed within full view of a detachment of Union cavalry, who simply watched from a distance. At Linney's Corners, about a mile from the bridge, however, 100 Union horsemen from the 5th Cavalry—Custer's former unit—waited in the road on the crest of a hill, ready for battle.

Stuart had the superior force and wasted no time contemplating strategy. "Form fours!" he ordered. "Draw sabers! Charge!"

His men, with Captain William Latane and his Essex Light Dragoons leading the way, surged forward, four abreast, yelling and waving their sabers. The sudden assault overwhelmed the blue-clad troopers, who scattered in confusion and fell back toward their camp in the village of Old Church.

During the skirmish, however, Captain Latane, who had ridden fifteen yards ahead of his men, was struck with two pistol shots and fell dead—the only Confederate cavalryman killed that day. Stuart's troops pressed onward into the village and captured or chased away the remaining enemy troops before burning the Union camp.

Jeb Stuart was now confronted with a difficult decision. His expedition had gathered enough intelligence to confirm that the Union right flank was unprotected and vulnerable to attack. But the area between his command and General Lee was blocked by the entire Union army. If he retraced his original route there was the possibility of calling attention to his mission, which would make the information useless. There was no question in his mind that the prudent decision would be to ride completely around McClellan's army. This circuitous route would perhaps disguise his true purpose and afford him additional opportunities to wreak havoc on the Federal supply lines.

Stuart ordered his column forward—south and east instead of west, where he could eventually cross the Chickahominy to Charles City on the James River, then northwest on the New Market Road to Richmond. Stuart advised his skeptical subordinates of his decision, and the column moved out.

Later that day, John Mosby, who was riding ahead to scout the unfamiliar terrain, happened upon a Union cavalry outpost near Tunstall Station.

Mosby had been observed and was aware that his horse was too tired to make a run for it. The Union troopers were not close enough to get a good look at him, so he resorted to a bluff. He drew his saber, turned his horse around, and motioned the Union horsemen forward. The puzzled Pennsylvania troopers sat in their saddles and watched Mosby. By that time, lead elements of Stuart's column came into view, and the Union cavalrymen fled down the road leading to their main base at White House, six miles away, to spread the alarm.

The Southern horsemen raced into Tunstall Station and overwhelmed the small detachment of Union infantry stationed there. Stuart's men had set to work cutting the telegraph wires when the shrill whistle of an approaching train could be heard. A crude barricade was quickly constructed across the rails, but the train blasted through the station while running a gauntlet of rifle fire. The cavalrymen then set fire to the railroad bridge over Black Creek and plundered and burned a wagon train. Although it was growing dark and his men were weary, Stuart pushed them on a five-and-a-half-mile ride to Talleysville.

The column, with 165 Union prisoners riding double on mules, straggled into Talleysville to discover a welcome prize—a well-stocked sutler's store. The hungry cavalrymen, according to John Esten Cooke, feasted on such delicacies as figs, beef tongue, pickles, candy, tomato catsup, preserves, lemons, cakes, sausages, molasses, crackers, and canned meats. "Never in my life," Heros Von Borcke later remarked, "have I enjoyed a bottle of wine so much."

By the time Stuart ordered them back into their saddles at midnight, appetites had been satisfied and spirits considerably lifted. Cooke wrote: "Those who in the morning had made me laugh by saying 'General Stuart is going to get this command destroyed—this movement is mad,' now regarded Stuart as the first of men; the raid as a feat of splendour and judicious daring which could not fail in terminating successfully. Such is the difference in the views of the military machine, unfed and fed."

Following an exhaustive nightlong ride with whole companies sleeping in the saddle, Stuart's cavalry reached the swollen Chickahominy River at 5 a.m. on June 14. Forge bridge had been destroyed, and heavy rains upstream had rendered the waterway uncrossable. Troopers cut down trees at the river's edge in an effort to construct a temporary bridge, but the trees were too short and were swept away by the current.

Stuart understood the precariousness of his situation. He was stalled on the riverbank, and the Union army, likely under the command of his father-in-law, was on his trail and closing fast. His scouts had located the ruins of an old bridge about a mile downstream. After examining what remained of the structure and noticing a warehouse nearby that could supply planks, Stuart decided that his only choice was to repair the bridge. Two of his men had some experience constructing bridges and came forward to supervise the rebuilding effort.

Three hours later, the bridge was completed. By one o'clock that after-noon, the entire column had crossed the river. The final horsemen to cross set the bridge on fire. While the timber burned and collapsed, a small group of Union cavalry appeared on the other side of the river. A few shots were fired as Stuart's men disappeared into the nearby woods, but the frustrated Yankees could do little more but sit and watch from the opposite bank.

Stuart's cavalry traveled another seven miles to Charles City Court House before a halt was called to allow the troops and horses rest. Stuart visited a nearby plantation and slept for several hours. At dusk, he left orders for the main column to resume its march at eleven o'clock and set out with two of his couriers for Richmond, twenty-eight miles away. During the night Stuart stopped only once for coffee, and on Sunday morning, June 15, he rode triumphantly into Richmond and made his report to General Robert E. Lee at Dabbs Farm.

Jeb Stuart had led his cavalrymen nearly 150 miles in three days on the raid around McClellan's army. He had obtained vital intelligence, confiscated or destroyed millions of dollars' worth of Union property, bloodied the enemy at will, and captured 165 prisoners and 260 horses and mules, all the while thoroughly embarrassing the Northern army. And he had lost only one man—Captain William Latane, who would become a martyr for the Confederate cause. Stuart's amazing feat was about to gain him overnight celebrity status in the South.

Beneath headlines such as "A Magnificent Achievement," "Brilliant Reconnaissance," and "Unparalleled Maneuver," Southern newspapers were filled with embellished accounts of this dangerous expedition called either the "Ride Around McClellan," "Chickahominy Raid," or "Pumunkey Expedition."

James Ewell Brown Stuart was hailed a hero by an adoring Confederate public to the extent that he was recognized while viewing a military drill. He obliged requests to make a speech from the steps of the Governor's Mansion, which was received "amidst the ring of deafening cheers." But perhaps the most significant praise came from General Lee, who called Stuart a "gallant officer" and expressed "his admiration of the courage and skill so conspicuously exhibited throughout" the raid that he proclaimed was "a brilliant exploit."

Stuart himself got into the spirit of the moment when writing his own report of the raid. The report read like a novel with such eloquent phrases as "There was something of the sublime in the implicit confidence and unquestioning trust of the rank and file in a leader guiding them straight into the very jaws of the enemy" with "the hope of striking a serious blow at a boastful and insolent foe, which would make him tremble in his shoes."

Jeb Stuart had been elevated to a lofty position rivaling that of a knight of the round table and held claim to the honorable appellation as the *Beau Sabeur* of the Confederacy. But most of all, he had bestowed upon Southern people the confidence that they could prevail in this conflict.

General Lee planned to act immediately on the intelligence that Stuart had provided. This would entail bringing Stonewall Jackson down from the Shenandoah Valley to join three other divisions which together would strike the vulnerable Federal right flank. Stuart's cavalry was dispatched to screen the left flank of Jackson's army during the movement.

General McClellan had abandoned his headquarters at White House and was in the process of moving twenty miles away to the James River by the time the Confederates attacked at Mechanicsville on June 26. The Rebels were without Jackson, who inexplicably continued to slowly march southward and failed to arrive according to his commander's wishes.

Captain George Armstrong Custer was sent by McClellan to determine the extent of the situation. He reported back and then was told by McClellan to pass the word to the beleaguered Pennsylvania Reserves to "maintain the honor of Pennsylvania." Custer then rode along the entire line repeating

McClellan's words of encouragement to each regiment he passed and was showered with cheers from the troops.

On the following day, Custer was conferring with McClellan when Stonewall Jackson finally arrived from the Valley to strike a corps five miles downstream from headquarters at Gaines Mills. Custer was asked by McClellan if he knew of any crossing sites suitable to send in reinforcements. When Custer replied that he did, McClellan sent him out to guide two brigades across the river, which was not completed until late that afternoon amidst a scene of confusion that reminded Custer of the mad scramble across Cub Run Bridge at Bull Run. McClellan kept his aide busy moving brigades into position and assisting in the removal of the wounded. Custer would later write to his sister that "I was in the saddle four consecutive nights and as many days. I generally had but one meal—coffee and hard bread—breakfast."

Stuart's cavalry was held in reserve on Jackson's left flank during the battle of Gaines Mill on June 27 but nonetheless contributed to the effort. John Pelham's artillery, with only one Napoleon gun, dueled with eight guns of the enemy and held his ground in what Stuart later called "one of the most gallant and heroic feats of the war." In a bloody battle, the Confederates eventually routed the Federals from the field, including Stuart's father-in-law, Philip St. George Cooke, who had ordered an ill-fated cavalry charge and was afterward relieved of his command for the duration of the war.

At this point, McClellan abandoned his advance on Richmond and began to withdraw down the James River. The next morning, Stuart was ordered by Lee to disrupt Union supply lines on the Pumunkey.

On the march, his men cut down telegraph wires and ripped up tracks on the Richmond and York River Railroad before halting within four miles of McClellan's main supply base, a plantation called White House that had previously been the home of Rooney Lee. That night, Stuart and a distressed Rooney Lee watched as the sky lit up as "vast clouds of smoke rose hundreds of feet in air, and explosions of shells and other ammunition" sounded like a battle. The Union soldiers had evidently set fire to their supply base.

At dawn on June 29, Stuart, owing to rumors that the base held 5,000 Union troops, cautiously approached the smoking ruins of White House.

He discovered that the troops had vacated the area, but a Union gunboat, the *USS Marblehead,* was tied up at the landing. He dispatched seventy-five troopers, who advanced within forty paces of the boat and peppered the deck with rifle fire. The Union navy countered by sending ashore a detachment of sharpshooters who offered stiff resistance. Finally, Stuart ordered up one of Pelham's howitzers, which quickly chased away both the Union skirmishers and the gunboat. Stuart was greatly amused by the fact that his horsemen had been victorious in a naval battle.

The Federal troops had left behind quite a supply of commissary supplies at White House, which the Southern cavalrymen put to good use. Stuart remained at White House resting both men and horses until July 1, when a courier from General Lee arrived with orders for the cavalry to rejoin Jackson's troops. Stuart spent a frustrating day trying to locate Jackson and missed the fierce battle of Malvern Hill, the last of the Seven Days Campaign. When the Federals withdrew, however, Stuart's cavalry harassed the rear guard and rounded up stragglers and collected abandoned weapons. Although this campaign had proved costly to both sides, Lee, who believed that he should have destroyed the Federal Army, had managed to successfully relieve pressure on Richmond, which was a victory in itself.

On July 25, James Ewell Brown Stuart received his commission as major general. The new two-star general, in accord with his rank, would command a division of cavalry comprised of two brigades. One brigade would be commanded by Stuart's warm friend, twenty-seven-year-old newly commissioned brigadier general Fitzhugh Lee, Robert's nephew, veteran of the Indian wars, and one of George Armstrong Custer's instructors at West Point. The other brigade went to new brigadier general Wade Hampton, a forty-four-year-old South Carolinian whose management of his family's plantations had made him one of the wealthiest men in the South. Stuart's division would be augmented the following month by the addition of another brigade commanded by thirty-six-year-old Brigadier General Beverly Robertson, whom Stuart would call "by far the most troublesome man I have to deal with."

While Stuart drilled his troops and held reviews, with ample time off to enjoy Sam Sweeney's banjo playing, Armstrong Custer was detailed by

General McClellan to accompany a reconnaissance mission toward Southern lines comprised of 300 cavalrymen under the command of Colonel William W. Averill.

By late morning on August 2, the patrol had traveled forty miles. Custer was scouting ahead when he came upon a regiment of Confederate cavalry near White Oak Swamp. He reported his discovery, and Colonel Averill ordered a charge. The surprised Rebels scattered in the face of the assault, many of them surrendering when realizing that their escape route was cut off. Custer, who had chased and overtaken a Confederate officer, called twice for the man to surrender. When there was no reply, Custer shot him from the saddle—the first man he had killed in the war.

Custer also captured a soldier and confiscated a double-barreled shotgun and a bright bay horse, which he planned to send home to his brother, Boston. Other accounts relate that Custer captured or was given a sword—a "Toledo Blade"—from the saddle of a riderless mount. This heavy blade was inscribed with the Spanish sentiment: *No ni tires sin razon, No mi envaines sin honra.* ("Draw me not without provocation. Sheathe me not without honor"). In the tradition of King Arthur's Excalibur, Custer was said to have been awarded the special sword by virtue of the fact that he was the only one strong enough to heft the blade above his head.

The raiding party returned without losing a man, and Custer was cited for "gallant and spirited conduct." But all was not well at headquarters when Custer reported back to General McClellan.

After McClellan's poor results in the Peninsular Campaign, President Lincoln decided to reorganize his army. McClellan's corps was recalled to the capital and would be combined with the armies of Generals Nathaniel Banks, John C. Fremont, and Irvin McDowell to create the Army of Virginia, under the command of Major General John Pope. McClellan predictably was opposed to the plan and lingered until mid-August before marching his troops toward Fort Monroe for transport to Washington.

When Custer arrived in Williamsburg with McClellan's staff, he learned that his Confederate friend Gimlet Lea, who was on parole and recuperating in that town, was about to be married. Custer, dressed in his blue uniform, served as groomsman during the ceremony and proudly stood beside his gray-clad friend. Lea would soon be exchanged and, according to Custer, "fighting for what he *supposes* to be right!"

General Lee understood that if McClellan's army managed to join Pope's troops in northern or central Virginia, the Confederates would face almost unbeatable odds. Lee decided to attack Pope with Stonewall Jackson's corps before the Federals could be reinforced. Stuart, with the brigades of Fitz Lee and Beverly Robertson, would support Jackson by riding east to Pope's rear and wreak havoc on Union supply lines and patrol retreat routes while Jackson attacked from the left rear.

On the night of August 17, Jeb Stuart had stopped at a farmhouse near Verdiersville and dispatched adjutant Major Norman Fitzhugh to ride down the road to seek the whereabouts of Fitz Lee's brigade, which was late in arriving. Before long, the sound of a cavalry column could be heard approaching the farmhouse from within the thick pre-dawn mist. Stuart walked to the fence by the road to greet Lee, perhaps with intentions of dressing him down for his tardiness. The oncoming horsemen appearing from the mist, however, were not Lee's brigade but the Union cavalry.

Pistol shots cracked behind him as Stuart leaped aboard his horse, jumped a picket fence, and headed for the woods. The general barely escaped capture, and, to his humiliation, the Yankees confiscated his prize plumed hat and other personal belongings. In a letter to his wife Stuart wrote, "I intend to make the Yankees pay dearly for that hat."

Worst yet, Major Fitzhugh, who had been carrying a signed copy of Lee's plan of attack, had been captured by that same cavalry unit. Pope responded to the information taken from Fitzhugh by withdrawing across the Rappahannock to escape Lee's trap.

The opportunity for Stuart to avenge the loss of his hat occurred on August 22. General Lee approved a proposal by Stuart to raid into the rear of Pope's army to disrupt supply and communications and destroy the railroad bridge over Cedar Run. Stuart and 1,500 horsemen, with Custer's close friend Tom Rosser commanding the lead regiment, swept into Pope's headquarters at Catlett's Railroad Station just after dark to face only token opposition.

The raiders rifled a payroll safe containing $500,000 in greenbacks and $20,000 in gold and appropriated a dispatch book filled with vital information about the location and disposition of the Union forces that was of great interest to General Lee. In addition, they confiscated General Pope's personal baggage, including his dress coat, which was put on display in Richmond, and rode off with about 300 Yankee prisoners. The only downside to the mission was that rain prevented them from destroying the bridge over Cedar Run. Otherwise, Stuart had satisfactorily restored the plume in his hat and had once again demonstrated the versatility and daring of his horsemen to the delight of the adoring Southern citizenry.

Stuart's raid had confirmed that the route to the Union rear was unopposed, and Lee decided to exploit that advantage by attempting yet another attack on Pope before he could be reinforced by McClellan. Stonewall Jackson marched on August 25, and in two days' time had severed Pope's connection to the Washington railroad, looted his supply depot at Manassas Junction, and entrenched his men on a ridge overlooking the Manassas, or Bull Run, battlefield—the place where the year before Jackson had earned his nickname, Stonewall. Pope turned his troops to face Jackson on August 29, and a vicious battle raged for two days.

Jeb Stuart's cavalry rode tirelessly throughout the engagement, gathering information and opening lines of communication with James Longstreet's command as it moved to support Jackson on the flank. At one point, Stuart executed a brilliant ploy by having his men tie pine branches on their halters and drag them along a road to create clouds of dust that convinced Union Major General Fitz John Porter that infantry was massing. Porter postponed his attack, and he later stood a court-martial and was dismissed from the service for his blunder.

On the final day, August 30, Stuart supported Longstreet's five divisions, with Tom Rosser admirably commanding four artillery batteries, and Pope's Union troops were beaten into an unorganized retreat to Centreville. The Confederates pursued, but Pope managed to extricate his army and cross the Potomac toward Washington with Lee hot on his heels.

Two days after this Second Battle of Bull Run, President Lincoln, in a move hailed by the rank and file troopers, restored General George McClellan to command of the Union army. With Lee invading Maryland,

McClellan quickly marched with his energized army to meet the challenge, arriving in Rockville on September 7.

Stuart's cavalry was assigned the duties of guarding Lee's twenty-mile front across Maryland and reporting about the enemy's strength, location, and intentions. His military tasks, however, did not prevent the fun-loving cavalry commander from enjoying himself along the way.

On September 8, Stuart organized a ball at Urbanna with music provided by the 18th Mississippi Infantry band. At about 11 p.m., the festivities were interrupted by artillery fire. Stuart and his men rode off to the sound of the guns. Pelham's cannons quickly ended the brief skirmish, and by 1 a.m. the cavalrymen had returned to resume dancing. Several had been wounded, however, and the ladies—"ministering angels," Blackford called them—still dressed in their elegant gowns, attended to their needs.

McClellan cautiously resumed his pursuit of Lee. By a quirk of fate, he acquired a copy—one of nine given to the various commanders—of Lee's Special Order No. 191, which outlined Confederate plans for the Maryland campaign. A Union private had discovered the orders wrapped around three cigars in a meadow where Confederate soldiers had previously camped. The wary McClellan thought it might be a trap and waited two days before confronting Lee's army. That hesitation on McClellan's part afforded Lee time to position his men on the crest of a four-mile ridge east of Sharpsburg, Maryland, beside a creek called Antietam.

The battle of Antietam on September 17 was the bloodiest single day of the war. Seventy thousand Union troops faced thirty-nine thousand Confederates. When calm was restored and the bloody storm subsided, the field was littered with more than 26,000 casualties—13,700 Confederates and 12,350 Union soldiers were dead, wounded, or missing.

McClellan received reinforcements on September 18 but hesitated again. This pause gave Lee time to escape across the Potomac into Virginia during the night. At one point in the battle, Stuart's troopers had fought dismounted alongside the infantry on the extreme left, but they now assumed the duty of screening Lee's retreat.

McClellan followed without much enthusiasm, never close enough to engage his enemy. While the Union army recuperated in the vicinity of

Sharpsburg, President Lincoln issued his preliminary Emancipation Proclamation, which for the Northerners meant another goal to attain in this conflict of states' rights and restoring the Union, that of human freedom.

At Antietam, Armstrong Custer had been kept busy at McClellan's headquarters. At one point, however, he and another aide, Lieutenant James P. Martin, were detailed to General Alfred Pleasonton and attached to the 8th Illinois at South Mountain. Near Boonsboro, Custer and a detachment were returning to headquarters when they encountered and captured several hundred Confederate stragglers and two abandoned cannons. Pleasonton cited Custer and Martin for heroism, and McClellan later reported the incident to President Lincoln.

On September 26, Custer escorted a group of paroled Confederate soldiers across the Potomac under a flag of truce and happened upon several of the enemy who had been classmates or friends. The gregarious Custer and his Rebel acquaintances "had an hour's social chat, discussing the war in a friendly way."

In his role as a general's aide, Custer was traveling on the fringes of danger, but he no doubt would have preferred to have been in the thick of the fighting. He wrote a letter of a curious nature to his cousin on October 3 while Lincoln visited the camp, which read in part: "I must say that I shall regret to see the war end. I would be willing, yes glad, to see a battle every day during my life."

Skeptics might comment that these words were merely the false bravado of a man who, due to his position with McClellan, had not endured the daily hardships of war when compared to the average cavalry officer. That opinion, however, fails to take into consideration the fact that Custer possessed the character of a natural-born cavalier—bold, daring, and ambitious almost to a fault. His revealing statement truly demonstrates how he yearned to prove his ability on the field of battle and that he feared that hostilities would end before he had the chance to attain the glory that he envisioned for himself.

There certainly had been no lack of battle experience for Jeb Stuart, but he did not intend to remain idle when the opportunity for further distinction was only an expedition away. On October 8, 1862, Lee approved a plan by Stuart to lead a raiding party to Chambersburg, Pennsylvania. The purpose of the mission, in addition to gathering "all information of the position, force, and probable intention of the enemy," was to collect horses, snatch hostages for exchange, if possible, and destroy the railroad bridge over Conococheague Creek. Stuart chose 600 men from each of his three brigades and John Pelham commanding four guns to join the expedition.

At dawn on October 10, Stuart's 1,800 horsemen crossed the Potomac at McCoy's Ford and headed north. By midmorning the column had entered Pennsylvania, and Stuart assigned 200 men from each brigade to visit farms along the way to appropriate horses. The day was dark and cloudy with intermittent rain, which had chased farmers inside their barns to thresh wheat and made the task of grabbing horses relatively easy. By 7 p.m., the Southern horsemen had traveled forty unopposed miles to reach Chambersburg, at the immediate rear of McClellan's army now at Harpers Ferry.

Stuart seized the town without any resistance, bivouacked for the night, and the following morning began sacking stores of arms and ammunition and military clothing. The cavalrymen burned the government depot, railroad machine shops, and a warehouse stocked with ammunition that continued to explode all morning. One brigade was sent to destroy the bridge over Conococheague Creek, but the structure had been built of iron and could not be burned or demolished with axes.

On the morning of October 11, Stuart surprised his men by directing them east out of Chambersburg, toward Gettysburg. He intended to employ the tactic of doing exactly the opposite of what he thought the enemy would expect. Yankee infantry would be looking for them on their former trail, and the terrain on this new route would be more advantageous to cavalry movement than the hilly country over which they had passed on their approach to Chambersburg. In other words, Stuart's cavalry would once again ride around McClellan's army on the return trip.

Stuart justified his decision to adjutant William Blackford with the preface: "I want to explain to you my reasons for selecting this route for return; and if I do not survive, I want you to vindicate my memory." Blackford assured Stuart that he understood and approved of the reasons and would certainly make them known should the need arise. This answer apparently satisfied Stuart that his actions would not be interpreted as simply a grandstand ploy to gain glory—whether true or not.

Stuart rode with the advance guard of a column that, on account of its sizeable herd of captured horses, stretched for almost five miles down the road. His couriers were kept on the move delivering his instructions to close up ranks. After a forty-five-mile march, Stuart crossed back into Maryland near Emmitsburg, where the local citizenry showered the cavalrymen with cheers, flowers, and gifts. From there the column traveled over back roads for thirty-three miles in a southerly direction until reaching Hyattstown at dawn on October 12. Only twelve miles separated them from Virginia soil, but standing in their way of crossing the Potomac at White's Ford was a line of entrenched Union infantrymen.

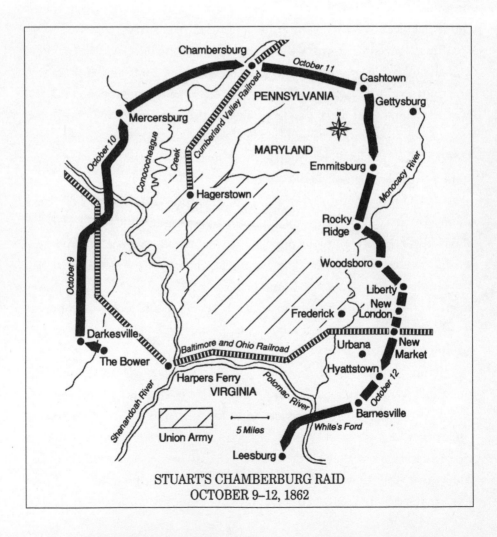

STUART'S CHAMBERBURG RAID
OCTOBER 9–12, 1862

General McClellan had been receiving reports of Stuart's movements and had dispatched Pleasonton's cavalry to intercept the Confederate column. Pleasonton executed an extraordinary march of seventy-eight miles in twenty-eight hours in a noble attempt to catch his enemy—once passing like ships in the night within four miles of Stuart—but to no avail. The only hope of stopping the Confederate raiders now would be in the hands of the infantry waiting near White's Ford on the Chesapeake and Ohio Canal.

Rooney Lee brought up his guns and dismounted some troops for an assault on the Union position until realizing the enormity of the task. He then borrowed a page from Stuart's book and tried a bluff. Lee dispatched a courier to the Federal commander demanding that he surrender, warning that he had sufficient troops to destroy the position. Following a few rounds from Pelham's guns for encouragement, the ruse worked, and the Yankees withdrew from their position.

The Southern cavalry uniformly crossed the river. Stuart had started his Chambersburg Raid with 1,800 men and led that exact number into Leesburg that afternoon, along with about 1,200 captured horses, having left in his wake at least $250,000 in damage. The mounted column had traveled 126 miles and covered the final ninety miles of their route in thirty-six hours without stopping.

Stuart had once again embarrassed McClellan and the Union army with a bold raid, and this fact was widely reported to his admiring public. "The country is once more cheered by Stuart's cavalry," wrote the *Richmond Examiner*. The *Dispatch* added, "All honor to General Stuart and the brave boys that assist in upholding his banner." General Lee called the raid "eminently successful . . . he deserves much credit for his prudence and enterprise."

Stuart himself officially commemorated the event with a grand ball, which was attended by his wife, Flora. He also received a gift of a pair of golden spurs from a woman in Baltimore. Stuart would adopt the sobriquet "The Knight of the Golden Spurs" and even sign some his correspondence with the abbreviation "K. G. S."

Stuart may have been celebrated as a national hero, but fame did not render him immune from personal tragedy. His five-year-old daughter, Flora, had been gravely ill, but duty had prevented him from traveling to visit her in Lynchburg. He was awakened during the wee hours of November 6 by Major Von Borcke with a telegram containing sad news. Little Flora had died three days earlier and had been buried the next day. Stuart was devastated by the loss. To his wife, he wrote: "God has shielded me thus far from bodily harm, but I feel perfect resignation to go at His bidding, and join my little Flora. I cannot write more." He later told John Esten Cooke: "I will never get over it—never."

Union General George McClellan was also the recipient of bad news on November 7. Word reached the general that two days earlier President Lincoln had replaced him as commander of the Army of the Potomac with Major General Ambrose E. Burnside. Farewells and a final review were held, and McClellan with his staff members boarded a special train to Washington.

The loyal Armstrong Custer was predictably saddened by this turn of events and, rather than recognize the military faults of his commander, blamed the politics of the Republican administration for deposing the Democrat McClellan. Regardless of the true reason, there was little for Custer to do but return to Monroe, Michigan, and await orders. His disappointment with McClellan's fate would quickly become secondary in importance when another special person would enter his life.

On Thanksgiving Day, Custer attended a party at Boyd's Seminary and was introduced to Elizabeth "Libbie" Bacon. Libbie was the only child of Judge Daniel S. Bacon, a descendant of the Plymouth Colony who had at one time or another been a farmer, schoolteacher, a member of the Territorial Legislature, losing candidate for Michigan lieutenant governor in 1837, a probate judge, and director of a bank and a railroad. Needless to say, Judge Bacon was one of Monroe's most influential and respected citizens. And Libbie, a slender, spirited twenty-year-old with chestnut brown hair and light blue-gray eyes, was considered the prettiest girl in town and did not lack for suitors.

Armstrong was immediately smitten with Libbie. He dreamed about her that night—a classic case of love at first sight. The Bacons, however, were members of the upper class, and Custer was the son of the village smithy, a boy from the other side of the tracks. Custer ignored this social disparity and relentlessly courted Libbie by showing up wherever she happened to be and continuously strolling past her home. Armstrong even began attending the local Presbyterian church and sat where the two could exchange glances during the services. Libbie admired his perseverance but was not quite sure what to make of this handsome army lieutenant and remained standoffish to his advances.

While Custer dallied in Monroe awaiting orders, Ambrose Burnside had moved his Army of the Potomac to the outskirts of Fredericksburg, where he planned to cross the Rappahannock River, seize the town, and move on to attack Richmond. Bridges across the river had been destroyed, and it was seventeen days until pontoon bridges had been positioned to ferry his 120,000 men across the river. This delay afforded the Confederate army time to evacuate Fredericksburg and deploy 78,000 soldiers in the surrounding hills.

Following two days of shelling, Burnside attacked on the morning of December 13. The Union soldiers advanced twelve times, and each time the Confederates held their ground. Stuart, who was unhurt when shot through his fur collar, covered the right flank and saw little action. His artillery batteries under the "Gallant" Major John Pelham, however, distinguished themselves by halting the advance of an entire Union division. The two-day battle, which Stuart later called a "tremendous slaughter," cost the Union army approximately 12,653 men and the Confederates 5,309, another devastating defeat for the North orchestrated by a blundering general whose absurd plan to cross a river into the waiting guns of the enemy should have been scrapped by the president.

Stuart spent Christmas enjoying a dinner attended by his family and General Lee but determined that the holidays could be best celebrated with another raid into enemy territory. On December 26, Stuart rode out with 1,800 troops—sending Wade Hampton to Ocoquan, Fitz Lee to south of Quantico, and Rooney Lee to Dumfries—and once again disrupted Union communication and supply lines. At Burke's Station on the Orange & Alexandria Railroad, just fifteen miles from Washington, the mischievous Stuart sent a telegram to the United States Quartermaster of the US Army, Major General Montgomery Meigs, that read: "Quality of mules lately furnished me very poor. Interferes seriously with movement of captured wagons. J. E. B. Stuart."

The column then completed a wide circuit to elude Yankee pursuit and returned to camp on New Year's Day with 200 prisoners, about 200 horses, and twenty wagons loaded with supplies. Stuart's raids had become so commonplace that the newspapers gave only scant attention to this one, other than the telegram, which was the source of great amusement.

Contrary to Stuart's habit of circling his enemy, Armstrong Custer had executed a frontal assault on two fronts. The first one, an attempt to secure the colonelcy of the 7th Michigan Cavalry, had fared poorly in its initial stages. The appointment involved political patronage, and the Republican governor took a dim view of Custer's Democratic views and associations. His pursuit of Libbie Bacon, on the other hand, had showed some promise.

Custer had pledged his undying love to Libbie, which she rebuffed. But his persistence had softened her heart to the extent that she wrote in her diary: "He is noble, brave and generous and he loves, I believe, with an intensity that few know of or as few ever can love. He tells me he would sacrifice every earthly hope to gain my love and I tell him if I could I would give it to him. I told him to forget me and he said he *never could* forget me and I told him I never should forget *him* and I wished to be his true friend through life but it is no use to offer myself as a friend for he will never think of me otherwise than his wife. Oh, *Love, love,* how many are made miserable as well as happy by the all powerful influence."

Judge Bacon, who had noticed Custer's interest in Libbie, did not fancy his only child married to a common military man, especially one whom he had witnessed in an intoxicated state the previous spring. The judge made Libbie promise to not see Custer again or write to him when he returned to duty. Libbie secretly gave Armstrong her ring at a party but soon afterward informed him that she must abide by her father's wishes and never see him again. Judge Bacon might have thought that he had succeeded in saving his daughter but had perhaps underestimated the determination of a young man in love—particularly a young man like Armstrong Custer who relished a challenge.

Jeb Stuart also suffered a painful loss in March 1863—one that would affect Custer as well. On the morning of March 17, Union Brigadier General William W. Averell and 2,100 cavalrymen crossed the Rappahannock at

Kelly's Ford and were advancing toward the Orange & Alexandria Railroad. Stuart's troops rushed to confront Averill, and during the ensuing engagement an artillery shell burst near Major John Pelham. Fragments from the shell struck Stuart's gallant artillery commander in the back of the head, and he died the following afternoon without regaining consciousness.

The resolute Federals had been repulsed, but Stuart had lost his beloved subordinate and Custer had lost his West Point friend. The Confederate cavalry commander wept over Pelham's body, then kissed his forehead and whispered an emotional "Farewell" before turning away in anguish. He ordered his troops to wear a black mourning cloth around their left arms and renamed his headquarters Camp Pelham.

On January 25, 1863, President Lincoln had reacted to the debacle at Fredericksburg by replacing Ambrose Burnside with Major General Joseph Hooker. The new commander would spend the next few months reorganizing and equipping his troops in preparation for a spring campaign.

Armstrong Custer's campaign in Monroe to win the heart of Libbie Bacon had continued with the stealth of a reconnaissance behind enemy lines. The two would share moments together at social gatherings or at church, and convinced Libbie's friend, Annette "Nettie" Humphrey, to serve as a go-between to pass notes and messages. By April 8, Libbie's twenty-first birthday, when Custer boarded a train to return to duty in Washington, love had blossomed between them, but the future of their relationship had not by any means been settled due to Judge Bacon's adamant opposition.

First Lieutenant Custer arrived in Washington on April 10 and was informed that General McClellan had requested his assistance in preparing the official reports of his tenure as commander. Custer traveled to New York where he lived in the Metropolitan Hotel while working at McClellan's "magnificently furnished" home. The task was completed by the end of the month, and Custer was assigned temporary office duty at the War Department.

By the end of April, "Fighting Joe" Hooker had planned an operation designed to outflank the Army of Northern Virginia. To that end, he marched his 75,000 troops across the Rappahannock River, through the second-growth forest known as the Wilderness, and established his headquarters near Chancellorsville. On April 28, Hooker sent three corps and cavalry to Kelly's Ford while General Stoneman's cavalry attempted to maneuver to the rear of the Confederate army.

General Lee countered Hooker by dispatching Stuart to gather intelligence and hinder the enemy's advance as much as possible while bringing up his own troops. On May 1, the 50,000-man Confederate infantry under Stonewall Jackson attacked its enemy in open country near Chancellorsville. Although the battle was going well for the Union, Hooker inexplicably ordered his men to break contact and withdraw into the timber encircling the crossroads of Chancellorsville.

That evening, Generals Lee and Jackson sat on cracker boxes while warming their hands over a campfire and discussed strategy. Stuart's cavalry had discovered that Hooker's right flank was unprotected. Lee decided to take advantage of that intelligence and devised an extremely risky and daring plan to divide his force. Jackson's 26,000 troops would march to the Union rear and attack, which in the meantime would leave only about 17,000 men at Lee's disposal to hold off an advance by Hooker. If successful, they could crush Hooker between them, but if Hooker detected the maneuver, he could turn on either fragmented force and likely overpower them. Lee decided that it was worth the gamble.

At 5 a.m. on May 2, Stuart's cavalry led Jackson's corps on its fourteen-mile all-day march through the Wilderness, around the Union army's vulnerable right flank. At twilight, Jackson's troops charged into their unsuspecting foe. The surprised Union infantrymen were quickly routed into a panicked retreat and disappeared into the darkness before Jackson could overtake them.

That evening, while on a reconnaissance mission between lines, the South suffered a tragedy. Jackson was mistakenly shot and severely wounded by members of his own 18th North Carolina. A. P. Hill, Jackson's second in command, had also been wounded earlier. Jeb Stuart was summoned to take command of Jackson's corps.

When the sun rose the following day, Stuart launched an attack into the dense undergrowth where the entrenched Union soldiers waited. Each charge of the Southerners was met with fierce opposition and repulsed.

At one critical juncture in the seesaw battle, Stuart, in the words of one infantryman, "leaped his horse over the breastworks near my company, and when he had reached a point about opposite the center of the brigade, while the men were loudly cheering him, he waved his hand toward the enemy and shouted, 'Forward men! Forward! Just follow me!' The men were wild with enthusiasm. The veriest coward on earth would have felt his blood thrill, and his heart leap with courage and resolution. The men poured over the breastworks after him like a wide raging torrent overcoming its barriers."

Stuart's horse, Chancellor, was shot out from beneath him, but he remounted and rallied a regiment that had wavered before the enemy onslaught by grabbing the regimental colors and leading a counter assault. He led his men on several more brazen charges, which dislodged the enemy from its positions and, supported by effective artillery fire, pushed the Union troops steadily backward.

"Stuart was all activity," an aide wrote, "and wherever the danger was greatest there was he to be found ... and in the midst of the hottest fire I heard him, to an old melody, hum the words, 'Old Joe Hooker, get out of the Wilderness.'"

Finally, Hooker, who was wounded in an artillery barrage, ordered his men to fall back toward the Rappahannock. The battle of Chancellorsville was perhaps Lee's greatest victory thus far, with much of the credit belonging to the Knight of the Golden Spurs.

Jeb Stuart had distinguished himself once more, this time as an infantry commander. He was also confident in the supremacy of his cavalry, which had not as yet come within two whoops and a holler of being challenged by Union horsemen. In fact, his troopers were now known as the Invincibles to the frustrated enemy.

On the other hand, George Armstrong Custer's participation in the war thus far had been that of a mere ambitious aide-de-camp to various generals, and presently an officer without a permanent assignment. This was not the scenario that he had envisioned when he had departed West Point, and he yearned to feel that he was making a difference for the Union.

The upcoming cavalry actions, however, would serve to alter the fortunes of both cavalrymen. By the time these operations had concluded, one would endure widespread criticism for the first time in the war; the other would be highly praised and stand on the threshold of extraordinary advancement.

CHAPTER FIVE

BRANDY STATION

IT WAS APPROPRIATE and perhaps predestined that James Ewell Brown Stuart and George Armstrong Custer both would be in the saddle on the same field in what would be the largest true cavalry engagement of the war.

The twenty-three-year-old Custer was offered the opportunity to be rescued from a dreary desk job at the War Department in Washington on May 6 when an official invitation arrived. Brigadier General Alfred Pleasonton, commander of the 1st Cavalry Division of the newly organized Cavalry Corps, requested that Custer serve as aide-de-camp on his staff.

Fighting Joe Hooker had reorganized the Union cavalry and its purpose in early 1863. McClellan had previously assigned mounted regiments to infantry brigades, which greatly diminished their effectiveness in battle. Hooker had placed the cavalry in a corps of three divisions under the command of Major General George Stoneman and employed independent tactics patterned after those of Stuart's cavalry.

The Federal horsemen had been dispatched on a raid against Lee's communication lines to Richmond during the Chancellorsville Campaign, and the absence had contributed to the Union defeat. Pleasonton, however, had personally distinguished himself in that engagement by routing a small band of Confederate infantry, and he was introduced several days later by Hooker to President Abraham Lincoln with the words: "Mr. President, this is General Pleasonton, who saved the Army of the Potomac the other night!" Soon after, when Stoneman journeyed to Washington to seek treatment for piles, Hooker seized the opportunity to replace his ineffective commander "temporarily" with the more aggressive Pleasonton.

Pleasonton, a West Pointer and veteran of the Mexican War and various frontier posts, had been promoted to brigadier general following the Seven

Days' Campaign, and had led a division at Antietam, Fredericksburg, and Chancellorsville. In the tradition of a cavalryman, he was a self-confident man, a fastidious dresser, and, perhaps more importantly, had the advantage of being politically well-connected.

His ambition, a trait that compelled some to observe that he had already risen beyond the level of his field competency, was no secret to anyone. Rumors about his lack of bravery under fire were also commonplace. He became known for embellishing his own role in a battle or blatantly taking credit for actions in which he did not participate. Postwar writers would dub him the "Knight of Romance" on account of his dispatches that were said to be full of "sound and fury, signifying nothing." To be fair, some criticism of Pleasonton likely stemmed from the fact that Winfield Scott Hancock had been the popular candidate for cavalry commander. Hancock, as commander of II Corps, would in the near future win great acclaim at Gettysburg.

Pleasonton had become acquainted with Custer's impetuosity and ability to relate accurate reconnaissance reports when both served with McClellan, and for that reason had requested his service as an aide-de-camp. In the words of Custer's future personal bugler, Joseph Fought: "Genl. Pleasonton, a very active officer, was always anxious to be posted about what was doing in front of him. He himself could not be in the front all the time, and in that respect his Trusties [aides] were more valuable to him than his brigade commanders. If Lt. Custer observed that it was important to make a movement or charge he would tell the commander to do it, would not dare question, because he knew Lt. Custer was working under Genl. Pleasonton who would confirm every one of his instructions and movements."

Custer had at first declined the invitation by Pleasonton out of loyalty to McClellan. But, after reconsidering that decision, he wholeheartedly transferred his fierce allegiance to his new commander. He termed Pleasonton "an excellent cavalry officer," and was quite pleased with his new position. The thirty-nine-year-old Pleasonton responded to Custer's fidelity with what could be called a paternal affection. Custer emulated Pleasonton in dress and mannerisms—studying in particular the art of self-promotion—and became known as "Pleasonton's pet."

Pleasonton's confidence in Custer was evidenced on May 20 when he dispatched his aide under orders from General Hooker on a dangerous mission into enemy territory.

Custer was assigned to accompany a squadron, two companies of seventy-five men each from the 3rd Indiana Cavalry, in an effort to intercept a party of Southern civilians from Richmond who were said to be traveling down the Rappahannock to Urbanna in possession of important Confederate mail and a large amount of money.

The Union detachment departed down the Potomac aboard two steamers after dark on the night of May 21 and arrived at eleven o'clock the following morning at Moon's Landing on the banks of the Yocomico River. They quickly mounted, rode forty miles in a little more than five hours to the vicinity of Urbanna, and concealed themselves in the woods until the next morning.

When an approaching Rebel sailing vessel was sighted, Custer and ten other men set out in pursuit. The chase was on for some ten miles until the vessel was forced to run aground. Custer and company captured the boat and passengers, whose identities were revealed as the ones they had been ordered to capture, and who indeed were in possession of a large sum of Confederate money.

Custer, accompanied by four men, went ashore and cautiously approached a nearby mansion. Custer observed a Confederate officer who was relaxing on the veranda engrossed in reading a copy of Shakespeare's *Hamlet*. This man was readily taken prisoner and, with apologies by Custer to the ladies of the house, removed to the boat as their captive.

Custer and twenty men in three small boats then visited Urbanna on the opposite bank. They burned two schooners and the bridge over Urbanna Bay, until finally returning to the north bank. There, they captured twelve more prisoners, boxes of Confederate supplies, and thirty horses, one of which, a blooded iron-gray stallion, Custer appropriated for himself and named Roanoke. The ambitious raiding party departed with their prisoners and returned home without suffering a casualty.

In a letter dated May 26, Custer related his account of the raid to Annette Humphrey, whom he knew would relay the thrilling tale to Libbie Bacon, and added, "General Hooker sent for me and complimented me very highly on the success of my expedition and the manner in which I had executed his orders. He said it could not have been better done."

Custer's achievement fueled his ambition for a command of his own. He was aware that some of his West Point classmates, particularly on the Confederate side, had already risen to field-officer status. His pursuit of the colonelcy of the 7th Michigan Brigades that had commenced while on furlough in Monroe continued when he mailed another request to Republican Governor Austin Blair on May 31. He had enclosed a letter of recommendation from General Pleasonton with an endorsement from General Hooker that read in part: "I cheerfully concur in the recommendation of Brig. Genl. Pleasonton. He [Custer] is a young officer of great promise and of uncommon merit."

It has been suggested that the audacious Custer went as far as to visit the camp of the 5th Michigan while its commander was absent and sought support in the form of a petition requesting his appointment from the brigade's officers, to no avail. The officers presumedly considered Custer too young for the command and likely resented the brashness of someone who would seek to dispose their commander in such an underhanded manner.

Another stumbling block in Custer's pathway to command a Michigan unit was that he had been branded a "McClellan Man," which was the kiss of death with any request to a Republican governor. McClellan, after all, had been rumored as the potential Democratic opponent to Lincoln in the next election.

Governor Blair predictably denied Custer's request on the grounds that the accepted custom was to award commissions to the men who had helped in the recruitment of the regiment. Privately, however, Blair informed Isaac Christiancy, founder of the state Republican party and a justice on the Michigan Supreme Court, that "His [Custer's] people are rebel Democrats. He himself is a McClellan man; indeed McClellan's fair-haired boy, I should say . . . I cannot place myself . . . whatever his qualifications."

Custer, much like Democrat George B. McClellan who had opposed policies of the Republican administration, had been a victim of politics. True, West Pointers his same age were colonels commanding Union regiments, but they were Republicans. He did not, however, intend to allow this minor setback to interfere with his pursuit of a command. Custer pledged to distinguish himself in such a manner that he could not be denied again. Little did he know that opportunity was within his reach just across the Rappahannock River.

Pleasanton reported to Hooker that Brigadier General David Gregg's division had been patrolling on May 28 within fifteen miles of Culpeper Court House and had noted that three Confederate cavalry brigades under Jeb Stuart had moved from Fredericksburg to that location. Pleasonton offered the opinion that Lee was assembling his troops for a major offensive in the North. Hooker was skeptical, but Pleasonton persisted. Reconnaissance balloons and additional reports appeared to confirm Pleasonton's theory. By June 4, Hooker was convinced, and informed the president that he intended to engage those Confederates under Stuart that were believed to be camped along the Rappahannock.

Hooker ordered Pleasonton to launch a June 9 two-pronged surprise attack—at Beverly Ford and at Kelly's Ford—comprised of 11,000 men, a number that included about 2,800 infantrymen and twelve pieces of artillery.

On the night of June 8, thirty-year-old Jeb Stuart went to sleep under only a tent fly on Fleetwood Hill without any notion that Union troops were gathering to assail his cavalry. His headquarters, which overlooked Brandy Station and the Rappahannock River northeast of Culpeper Court House, was uncommonly spartan. Earlier in the evening, wagons laden with headquarters baggage and equipment had been dispatched to Culpeper, while others sat loaded and ready to roll.

Orders had been issued by General Robert E. Lee that would require Stuart to move all remaining equipment and troops to Culpeper in the morning. With that plan in mind, Stuart had placed his five brigades on passable roads near the river. His cavalry was prepared to march but not by any means deployed in strategically defensive positions.

Rooney Lee's brigade was camped two miles north at Welford; Fitz Lee's brigade, presently commanded by Thomas T. Munford due to an attack of rheumatism that plagued Lee, could be found seven and a half miles northwest at Oak Shade Church; the brigade commanded by Grumble Jones camped between Stuart and the Rappahannock near St. James

Church; Beverly Robertson was about three miles away on a private farm; and Wade Hampton had been placed near Stevensburg, five miles south. The Horse Artillery, now under the command of Major Robert F. Beckham, had assumed a favorable position between Jones and the river.

The Army of Northern Virginia was poised to embark on a mission of great importance. General Lee had intentions of taking advantage of his stunning victory at Chancellorsville. To that end, he had obtained permission from Richmond for an invasion of the North that would put pressure on the major population centers of Washington, Baltimore, and Philadelphia. Lee had established his headquarters at Culpeper on June 3 and began withdrawing his army from the vicinity of Fredericksburg to rendezvous around his location.

In less than two days, on June 10, 72,000 Confederate troops would move out in earnest for the march north. This was Lee's most ambitious undertaking yet and was designed to accomplish a dual purpose by also drawing away Union General Joseph Hooker's massive army from posing a threat to Virginia.

The fact that the Confederate cavalry would not be prepared to fight when the Union borrowed a page from Stuart's book about attacking by surprise at several points at once partially can be attributed to a recent reconnaissance of Hooker's lines along the Rappahannock by Hampton's brigade. The result of this mission had convinced Lee that Union forces appeared to have no aggressive plans for the near future.

In addition, the threat to Richmond had been somewhat alleviated when word came that 5,000 infantry, 100 cavalry, and two batteries of artillery had vacated West Point, which was only thirty-five miles east of the Confederate capital. This conclusion by Lee, coupled with the Confederacy's recent domination of its enemy, likely had influenced the rather cavalier attitude displayed by Stuart when deploying his men.

Granted, the war was on course and the future held great promise. But the past month had been somewhat vexatious for Jeb Stuart.

His petition for the command of a corps and promotion to lieutenant general after Stonewall Jackson had died from his wounds on May 10 had been politely denied by Lee. Some measure of conciliation and recognition, however, came when Stuart was granted a larger force. Lee was aware that Hooker had consolidated his cavalry, and for that reason he had decided to expand the role of his own horsemen.

Lee had summoned the brigades of Grumble Jones from the Valley and Beverly Robertson from North Carolina, which now gave Stuart three brigades—9,536 men—the largest number that he had ever commanded. During this lull in the fighting after Chancellorsville, Lee suggested that Stuart gather his cavalry and "give them some breathing time, so as when you do strike, Stoneman may feel you."

Stuart made good use of this breathing time by assembling and drilling his troops, as well as assuring that arms and equipment were in proper condition. One notable change in his staff came when he chose Major Henry B. McClellan—first cousin of former Union commander George B. McClellan—as his adjutant to succeed Channing Price, who had bled to death at Chancellorsville when a shell fragment had severed one of his arteries. McClellan's quick thinking and coolness under fire during the upcoming battle at Brandy Station would salvage a portion of the day for the Confederates.

Stuart had moved his headquarters to the pleasant wooded hilltop near Culpeper Court House on May 20 and two days later held a grand review of the three brigades commanded by Wade Hampton and Fitz and Rooney Lee. This brilliant display of almost half of his troops prompted Stuart to envision an even more impressive performance.

In the tradition of a master showman, Stuart seized on the idea of assembling all of his command and staged an exhibition of such grandeur that it would surpass in spectacle any military review ever before known. This extravaganza, Stuart vowed, would render the viewers breathless and inspired by the strength and readiness of his troops—not to mention accolades for their commander who was never one to pass up the chance to promote himself.

The grand review was scheduled for the morning of June 5 at Brandy Station. Formal invitations were hastily dispatched to friends, relatives, and associates. Special trains were obtained to bring visitors from Richmond, Charlottesville, and the surrounding area. Adequate accommodations for expected guests were secured nearby. A glorious ball featuring music performed by the regimental band would be held on the evening before the grand review to entertain officers in their fancy dress uniforms and the female guests who would be adorned for the special occasion in their finest elegant gowns. General Lee had of course been invited to the festivities but had declined due to the necessity of putting the final touches on his Northern strategy.

The troops were caught up in the enthusiasm of their commander, especially after new uniforms had been issued, and set to work shining, polishing, and cleaning saddles, buckles, boots, scabbards, weapons, and other equipment with a zeal that would guarantee passing the most scrutinizing of inspections. The officers, with the exception of Grumble Jones, who refused to exchange his normal attire for a dress uniform, were as fervent as Stuart in their anticipation of this momentous event.

An escort of carriages, military wagons, and ambulances met each arriving train on the afternoon of June 4, and it soon became apparent that the response was so overwhelming that additional rooms in private homes and even tents pitched near Stuart's headquarters would be required to accommodate the throng of excited guests. This was but a minor inconvenience for those who considered it a privilege and honor to attend the gala performance at the invitation of the South's famous, swashbuckling living legend. That night, a ball was held in the poorly illuminated Town Hall, which was soon moved outside on the veranda under the moon.

The morning of June 5 dawned clear and sunny—perfect springtime weather for the occasion. Stuart and his staff departed Culpeper at eight o'clock for the short jaunt to Brandy Station. His arrival at the top of the knoll that would serve as the reviewing stand, which by now was crowded with spectators, was greeted by buglers sounding flourishes which inspired the cheers of his men.

Stuart sat regally atop his horse, the buttons on his jacket in danger of popping with pride, and surveyed the magnificent line of assembled troops that stretched in front of him for a mile and a half. His dramatic appearance was described by artilleryman George Neese: "The trappings of his proud, prancing horse all looked bright and new, and his sidearms gleamed in the morning sun like burnished silver. A long, black ostrich feather waved grace-fully from a black slouched hat cocked upon one side, and was held with a golden clasp which also stayed the plume."

Stuart bathed in this outpouring of adulation for a moment, then spurred his mount and galloped away, with his subordinates trailing behind, to personally review his troops. He returned to the knoll and, in the role of the military maestro that he had been born to play, gestured to the buglers and set in motion this masterpiece that he had orchestrated.

The regiments first moved forward in a column of fours to pass by the reviewing stand. The headquarters band played, and ladies rushed from the audience to lay flowers in the pathway of these gallant horsemen. Major Heros Von Borcke described the scene: "The magnificent spectacle of so many thousand troopers splendidly mounted made the heart swell with pride, and impressed one with the conviction that nothing could resist the attack of such a body of troops."

Stuart then topped off the performance by calling for maneuvers, which included a mock battle against an imaginary enemy. His cavalry began in a trot, then, when "Charge!" was sounded by the buglers, thundered past with sabers drawn to "attack" designated artillery batteries. Rebel yells split the air; the artillery unloaded a twenty-gun salute with blank charges; horses hooves sent turf flying; and, in the midst of it all, Jeb Stuart's ears were tuned to the exclamations and squeals from the onlookers, whose hearts soared with admiration at the impressive sight.

Stuart's officers, who were accustomed to such spectacles, reacted in much the same manner as the other observers and were moved to emotion as the Invincibles roared past to a serenade of cannon fire. Young ladies col-lapsed in a faint into the arms of their escorts, either truly overcome or act-ing out of appreciation and respect for the proceedings. As a grand finale, another dance was held that night under the stars, illuminated by the light of lanterns and bonfires. And presiding over it all was a jovial, perhaps even giddy, Jeb Stuart, who reveled in the demonstration of military magnificence that he had scripted.

Stuart was even more puffed with pride when he received word that General Lee would be pleased to attend an encore grand review performance on June 8. This time, however, Lee requested that Stuart conserve gunpowder and eliminate the artillery salute. Despite the omission of bombs bursting in air, the review, which was also attended by Stuart's friendly nemesis, infantry General John Bell Hood, who had been invited with his staff and instead brought his 10,000-man division, was a resounding success. Lee later wrote to his wife: "It was a splendid sight. The men & horses looked well . . . Stuart was in all his glory."

There was, however, widespread grumbling from rank and file troops about this second rendition. The cavalrymen complained that they had already had their fill of pageantry the first time around. They were tired and had been compelled to once again tend to uniforms, equipment, and horses for the sole purpose of appeasing the vanity of their commander.

Not everyone in the South was impressed with Stuart's performance. Richmond newspapers ridiculed what they termed "military foppery." President Jefferson Davis received a letter from an anonymous woman, which read in part: "President, allow a rude Southern lady to say that General Stuart's conduct since Culpeper is perfectly ridiculous, having repeated reviews for the benefit of his lady friends, he riding up and down the line thronged with those ladies, he decorated with flowers, apparently a monkey show on hand and he the monkey." Perhaps this woman's personal invitation to Stuart's ball and grand review had been lost in the mail.

None of this criticism affected Jeb Stuart. He retired to his fly tent on Fleetwood Hill on the night of June 8 with the satisfaction and confidence of a man who had advanced his claim to the title of the South's reigning knight in shining armor. The war was headed north, and final victory, or at the very least additional tributes, were in his future. He was on top of the world and having the time of his life.

There was only one problem. While Jeb Stuart slept, the Union cavalry was on the move and within hours would splash across the Rappahannock to temporarily douse the major general's aspirations.

On the night before the impending battle, Pleasonton had established his headquarters about a mile from Beverly Ford at a private residence. Armstrong Custer, who was officer of the day, paused from his rounds of the camp to write a letter to his sister stating that "I never was in better spirits than I am at this moment." But, with a flair for the dramatic, he added that he could be killed the following day: "In case anything happens to me," he wrote, "my trunk is to go to you. Burn all my letters."

The cavalrymen were already in place when Custer awoke General Pleasonton at 2 a.m. for the planned 4 a.m. crossing of the Rappahannock. Brigadier General John Buford's 1st Division was poised to cross at Beverly Ford while a combined force of the 3rd Division under Brigadier General David Gregg and Colonel Alfred Duffie's 2nd Division would strike at Kelly's Ford.

Buford and Gregg were both West Pointers, respected by their peers and subordinates, and had the reputation of both being tough as old boots. Duffie, on the other hand, had been born in France, had fought in the Crimean War, and, perhaps due to his training in European heavy-cavalry tactics, had been saddled with the tag of someone who had been promoted beyond his capabilities. Pleasonton personally disliked foreigners, and Duffie in particular, and hoped that the colonel would eventually furnish a reason to replace him.

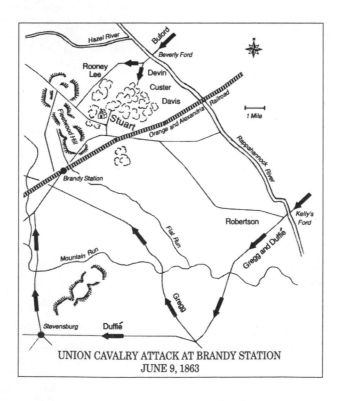

UNION CAVALRY ATTACK AT BRANDY STATION
JUNE 9, 1863

Lieutenant Custer, at the direction of Pleasonton, accompanied a brigade of Buford's division commanded by Alabama-born and Mississippi-reared Colonel Benjamin F. "Grimes" Davis that would lead the way across the foggy river near Beverly Ford at 5 a.m. Davis, a West Pointer who had escaped Harpers Ferry before the Union had surrendered, solemnly passed the word: "Stand ready, men, and begin firing as soon as you see anything!"

When the first shots of the battle were fired by startled Confederate pickets with Company A of the 6th Virginia, Davis, with Custer at his side, rode to the front of the 8th New York Regiment, unsheathed his saber, and charged to engage the enemy.

On Fleetwood Hill, Jeb Stuart was either asleep or had just awakened when he heard the distant sound of gunfire. Within moments, a courier from Grumble Jones reported with word of the attack at Beverly Ford. Stuart did not panic, but without precise knowledge of the size of the force of Federal cavalry, he was unable to formulate any specific strategy. He simply ordered his men to fight. He did, to his credit, have the presence of mind to dispatch a courier directing General Beverly Robertson's brigade toward Kelly's Ford, which he had correctly assumed might be struck as well.

General Wade Hampton's brigade hurried from Brandy Station to reinforce Jones at the point of attack. Rooney Lee took a position on Buford's right flank behind a stone fence and was supported by Munford commanding Fitz Lee's brigade.

Stuart himself remained on Fleetwood Hill and attempted to gather enough intelligence to adequately deploy his cavalry. But he was dismayed to admit the element of surprise by the Union had succeeded, and his men likely would be in for the fight of their lives.

Buford's division, led by Grimes Davis and his brigade, had charged into those Rebels camped at Beverly Ford and virtually trampled them beneath their horse's hooves while firing at will and slashing them apart with swinging sabers. Stuart's shocked men, who had been sound asleep or huddled in front of small fires, most in various stages of dress, were unable to offer much immediate resistance to the charging horsemen. They were far more concerned with mounting their own skittish horses or dashing on foot into the nearby timber to escape this unexpected tumult. A small number of Confederate cavalrymen paused at the tree line in an effort to provide a base of fire to assist their beleaguered comrades in this every-man-for-himself retreat.

The banks along the Rappahannock were the scene of mass chaos as thousands of unyielding Federal cavalrymen swooped down upon their unsuspecting prey. The early morning was ablaze with discharges of gunfire—the plumes of smoke and pungent odor of sulfur stinging eyes, irritating nostrils, causing voices to be harsh and barely audible above the din. Running men were cut down with savage saber strokes; others toppled from their horses in the same manner. The dewy ground was soon littered with writhing, torn bodies, wounded and dying. Cries of agony, terror, triumph, and surrender combined with bugle calls, urgently shouted orders, and the high-pitched whinnies of frightened, bolting horses to create a macabre quality that would forever be etched into the memories of the participants.

Colonel Davis directed his men into the woods to chase the fleeing Rebels. The Union horsemen dashed through the trees, wreaking havoc upon their enemy as they passed, and emerged to view a cleared area several hundred yards in length that ran almost to St. James Church. At the far edge of this clearing, beyond the scrambling Confederates that had been overrun, several pieces of Rebel artillery could be observed.

It was well known that thus far during the course of the war, Jeb Stuart had not lost even one cannon to his enemy. An exhilarated Grimes Davis immediately called for a charge of this gun emplacement. His men, including Armstrong Custer, responded by pounding across the meadow to attack the seemingly exposed South Carolina battery commanded by Captain James F. Hart.

The Union cavalrymen were nearing their objective when out of the woods on their flank burst a countercharge of at least 150 of Stuart's horsemen under Major Cabell E. Flourney. The surprised Union troops frantically yanked on their reins to restrain their mounts and abort the charge. Many were thrown from the saddle, scrambling to leap aboard a loose mount or escape on foot in order to avoid the resolute Confederate assault. Numerous casualties were inflicted as the Union force commenced a hasty retreat to the relative safety of the timber.

There was one exception to that sudden retreat. Colonel Benjamin Davis, defiant and gallant, stood his ground. When the colonel had emptied his pistol at his oncoming enemy, he resorted to the saber. It had been said of Davis by a member of the 8th New York: "When Colonel Davis found the Rebels he did not stop at anything, but went for them heavy. I Believe he liked to fight the Rebels as well as he liked to eat." In this case, however, his determination perhaps overruled prudence.

Virginia cavalry lieutenant R. O. Allen targeted Davis, and cautiously approached by hugging his horse's neck to evade the blade of the colonel's saber. Allen closed the distance between them, raised his pistol, and fired three shots point-blank at Grimes Davis. The third bullet struck Davis in the forehead, knocking him from his horse to the ground and killing him instantly.

The withdrawal of the 8th New York to the woods thwarted the advance of the 8th Illinois, which had been following closely behind. The troopers dismounted at the tree line to fire their carbines and were augmented by barrages from Captain James M. Robertson's artillery battery. This action eventually discouraged the Rebel counterattack and exacted a toll of at least thirty of Flourney's men. The Union cavalrymen could not take advantage, however, because four Confederate brigades had assembled to keep them pinned in the timber.

The role that George Armstrong Custer played in events that immediately followed the death of Grimes Davis could be called a matter of interpretation. Some biographers have related that Custer, despite being subordinate on the field to Major William McClure of the 3rd Indiana Cavalry, at that point assumed command of the three brigades. This may or may not be correct. No official documentation has been located to confirm or debunk the story.

There exists the distinct possibility, however, that Custer by virtue of his actions became de facto leader of the entire brigade or at least some individual detachment. It was well known that Custer had a zeal for active battlefield leadership, which had been demonstrated in past engagements, and could conceivably have taken charge in this instance as well. He had, for example, displayed this tendency at Williamsburg, Pennsylvania, in May

1862, when on impulse he spurred his horse and rallied hesitant Union troops against the enemy.

By some accounts, Custer was said to have led a series of charges that day at Brandy Station, one of which caused his outnumbered force to be surrounded, a predicament that he remedied by eventually fighting his way through the enemy. During the action, Custer allegedly had two horses shot out from beneath him, and a bullet tore through his boot.

At some point, however, Custer was prevented from leading anyone—his horse had bolted and slammed into a fence, where it huddled in fright and could not be coaxed to move. Custer dismounted, wrestled with the frightened animal, and finally managed to mount just as it raced away. To the immediate front loomed a stone wall, which the terrified horse maladroitly toppled over, tossing Custer bootheels over tea kettle. Custer was dazed but unhurt and quickly remounted to dash away and take refuge with a friendly artillery battery.

There can be no question that Custer in some manner distinguished himself during the charges and countercharges at St. James Church. General Pleasonton, who had established his headquarters at a nearby residence, had apparently observed or been informed about Custer's actions. Pleasonton singled out his aide for "gallantry throughout the fight" in his dispatches. Custer, who had reported back to Pleasonton before noon, was chosen to personally deliver to General Hooker these dispatches along with a list of prisoners and a battle flag captured from the 12th Virginia Cavalry.

To describe Jeb Stuart as being in a foul mood over events would be an understatement. The cavalry commander was livid and could not fathom that his Invincibles were being contested by an enemy that he had without exception dominated throughout the war. It was Stuart who had always pressed the attack, striking when and where he chose, sending his enemy to retreat or defeat. His cavalry was the eyes and ears of the army, yet they had been blindsided, surprised by the upstart Yankee horsemen. And, to add insult to injury, Stuart was now in the unaccustomed position of having to plot a *defensive* strategy.

The Union offensive might have been more effective had it not been for the unexplained delay by Colonel Duffie in crossing the Rappahannock at

Kelly's Ford. Duffie's tardiness had cost General Gregg four hours and could have been disastrous had it not been for the questionable actions of Beverly Robertson, whose brigade Stuart had earlier dispatched to that location.

Robertson's position in the woods was noted by Gregg, who avoided direct conflict and simply bypassed the Confederate line by marching in a southerly direction down a road that led to Stevensburg. Robertson watched Gregg pass but inexplicably made no effort to attack or even to inform Stuart about the movement. Duffie then continued on to Stevensburg while Gregg took a circuitous route heading northwest back toward Brandy Station.

Stuart departed Fleetwood Hill with his staff at about midmorning, leaving only adjutant Henry McClellan and a few orderlies behind, and ventured to St. James Church. Grumble Jones, Rooney Lee, and Wade Hampton had arrived to reinforce the artillery batteries, and the threat at that location had been contained for the time being. In fact, there appeared to be a lull in the fighting.

That was, until word arrived from Grumble Jones that Union troops were crossing at Kelly's Ford, six miles south. Stuart was incredulous and hesitant to believe the courier. "Tell General Jones to attend to the Yankees in his front," he snapped, "and I'll watch the flanks!" Jones responded to the curt message with enough venom to kill ten major generals: "So he thinks they ain't coming does he? Well, let him alone; he'll damned soon see for himself!"

The response of both men was typical. A mutual dislike had developed between the two from their first meeting, perhaps initiated by Jones, who was older and West Point educated and resented, even despised Stuart for his superior rank and position. This relationship paralleled that which Custer would endure with Captain Frederick Benteen years later in the 7th Cavalry.

It was about noon when Major McClellan dispatched a courier to advise Stuart that a long column of Federal cavalry was preparing to advance up Fleetwood Hill. Stuart realized that it would be devastating for the entire Confederate command if Union troops supported by artillery succeeded in capturing that strategic position. The general, however, remained skeptical, and he sent an artillery captain to confirm the report. Within moments, another anxious courier from McClellan appeared and reported, "General, the

Yankees are at Brandy!" The sounds of a raging battle from that direction were now quite distinct, and Stuart understood that he must respond quickly, or all would be lost.

Meanwhile, Henry McClellan remained atop Fleetwood Hill with only several couriers and an artillery piece with little ammunition and watched as the long line of Yankee cavalry advanced toward him. Gregg, who had encountered no opposition, had targeted Fleetwood Hill as the place where he could command the entire field, and the likely position where the Rebels would make a stand.

The courageous McClellan attempted to bluff Gregg into thinking that Fleetwood Hill was adequately defended by ordering his men to commence firing the six-pounder at a slow rate. The ruse stopped Gregg in his tracks and compelled the general to return fire from below in order to prepare his horsemen for a major assault.

Shells rained down on McClellan, who had fired the last of his ammunition, and forced him to abandon the headquarters. Stuart's gallant adjutant mounted and raced toward the 12th Virginia that, oddly enough, was approaching at a trot. McClellan prodded the troops forward, and the unit responded at the gallop.

Union troops under Colonel Percy Wyndham were only fifty feet away from the crest of Fleetwood Hill when the 12th Virginia reached the top. The Confederates crashed into Wyndham's men and, by sheer force of their momentum, passed right on through the Yankees and down the opposite slope. Wyndham, for the moment, had control of Fleetwood Hill and waited for reinforcements.

Jeb Stuart, who had been skeptical about the seriousness of the threat to Fleetwood Hill, had initially dispatched only two regiments. Due to the urgency of the messages and the intensity of the firing, he decided to ride to his headquarters and see for himself exactly what was happening. He quickly sized up the situation and realized that he had underestimated his enemy.

Stuart ordered William Blackford to "gallop along the line and order every commanding officer of a regiment to move on Fleetwood at a gallop." Stuart also ordered Blackford to then ride to Culpeper and summon into the fray the infantry assembled there for the impending move north.

Possession of Fleetwood Hill changed numerous times in the ensuing battle as the opponents in units from company to regimental size charged and countercharged to gain the upper hand. The issue was finally settled when Wade Hampton's brigade, reinforced by elements from Grumble Jones, gradually drove the Union cavalrymen back to Brandy Station in a running battle fought for the most part hand-to-hand or with sabers. Stuart quickly took advantage of what he could presume would only be momentary upper hand and concentrated his command around Fleetwood Hill to strengthen his hold on that coveted position.

Sporadic fighting raged for some time on the flanks. Some miles north, Duffie had engaged the 2nd South Carolina and the 4th Virginia. He had in some measure redeemed himself by doing quite well, but the skirmish prevented him from assisting at Fleetwood Hill, which might have made a difference in the outcome.

General Lee, whose headquarters was only about a half mile from the fighting, arrived on the field in time to observe his son, Rooney, being carried away on a stretcher. Rooney Lee had suffered a bullet wound in the thigh while leading a charge against Captain Wesley Merritt's men who were attempting to flank the Confederate line near the Cunningham farm.

At about five o'clock, General Pleasonton determined that, with the loss of Fleetwood Hill, it was time to withdraw his weary troops back across the Rappahannock. Pleasonton had apparently caught the scent of the Confederate infantry's advance and understood that after a day of fighting, his troops were in no condition to continue the battle against greater odds. The Union cavalry, to their credit, had conducted themselves courageously and gathered vital intelligence, which had been a primary purpose of their mission.

Jeb Stuart, the consummate aggressor, did not press whatever advantage he might have gained by holding Fleetwood Hill. Instead, he permitted his enemy to gradually withdraw without any pursuit. This had been a close call, and Stuart was wise enough to circle his wagons and assess the situation before rushing off into what could be another surprise.

The battle at Brandy Station, also known as Fleetwood Hill or Beverly Ford, the greatest cavalry engagement of the century, had concluded. Both sides, as might be expected, claimed victory. In truth, the battle was tactically and statistically won by the Army of Northern Virginia. The Confederates had held the field and sustained fewer casualties—estimates ranged anywhere from 866 to 936 for the Union, although many were said to have later rejoined their units, and less than 500 to 523 for the South.

Victory, however, must at times be judged by elements that have little to do with field position or casualty estimates. In the case of the Union cavalry, this had been a moral victory and, at least in the minds of the troopers, a military one as well. This shining success was an affirmation that Stuart's Invincibles were no longer quite as invincible. That in itself, after two years of devastating defeats at the hands of Rebel horsemen, was reason enough to celebrate. A Federal artillery officer summed up these sentiments when he said: "The affair at Brandy Station certainly did a great deal to improve the morale of our cavalry, so that they are not now afraid to meet the 'rebs' on equal terms."

The Confederates, on the other hand, had reason to be concerned. And Jeb Stuart was the person on whose shoulders the heaviest burden of criticism was placed.

William Blackford's brother, Charles, wrote: "The cavalry battle at Brandy Station can hardly be called a *victory*. Stuart was certainly surprised and but for the supreme gallantry of his subordinate officers and men in his command it would have been a day of disaster and disgrace ... Stuart is blamed very much, but whether or not fairly I am not sufficiently well informed to say." A clerk in the Confederate War Department said, "The surprise of Stuart, on the Rappahannock, has chilled every heart." The military point of view was best stated by Major Henry McClellan, whose heroic actions had likely saved the day for Stuart: "One result of incalculable importance certainly will follow this battle—it *made* the Federal Cavalry."

Southern newspapers in particular took the general to task. The *Richmond Dispatch* called the battle a near rout, avoided by the sheerest of luck. The *Richmond Whig*, normally a Stuart supporter, blamed the affair on overconfidence and encouraged Stuart to attack Pleasonton as soon as possible in order to restore his lost honor and prestige. The *Charleston Mercury* called it an "ugly surprise" and blamed Stuart for "rollicking, frolicking and running after girls." Other newspapers weighed in with opinions that the fire had formed a vicious ring around Jeb Stuart. The *Mobile Daily Advertiser and Register*: "disastrous affair;" *Memphis Appeal*: "Needless slaughter;" and the *Richmond Examiner*: "consequences of negligence and bad management."

The opinion that mattered most to Stuart, however, belonged to his commanding officer, Robert E. Lee, who, true to character, was restrained but offered praise. "The dispositions made by you to meet the strong attack of the enemy," Lee wrote, "appear to have been judicious and well planned. The troops were well and skillfully managed." Lee was known for his motivational praise rather than his scorn, in most cases, but he knew what had really happened at Brandy Station and could not be too happy with Jeb Stuart about it.

Stuart promptly moved his headquarters from the carnage of human and equine corpses that had drawn flocks of buzzards to Fleetwood Hill. He assembled and addressed his men following the battle and employed the grandiloquent statements that had served him well in the past in an effort to convince them that a great victory had been won. "Your saber blows," Stuart told them, "inflicted on that glorious day, have taught them again the weight of Southern vengeance."

Perhaps Stuart believed his words most likely he did—when taking into consideration his massive ego and tendency for embellishment. But to a vast majority of Southerners, a portion of the luster on the shining armor of this gallant knight had been tarnished at Brandy Station.

On the Union side of the line, the *New York Tribune* summarized the ecstatic reaction of the North when it wrote: "The Confederates begin to find that their boasted cavalry is being overmatched by the Union horsemen. Our troops . . . will make as fine cavalry as can be found in the world."

And from the arbitrament of the saber at Brandy Station a new hero was about to emerge to help lead this fine Union cavalry. Twenty-three-year-old George Armstrong Custer, the West Point class clown, was on the verge of rising from relative obscurity into the spotlight of glory that he so craved.

CHAPTER SIX

ON *to* GETTYSBURG

NEITHER ARMY LINGERED for any length of time on the battlefield following hostilities at Brandy Station. On June 10, Robert E. Lee resumed his mission to invade the North and dispatched Ewell down the Shenandoah, Longstreet east of the Blue Ridge Mountains, and Ambrose Hill trailing Ewell. Jeb Stuart's duty was to screen this Confederate three corps movement and guard the mountain gaps of the Blue Ridge against attack as the army moved to a planned crossing of the Potomac at Harpers Ferry.

On June 17, the two opposing cavalries would collide in the Virginia Piedmont at Aldie, which was strategically located at the western end of a gap in the Bull Run Mountains and at the fork of two roads leading to Winchester.

Fitz Lee's brigade, commanded by Colonel Thomas Munford in Lee's absence, had been sent ahead to guard Aldie. Munford moved from Upperville through Middleburg, deployed pickets east of Aldie, and continued on to procure supplies at a local residence.

Stuart and his staff retired to the picturesque village of Middleburg to engage in what had become the cavalry commander's favorite pastime—entertaining the young ladies, many of whom could be termed camp followers, with music and tales of daring. For the second time in just over a week, Stuart's cavalry, the eyes and ears of the Army of Northern Virginia, would be taken by surprise when Pleasonton and three brigades of Gregg's 2nd Division arrived at Aldie about four o'clock that afternoon to attack Munford.

Riding with Pleasonton and Gregg was aide-de-camp Armstrong Custer, who had made himself conspicuous just prior to the assault by soaking himself in a river after watering his horse. Custer had been urging his mount up a steep bank when the animal toppled over backwards, spilling him into the water. One of Gregg's staff quipped that when Custer emerged from his impromptu bath, the dust "settled on his wet clothes and wet hair, [and] Custer was an object that one can better imagine than I can describe." Fortunately for the embarrassed lieutenant, this incident would be a mere footnote to his actions that day.

The battle commenced when Hugh Judson Kilpatrick's brigade stormed into Aldie and sent Munford's pickets reeling into a hasty retreat. Custer's former West Point classmate and close friend Colonel Tom Rosser rallied his 5th Virginia with a bold saber charge, then posted sharpshooters behind haystacks on the right of the Snickersville Road and held firm against Kilpatrick's advance. The two cavalries charged and countercharged as the fighting raged west of Aldie, with neither side gaining a clear advantage.

Stuart's flirtatious dallying was abruptly interrupted when frantic pickets ran down the street yelling, "The Yankees are coming! The Yankees are coming!"

Stuart and his staff leaped aboard their horses and raced away just as a regiment of Duffie's cavalry approached at the gallop. Adjutant Henry McClellan described the getaway as "a retreat more rapid than was consistent with dignity and comfort." Stuart joined Beverly Robertson's brigade and dispatched a message at about dusk calling for Munford to fall back to Middleburg.

Munford complied with Stuart's order, and a running battle ensued as Kilpatrick chased the stubborn Confederates down the road leading into the village proper.

Lieutenant Custer had been occupied with carrying dispatches for General Pleasonton throughout the initial stages of the battle. Late in the day, he arrived at Kilpatrick's position. Kilpatrick was one of those officers who was the subject of Custer's envy. Kilpatrick had been only one year ahead of Custer at West Point but already was in command of a brigade. Custer, who was always eager for combat experience, asked for and was granted Kilpatrick's permission to enter the fray. Custer would certainly have been anxious to impress Kilpatrick, not to mention Pleasonton, with his competence under fire whenever the opportunity arose to trade his aide functions for a combat role. In this instance, however, it would not necessarily be the ability of Custer that would turn heads but allegedly the initiative of a runaway horse that would gain its rider instant fame.

Custer was becoming widely known, and likely ridiculed, for his skittish horses—first at Brandy Station and then earlier in the day when he had taken the dunking. These episodes in no way reflected a true picture of his skill in the saddle. As evidenced by his ability at West Point, he was a natural-born equestrian, and very few could compare to him when it came to horsemanship. Perhaps it was poetic justice to compensate for the other mishaps that this occasion would provide more positive results.

Custer rode a black horse that he had named Harry in honor of his five-year-old nephew—who, incidentally, would be nicknamed Autie in honor of Custer and would die with his famous uncle at the Little Bighorn.

Harry the horse became unnerved by the din of battle and bolted—straight toward the enemy. Custer fought to restrain his mount but was unable to rein up the terrified animal. Before long, Harry had carried his hapless rider directly into the midst of Munford's cavalry.

Two Rebel cavalrymen quickly targeted Custer and closed in for the kill. Custer instinctively drew his blade. The Confederate horsemen were greeted with Custer's heavy saber, and one was cut from the saddle. Harry then treated Custer to a wild, harrowing ride for at least a mile through enemy lines. Finally, Custer managed to control his horse, escaped out a flank, and circled the entire field at a gallop to return safely to Kilpatrick's headquarters.

Custer claimed that his deliverance could be attributed to his soft, felt, Confederate-style hat, which best protected his fair skin from the sun. He wrote in a letter to his sister dated June 25: "I was surrounded by rebels, and cut off from my own men, but I had made my way out safely, and all owing to my <u>hat</u>, which is a large broad brim, exactly like that worn by rebels. Everyone tells me I look like a rebel more than our own men. The rebels at first thought I was one of their own men, and did not attack me, except one, who rushed at me with his sabre, but I struck him across the face with my sabre, knocking him off his horse. I then put the spurs to 'Harry' and made my escape."

Despite Custer's protestations to the contrary, which was a rarity for such a masterful self-promoter, many observers were of the opinion that he had intended to charge right through the whole Confederate army. Newspaper correspondents knew a good story when they saw one and embellished the "charge" into enemy lines to depict Custer as the hero of the battle.

One Michigan newspaper later reported in part: "Outstripping his men in pursuit of the enemy, one of them turned, fired, but missed, his revolver being knocked by a sword blow that sent the rider toppling to the ground. Another enemy trooper tore alongside, but Custer, giving his horse a sudden check, let the man go shooting by. Then face to face they fought it out, gray going down before blue."

Artist A. R. Waud of *Harper's Weekly* rendered a sketch of this valorous charge by Custer which several months later would grace the cover of that prestigious national magazine.

Perhaps more consequential to Custer at the time was the news that as a result of the battle at Aldie, Pleasonton had been promoted to major general. This meant that Custer could once more assume the brevet rank of captain. But unbeknownst to anyone at present, he would barely have time to get accustomed to his new rank before Dame Fortune would smile upon him with a much more significant promotion.

Two days later, the Union cavalry struck Middleburg again. Duffie led the charge, which pushed the Confederate troops further west to near Upperville. The skirmishing between detachments of the two armies raged on in earnest, but Jeb Stuart had wisely positioned his men in a long line from Middleburg to Upperville, which maintained his ability to protect the gaps for Lee's advancing army.

Stuart was saddened to witness the wounding of Heros Von Borcke by a sharpshooter in that June 19 attack. The Prussian staff officer had been struck in the neck by a bullet, a severe wound that at first had been diagnosed as likely fatal. The tough Von Borcke would survive but would never fight again.

Pleasonton continued to sporadically probe Stuart's line but remained contently settled in for the time being around Middleburg. The new major general was confident that his men were in the process of delivering a Union victory, but there was one exception. Duffie's regiment had been cut to ribbons, losing nearly two-thirds of its men. Duffie, likely over Pleasonton's objections, had been promoted to brigadier general a few days earlier. Now

Pleasonton finally had reason to remove the Frenchman. At his urging, Hooker reassigned Duffie to Washington.

Union artillery shells were bombarding the streets of Upperville, and Stuart decided out of regard for the women and children who resided there to withdraw to Ashley's Gap in the Blue Ridge Mountains. Stuart was quite conscious that his presence placed the civilian populace under a threat and always attempted to draw the battle away from towns. Soon after, Pleasonton fell back to Aldie. Stuart, satisfied that he had won a victory, returned to his position before Aldie.

During the four days of skirmishing, the Union had suffered an estimated 800 to 827 casualties to an estimated 510 to 660 for the Confederate army—numbers comparable to those at Brandy Station. Stuart's cavalry had fought with resolve and won the statistical battle; the Union horsemen, however, had for the second straight time proven themselves a worthy opponent. But there was a dark side for Jeb Stuart. He had once again been caught with his pants down, figuratively if not literally, and owed any success primarily to the efforts of Munford and Rosser, who had outdueled Gregg and Kilpatrick.

More puzzling was the fact that Stuart, who was known for riding to the front lines and directing traffic, was conspicuously absent during much of the fighting. He had opted to issue orders to subordinates and remain physically detached. Munford and Rosser had gallantly responded of their own volition, as had McClellan at Brandy Station when Stuart refused to believe reports and issue timely orders for the defense of Fleetwood Hill.

Officers and rank and file troops both asked the question: what could have brought about this sudden change in Stuart's style of commanding his cavalry? The most troubling and thought-provoking theory—and far-fetched—would be that the *Beau Sabreur* had temporarily lost his zest for combat and penchant for playing to the galleries. Could the deaths of Stonewall Jackson and the gallant John Pelham, combined with the recent wounding of Heros Von Borcke, have made an impression on Stuart about his own mortality and compelled him to be more cautious?

Not likely. Although detractors had bandied about the question, Stuart could never be accused of losing his nerve or confidence. Those traits were firmly imbedded in his character. According the Major Henry McClellan,

Stuart related that his willingness to delegate authority to his field officers was an intentional act, one that would benefit his subordinates with the opportunity to gain experience from the added responsibility. Perhaps in the back of his mind, Stuart the patriot had a more noble purpose—the Confederacy itself. Now that the Union cavalry had proved its competency, he tendered the concern and desire to prepare others to take command in the event of his own death.

While Longstreet and Hill advanced down the Valley and Ewell was on his way into Pennsylvania, Stuart reestablished his headquarters near Middleburg at Rector's Cross Roads. He had sent proposals to General Lee in recent days pertaining to an independent cavalry reconnaissance intended to slow Hooker's movements by harassing him, confusing him as to the whereabouts of Lee's army, cutting communications, and providing vital intelligence. Lee recognized the value of Stuart's reasoning and agreed with his request.

The following orders were issued regarding this extensive cavalry operation:

Headquarters
June 22, 1863
Maj. Gen. J. E. B. Stuart, Commanding Cavalry

General: I have just received your note of 7:45 this morning to General Longstreet. I judge the efforts of the enemy yesterday were to arrest our progress and ascertain our whereabouts. Perhaps he is satisfied. Do you know where he is and what he is doing? I fear he will steal a march on us, and get across the Potomac before we are aware. If you find he is moving northward, and that two brigades can guard the Blue Ridge and take care of your rear, you can move with the other three into Maryland, and take position on General Ewell's right, place yourself in communication with him, guard his flank, keep him informed of the enemy's movements, and collect all the supplies you can for use of the army. One column of General Ewell's army will probably move toward the Susquehanna by the Emmitsburg route; another by Chambersburg. Accounts from him last night state that there was no enemy west of Frederick. A cavalry force [about 100] guarded the Moncracy Bridge, which was barricaded. You will, of course, take charge of

[A. G.] Jenkins' brigade, and give him necessary instructions. All supplies taken in Maryland must be by authorized staff officers for their respective departments—by no one else. They will be paid for, or receipts for the same given to the owners. I will send you a general order on this subject, which I wish you to see is strictly complied with.

I am very respectfully, your obt sevt,
R. E. Lee, Genl.

The above order was delivered by and with the following endorsement by Lieutenant General James Longstreet, to whose command Stuart's cavalry was attached:

Headquarters
Millwood, June 22, 1863—7 P.M.
Maj. Gen. J. E. B. Stuart, Commanding cavalry

General: General Lee has enclosed to me this letter to you, to be forwarded to you, provided you can be spared from my front, and provided I think that you can move across the Potomac without disclosing our plans. He speaks of your leaving, via Hopewell Gap, and passing by the rear of the enemy. If you can get through by that route, I think that you will be less likely to indicate what our plans are than if you should cross by passing to our rear. I forward the letter of instructions with these suggestions. Please advise me of the condition of affairs before you leave, and order General Hampton—whom I suppose you will leave here in command—to report to me at Millwood, either by letter or in person, as may be most agreeable to him.

Most respectfully,
James Longstreet, Lieutenant-General

N. B.—I think that your passage of the Potomac by our rear at the present will, in a measure, disclose our plans. You had better not leave us, therefore, unless you can take the proposed route in rear of the enemy.

Lee's second set of orders to Stuart, issued on the afternoon of June 23, reads as follows:

Headquarters Army of Northern Virginia
June 23, 1863—5 p.m.
Maj. Gen. J. E. B. Stuart, Commanding cavalry

*General: Your notes of 9 and 10:30 a.m. to-day have just been received.
As regards the purchase of tobacco for your men, supposing that
Confederate money will not be taken, I am willing for your commissaries or
quartermasters to purchase this tobacco and let the men get it from them,
but I can have nothing seized by the men.*

*If General Hooker's army remains inactive, you can leave two brigades
to watch him, and withdraw with the three others, but should he not appear
to be moving northward, I think you had better withdraw this side of the
mountain to-morrow night, cross at Shepherdstown next day, and move over
to Fredericktown.*

*You will, however, be able to judge whether you can pass around their
army without hinderance, doing them all the damage you can, and cross
the river east of the mountains. In either case, after crossing the river, you
must move on and feel the right of Ewell's troops, collecting information,
provisions, &c.*

*Give instructions to the commander of the brigade left behind, to watch
the flank and rear of the army, and (in the event of the enemy leaving their
front) retire from the mountains west of the Shenandoah, leaving sufficient
pickets to guard the passes, and bringing everything clean along the valley,
closing upon the rear of the army.*

*As regards the movements of the two brigades of the enemy moving
toward Warrentown, the commander of the brigades to be left in the
mountains must do what he can to counteract them, but I think the sooner
you cross into Maryland, after, to-morrow, the better.*

*The movements of Ewell's corps are as stated in my former letter. Hills
First Division will reach the Potomac to-day, and Longstreet will follow to-
morrow.*

Be watchful and circumspect in all your movements.

I am, very respectfully and truly, yours,
R. E. Lee, Genl

These orders with the implication that he would be required to ride around the enemy army or risk disclosing Lee's plans were accepted by Stuart at the time as standard operating procedure. The intentions of both messages, along with Longstreet's endorsement, however, would later become highly controversial in the career of Jeb Stuart, which is why they are reproduced here. Lee's orders would raise the question—and, to offer a harsher sentiment, the accusation—about whether or not Stuart willingly disobeyed orders and thereby contributed to the vulnerability of the Army of Northern Virginia during the upcoming Gettysburg campaign.

Coincidentally (or another act of fate), thirteen years later—to *the day*—on June 22, 1876, Lieutenant Colonel George Armstrong Custer would receive written orders from Brigadier General Alfred Terry during the Little Bighorn Campaign. These orders, delivered at the mouth of the Rosebud in Montana Territory, would ignite a controversy similar to the one Stuart would face that has been debated to this day regarding Custer's engagement of Sitting Bull's hostiles camped along the Little Bighorn River.

A summation of Lee's messages reveals that Stuart was assigned four separate missions as he ventured into enemy territory: guard the flank of General Richard Ewell, inform Ewell about enemy movements, confiscate any provisions that the army could use, and strike the enemy whenever and wherever possible. Few limitations pertaining to specific deadlines, timetables, or locations were stated by Lee, and it would appear that much of the mission had been left to the discretion of Stuart.

Jeb Stuart assembled the troops for his reconnaissance at Salem, about ten miles south of Rector's Cross Roads. His cavalry for the march would be comprised of the brigades commanded by Wade Hampton, Fitz Lee (back in the saddle), Colonel John Chambliss (commanding wounded Rooney Lee's brigade), and one six-gun battery. Beverly Robertson and Grumble Jones, with the rest of the horse artillery, would remain behind to guard the rear and flanks of the main army. Major John S. Mosby would not accompany Stuart but rather was sent north toward Dranesville to keep watch on the enemy and report any movement.

At one o'clock in the morning on June 25—with the rattle of spurs and creaking of saddle leather—Stuart's 6,000-man column rode south and east to set the operation in motion. By noon, the force was stopped in its tracks by the enemy along the Warrenton-Centreville Turnpike as it approached the village of Haymarket, which effectively blocked passage through the Bull Run Mountains. This corps of Union infantry commanded by Winfield Scott Hancock would end Stuart's planned march should it threaten Lee's rear. According to orders, Stuart would in that case be obliged to rejoin the infantry on the other side of the Blue Ridge.

Jeb Stuart had no intention of aborting his mission and decided to fire on Hancock with artillery, an action that was authorized by his orders. Hancock returned fire, but before his guns could enfilade the Rebel position, Stuart withdrew and rode five miles around his enemy to escape unscathed. Stuart camped at Buckland and grazed the horses for the remainder of the day. A courier was dispatched to inform General Lee that Hancock was heading to points leading to the Potomac. For some unknown reason, that message was never delivered, and Lee would remain unaware of the Federal pursuit.

On the morning of June 26, Stuart continued his movement east and south through Bristoe Station and Brentsville. By nightfall, he had arrived just north of Bull Run, a march of only a disappointing thirty-five miles in forty-eight hours due to the necessity of the detour.

The following day, Saturday, the main force continued on toward Fairfax Court House while Fitz Lee detoured east to tear up railroad track and cut telegraph lines at Burke's Station. Fairfax Station was found to be held by eighty-six troops from Companies B and C of the 11th New York Cavalry, who were on duty there for the purpose of guarding army stores.

Stuart, demonstrating his old form, galloped ahead of Hampton's brigade and brazenly charged alone—directly into point-blank rifle fire from the Yankees. At the last moment, Stuart spurred his horse and dashed away with the urgency of a man chased by the haunts to narrowly escape through a hail of bullets.

In the ensuing brief skirmish, the New Yorkers were able to inflict a number of casualties before twenty-six of them were either killed or taken prisoner while all the others fled into the nearby timber. The sutler's store was then sacked and provided Stuart's men with new hats, gloves, and boots, as well as a variety of edible delicacies and alcoholic beverages.

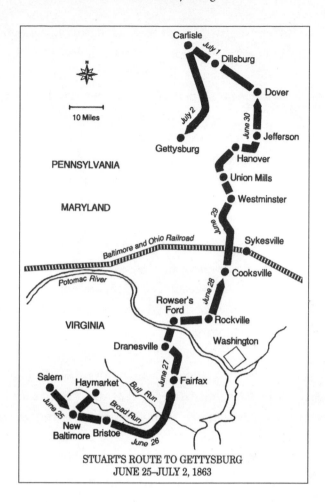

STUART'S ROUTE TO GETTYSBURG
JUNE 25–JULY 2, 1863

Stuart had intended to cross the Potomac at Seneca Ford, but recent rains had swelled the river by two feet above normal depth. A local civilian's recommendation to cross at Rowser's Ford above Dranesville was found to be an acceptable location. Wade Hampton's brigade led the way across the mile-wide river, followed by Stuart with the main force, then the artillery, which was floated across aboard flatboats. Ammunition was carried across in the hands of the cavalrymen.

It was not until three o'clock in the morning on June 28 when all the men and equipment finally made it across. Stuart immediately put his men to work until dawn destroying property along the Chesapeake and Ohio Canal and capturing additional stores, including several barrels of whisky.

The men were then rewarded by their commander with the opportunity to rest; the march would not resume until later that morning.

On the Union side of the line, Fighting Joe Hooker, who had been the subject of dissatisfaction since Chancellorsville, tendered his resignation. On June 28, President Lincoln accepted and subsequently appointed General George Meade to replace Hooker.

Major General Alfred Pleasonton sought an audience with Meade on the afternoon of the new commander's first day at the office. The purpose of Pleasonton's visit was to recommend a reorganization of the cavalry corps. Meade had been authorized by the president to replace or promote any officer deemed necessary to improve the effectiveness of his army.

Pleasonton made the request that Major General Julius Stahel, who outranked Pleasonton and was a native of Hungary—another foreigner—be relieved of duty, in addition to Brigadier General Joseph Copeland, commander of the Michigan Brigade.

Pleasonton also recommended the promotions to brigadier general of three officers, with June 29 as the official date of rank: Captain Elon Farnsworth, whose uncle, Congressman John Farnsworth, was a political ally; capable Captain Wesley Merritt; and Lieutenant, brevet captain, *George Armstrong Custer*.

Various versions over the years about how Custer received and reacted to the astounding news of his promotion have created more legend than fact. In one of the more popular and amusing accounts, Custer had returned to his tent following an inspection tour of pickets while enduring the rain and mud. His tentmates greeted his arrival by announcing, "Gentlemen, General Custer!" The banter continued with phrases such as "You're looking well, General," and "How are you, General Custer?" Custer was somewhat embarrassed and rebutted with the promise that they may laugh now but someday he *would* be a general. He was then directed to an envelope addressed to "Brigadier General George Armstrong Custer, U. S. Vols." Custer was allegedly mortified, chagrined, and on the verge of tears.

Whether or not the above account contains any truth would be a matter of conjecture. More than likely, Pleasonton, who regarded Custer as a surrogate son, would have desired to personally break the news. In a letter to

Isaac Christiancy dated July 26, 1863, Custer wrote that he had been summoned to cavalry headquarters at three o'clock on the afternoon of Pleasonton's meeting with Meade. It was at that time that the announcement was made that would stun Custer and confound and infuriate veteran officers. "I had not the remote idea that the president would appoint me," Custer wrote, "because I considered my youth, my low rank and what is of great importance at times & recollected that I have not a single 'friend at court.' To say I was elated," he added, "would faintly express my feelings."

At the tender age of twenty-three, Brigadier General George Armstrong Custer was now the youngest general in the Union army. Bugler Joseph Fought described the reaction to the promotion: "All the other officers were exceedingly jealous of him. Not one of them but would have thrown a stone his way to make him lose his prestige. He was way ahead of them as a soldier, and that made them angry."

Pleasonton would respond to any criticism of his choice by saying: "Custer is the best cavalry general in the world and I have given him the best brigade to command."

Not only was the promotion itself remarkable, but the accompanying assignment was almost equally astonishing. Pleasonton placed his new general in command of the 2nd Brigade of Brigadier General Hugh Judson Kilpatrick's 3rd Cavalry Division. This brigade consisted of the 1st, 5th, 6th, and 7th Michigan Volunteer Cavalry Regiments. Custer had earlier exercised every possible act within his power, from upstanding to conniving, to be appointed colonel of any one of the Michigan regiments. Now he commanded them all. The appointment certainly enabled Custer to exact some measure of sweet revenge on the Republicans in his home state.

Apparently not only fellow officers were surprised and baffled by Custer's promotion. The Monroe, Michigan, *Commercial*, Custer's hometown newspaper, was initially skeptical: "Upon the first appearance of the report that Captain Custer had been made a brigadier general of Cavalry, we were in some doubt as to its genuineness: but it proved to be a bona-fide appointment. He had fairly earned his promotion to this position, and it is an honor which Monroe citizens should be proud of. He will no doubt prove fully capable and efficient."

The first order of business for the fashion-conscious Custer was to properly display his new rank. He was in possession of a flashy uniform but locating a pair of stars would be a challenge. He dispatched bugler Fought on a scavenger hunt, which finally late into the night was successful when two silver cloth stars were purchased from an army sutler.

Fought sewed on the stars to complete the uniform that he described as "a velveteen jacket with five gold loops on each sleeve, and a sailor shirt with a very large collar that he got from a gunboat on the James. The shirt was dark blue, and with it he wore a conspicuous red tie—top boots, a soft hat, Confederate, that he had picked up on the field, and his hair was long and in curls almost to his shoulders."

Not everyone was impressed with Custer's homemade costume. One of General Gregg's staff officers quipped that Custer looked like a "circus rider gone mad." This was the distinctive uniform, however, that Custer would be known by for the remainder of the war.

While Custer was coming to terms with his promotion and preparing himself to ride out early the following morning and introduce himself to his new command, Jeb Stuart and his three brigades were riding and raiding through the lush Maryland countryside.

Stuart had crossed the Potomac to arrive on the outskirts of Rockville at about noon on June 28 and was delighted to be welcomed by an adoring group of young ladies from a local female academy. The flirtatious girls embraced the cavalrymen, happily pinning ribbons on them, cutting off locks of their hair for souvenirs in trade for uniform buttons, and serving a buffet of food. Captain John Esten Cooke wrote that the troops were enthralled by the attention offered by "the beautiful girls in their fresh gaily coloured dresses, low necks, bare arms, and wilderness of braids and curls. Every eye flashed, every voice exclaimed; every rosy lip laughed."

The enjoyment of the company of these fair maidens was interrupted when Wade Hampton relayed word that he had spotted a Union wagon train. This supply train, comprised of 150 wagons and 900 mules that stretched for eight miles in length, had earlier departed Washington bound for Meade's army.

Stuart and his troops swooped down on the unsuspecting wagons, which Cooke described: "Every team in full gallop, every wagon whirling onward, rebounding from rocks, and darting into the air—one crashing against another 'with the noise of thunder'—here one overturned, and lying with wheels upward, the mules struggling and kicking in the harness; then one toppling over a steep bank, and falling with a loud crash: others burning, others still dashing for shelter to the woods, the drivers cursing, yelling, lashing, blaspheming, howling amid the bang of carbines, the clatter of hooves, and cries of 'Halt! halt! halt!'"

Stuart burst into laughter and exclaimed: "Did you ever see anything like that in all your life!"

The Southern horsemen captured 125 wagons, losing only those that overturned and the few that evaded them by detouring onto side roads. Stuart confiscated the generous load of supplies, which included delicacies such as ham, sugar, and whisky, then paroled the 400 teamsters. Perhaps more importantly, most of the wagons contained oats, a boon to the horses, which were in poor condition. The column re-formed at Cookeville to camp for the night.

Brigadier General George Armstrong Custer rode out before dawn on June 29 to take command of his brigade, which was encamped forty-five miles away at Abbotstown, a few miles north of Hanover.

Custer immediately assessed that his troops were poorly disciplined by officers who had been lax in enforcing regulations. Many of these subordinates had been field officers while Custer was a West Point cadet, but he refused to treat them ingratiatingly or even cordially, which he considered a sign of weakness. Instead, he acted cold and aloof while issuing orders to improve readiness—and to let everyone know who was now in charge.

Custer summed up his sentiments by later writing: "From the very nature of the military rule which governs and directs the movements and operations of an army in time of war, it is essentially requisite to success that the will of the general in command shall be supreme, whether or not he possesses the confidence of his subordinates. To enforce obedience to his authority, no penalty should be deemed too severe."

Custer understood that his officers and troops may dislike him at first, but he pledged to change their minds when the opportunity to lead them into battle presented itself. "I should soon have them clapping me on the back and giving me advice," he wrote.

The 5th and 6th Michigan earlier had been detailed on a scouting mission. The remainder of Custer's brigade, which included Battery M, 2nd United States Artillery, rode out later that day toward Littlestown to spearhead the main body of Meade's army across the Pennsylvania state line. Meade intended to remain between Lee and the city of Washington. Unknown at that time to either side was that Meade's objective would put his army on a collision course with Lee's army that would climax in the rolling hills of southern Pennsylvania near the town of Gettysburg in a battle for the ages.

At the same time that Custer was assuming command for the first time, Jeb Stuart was riding on a northerly route through Maryland toward Pennsylvania. His cavalry had been slowed by the newly captured wagons, which adjutant Henry McClellan had to no avail urged Stuart to burn, and bore an additional burden of dragging along the Yankee prisoners. But Stuart justified his decision not to abandon the wagons by citing Lee's instructions to "collect all the supplies you can for the use of the army." Stuart had also to some extent lost his bearings and was not entirely certain about the exact location of Lee's army but believed it to be to the west near Frederick.

Along the way, Stuart's men destroyed telegraph lines that effectively severed communication between Washington and points north and west, tore up track along the Baltimore and Ohio Railroad, and wrecked a bridge at Sykesville. Late in the afternoon, after attempting without success to intercept trains on the B & O, Stuart moved on and encountered some resistance from two companies of the Delaware cavalry at Westminster.

The ninety-five Union troopers were stubborn—charging several times and inflicting moderate casualties on the ranks of the Invincibles. Finally, Stuart personally led a counterattack by the 4th Virginia and overcame the opposition, which lost sixty-seven killed, wounded, or captured. Stuart lost two officers and gained more prisoners, and perhaps more importantly, the skirmish created another delay in his progress.

By five o'clock, Stuart's command with its 125 wagons extended for five miles northward to Union Mills, and he made the decision to camp for the night. He dispatched scouting patrols, found forage for the animals, and tended to the casualties from the skirmish with the Delaware cavalry. Stuart himself remained in Westminster, settled into a chair propped against a private residence, and slept without the knowledge that Custer and his troops were bivouacked less than eight miles away.

At daylight, Stuart was back in the saddle, unaware that he was riding directly into the middle of the Union army—41,000 Federal troops were ahead of him, and an equal number close behind. He was somewhat concerned that, due to the delays caused by the impediment of the captured wagon train, he had lost contact with Ewell. Apparently, he was not *too* concerned. He managed to find the time to stop over in Union Mills at the home of Confederate patriot William Shriver. Stuart consumed a leisurely breakfast followed by an hour or so of singing his favorite songs, including "Jine the Cavalry," with his staff around the Shriver family Steinway piano.

General George Armstrong Custer's men were also treated to an unaccustomed breakfast from sympathizers. His regiment had led the way for Kilpatrick on the ride that rainy morning that brought them to Hanover at about eight o'clock. Hanover was fearing a siege by the enemy and had taken appropriate precautions. According to Reverend William K. Zieber, pastor of the Emmanuel Reformed Church, "Bank deposits and valuable articles owned by private citizens were sent away. Some people concealed their treasures in their houses or buried them in their yards or gardens."

For that reason, the Union cavalrymen were greeted like conquering heroes and lauded with hardy applause and cheering as well as a serenade by young girls in front of the Lutheran church parsonage. Gifts of cigars, loose tobacco, and baskets of flowers were presented. Word was passed around town by Reverend Zieber that the troops were hungry and had little food. The locals responded with enthusiasm, and before long the men were enjoying a fine meal. Custer and his cavalrymen remained in town for almost two hours enjoying the hospitality before departing toward Abbottstown out the York Pike.

Jeb Stuart's entertainment at the Shriver home was interrupted when scouts rushed in to inform him that a large contingent of the Army of the Potomac had been sighted seven miles to the north near Littlestown.

Shriver's son, Herbert, volunteered to lead Stuart's men on a back road that would permit them to ride around those Union forces. The general was now greatly concerned. A detour around Littlestown would further delay his rendezvous with the infantry. But, taking into consideration the encumberment of the wagons, he was compelled to avoid a battle if at all possible.

Stuart immediately set out with Herbert Shriver as guide in an effort to evade the Union troops by moving in the direction of Hanover. Five miles later, the column crossed the Mason-Dixon line into enemy territory, which evoked cheering throughout the ranks. Confederate troops had a habit of reacting in this manner whenever stepping onto enemy soil.

The plan to dodge the enemy was dashed when at about ten o'clock, Stuart's advance guard led by Colonel Chambliss's brigade ventured into Hanover and stumbled upon elements of the 18th Pennsylvania Cavalry. The Federals, under General Farnsworth, had followed Custer into town and had received the same gracious welcome.

Without waiting for orders, Chambliss's 2nd North Carolina Regiment charged into Farnsworth's troops and drove the Pennsylvanians back through the town. Farnsworth and the 5th New York mounted a counter attack and quickly routed the Confederate troops.

Jeb Stuart rode to the sound of firing just as his 2nd North Carolina, the "Black Horse Cavalry," under Colonel W. H. Payne, was sent into a panicked retreat out the Littlestown Pike with Federal horsemen in hot pursuit. Stuart watched for a moment as his men thundered past him while others engaged in hand-to-hand combat and saber duels. Then, with the threat of capture, or worse, mounting with every second, the cavalry commander, "waving his sabre with a merry laugh," according to William Blackford, leaped aboard his mare, Virginia, and jumped a hedge to escape into what he presumed was an open field. That particular field, unfortunately for Stuart and Blackford, who was riding alongside, happened to be occupied by Union troops.

Captain Blackford related: "As we alighted in the field, we found ourselves within ten paces of the front of a flanking party which was accompanying the charging regiment, and they called us to halt; but as we let our two thorough-breds out, they followed in hot pursuit, firing as fast as they could cock their pistols. A huge gulley fifteen feet wide and as many deep stretched across our path. There were only a couple of strides of distance for our horses to regulate their step. Stuart and myself were riding side by side and I turned my head to see how Virginia had done it, and I shall never forget the glimpse I then saw of this beautiful animal away up in mid-air over the [twenty-seven-foot] chasm and Stuart's fine figure sitting erect and firm in the saddle. The moment our horses rose, our pursuers saw that there was something there, and it was with difficulty they could pull up in time to avoid plunging headlong into it."

Stuart regrouped from his close call on a ridge southeast of Hanover, which afforded him a commanding position for his troops. He discouraged the enemy from advancing with accurate artillery barrages while waiting for Hampton's and Fitz Lee's brigades to move up.

Kilpatrick, with Custer hot on his heels, raced back to Hanover and set up a command post on the square in the Central Hotel. The terrified citizens of Hanover had barricaded the streets to the south with store boxes, wagons, hay ladders, fence rails, barrels, bar irons, and anything else that would prevent the enemy from dashing into town. Kilpatrick quickly dispatched Custer to deploy his regiments and two six-gun batteries on a ridge northwest of town known as Bunker Hill.

Custer's 5th and 6th Michigan, the regiments that had been out scouting, now approached Hanover from the south and west and stumbled into Lee's brigade. Colonel George Gray of the 6th Michigan understood that his men would be overwhelmed by the superior Rebel force. He deployed a line of skirmishers to hold Lee at bay and escaped by riding northwest. Just after noon, the two regiments were united with Custer on the Union right, which enlarged the Boy General's command to about 2,300 men.

The two sides engaged in dueling cannons for the better part of the afternoon. This stalemate was finally broken when Custer moved about 600 of Colonel Gray's troopers west of Hanover to face the position occupied by Fitz Lee's artillery.

Custer dismounted his men and led them across the pasture of a farm, at times crawling on hands and knees, to a position within 300 yards of the enemy. Custer then ordered a barrage of Spencer rifle and Colt pistols, which effectively rousted the Confederates from their cannons. Lee rushed up reinforcements in an effort to hold the position. Custer countered by calling for another barrage. It was evident that Custer's cavalrymen would be unable to seize the position, but they accomplished the next best thing by successfully assuming vantage points that discouraged Stuart from committing himself to an attack.

George Armstrong Custer, on his second official day as a brigadier general, had proven himself an effective, take-charge leader. In the words of cavalryman James H. Kidd of the 6th Michigan: "It was here that the brigade first saw Custer. As the men of the 6th, armed with Spencer rifles, were deploying forward across the railroad into a wheatfield beyond, I heard a voice new to me, directly in the rear of the portion of the line where I was, giving directions for the movement, in clear resonant tones, and in a calm, confident manner, at once resolute and reassuring. Looking back to see whence it came, my eyes were instantly riveted upon a figure only a few feet distant, whose appearance amazed if it did not for the moment amuse me . . . an officer superbly mounted who sat his charger as if to the manor born. Tall, lithe, active, muscular, straight as an Indian and as quick in his movements, he had the fair complexion of a school girl . . . It was he who was giving the orders. At first, I thought he might be a staff officer, conveying the commands of his chief. But it was at once apparent that he was giving orders, not delivering them, and that he was in command of the line."

Jeb Stuart bided his time until sundown and then commenced a quiet withdrawal heading eastward beyond the Union left flank, then turning north. He would march his exhausted men and animals, along with the wagon train and about 400 prisoners, throughout the night without any definite knowledge of the location of the Army of Northern Virginia.

Tomorrow would be July 1, 1863. The most monumental and pivotal battle ever waged on American soil would commence. And James Ewell Brown Stuart and George Armstrong Custer had an appointment with destiny.

CHAPTER SEVEN

EAST *of* GETTYSBURG

KILPATRICK WAS QUITE PLEASED with the performance of his troops. Farnsworth and Custer in particular had distinguished themselves by respectively driving Stuart out of Hanover and crushing the Confederate left. His cavalry might have lost over 200 men in the standoff affair, which was likely about fifty more than his enemy, but Stuart's withdrawal was sufficient evidence of another Union victory.

For reasons known only to himself, however, the man known as Kil-Cavalry for his aggressive tendencies stepped out of character and decided not to initiate an aggressive pursuit. Instead, he sent out a few patrols and ordered his men into bivouac along the Abbotstown Pike.

Stuart with his three brigades, prisoners, horse herd, and 125 wagons, pulled by mules that had not been fed or watered for three days, trudged along for twenty miles through the darkness. The troops were short on rations and battle weary. The mules, which had been assigned to Fitz Lee, were a "source of unmitigated annoyance" according to William Blackford. To complicate matters, there was the additional burden of 100 captured horses, mostly of the draft variety, which were naturally plodding, and the 400 prisoners that had been rounded up.

Stuart later reported: "Whole regiments slept in the saddle, their faithful animals keeping the road unguided. In some instances they fell from their horses, overcome with physical fatigue and sleeplessness."

While Lee's and Meade's armies marched on a collision course that would rendezvous the next morning at Gettysburg, Stuart maintained his pace through Jefferson toward Dover. When the gray cavalry column reached New Salem, Stuart ordered John Esten Cooke to wait for Wade Hampton and direct the general to Dover. Hampton followed and rode until almost dawn, when he halted to catch forty winks in a haystack beside the road. Hampton, however, arrived in Dover by daylight on July 1 to greet the main column. Stuart at that point granted his men a well-deserved, albeit brief, rest.

Fitz Lee had in the meantime crossed the main road from York to Gettysburg and reported that Jubal Early had marched west. Stuart, however, found recent Yankee newspapers at Dover that gave him the impression that the army he was seeking was concentrating around Shippensburg. Lee encouraged Jeb to follow Early's trail, which should lead them to the as yet unknown position of Lee's army. Instead, the cavalry commander dispatched Major Andrew R. Venable with orders to discern the exact location of General Early.

Then, inexplicably, Stuart mounted his troops and resumed his march toward Carlisle Barracks with the hope of locating rations and fodder. This mistake would cost Stuart a full day's ride, further test the endurance of his men and animals, and result in serious consequences to his reputation.

Kilpatrick had no knowledge of Stuart's ambitious ride toward Carlisle. He roused his division early on the morning of July 1 and marched back through Abbotstown then north to East Berlin in a futile search for his elusive enemy around that area. Before long, barrages of rifle and artillery fire could be heard originating from the direction of Gettysburg, about nine miles to the west of Kilpatrick's position.

A Confederate division commanded by Major General Henry Heth, who was seeking boots and shoes for his men, had encountered Union cavalry under Brigadier General John Buford about four miles west of that strategically important town where nine roads converged. Heth's men mounted several charges on the dismounted cavalrymen but were repulsed each time. Both armies hurried to reinforce the field, and the ferocious battle for possession of Gettysburg commenced.

Jeb Stuart's absence during this critical time was a source of great consternation for his commander. General Lee had apparently expected the arrival of his cavalry by then and expressed his anxiety to Major General Richard Anderson. "I cannot think what has become of Stuart," Lee said. "I ought to have heard from him long before now. He may have met with disaster, but I hope not. In the absence of reports from him, I am ignorant of what we have in front of us here. It may be the whole Federal army, or it may be only a detachment."

Major G. Campbell Brown, an aide to General Ewell, reported to Lee that afternoon with dispatches confirming that Ewell's divisions were on their way to Gettysburg. According to Brown, Lee asked him "with a peculiar searching, almost querulous impatience, which I never saw in him before but twice afterward" whether Ewell had heard from Stuart. There had been no word for three days, Brown reported, although it was acknowledged that Stuart's instructions would have placed him on Ewell's right. Lee then ordered that patrols be dispatched in an effort to contact Stuart.

That morning's chance encounter between the blue and gray armies would ignite an escalating firestorm of sound and fury on the field. Custer and his comrades, who must have been chomping at the bit to enter the fight, would endure the uproar created by this major engagement throughout the day without receiving orders to move. While Kilpatrick's anxious men rested, Lee would successfully drive the Union troops onto Cemetery Ridge and Culp's Hill on the high ground south of town and celebrate a temporary victory. Word passed through the ranks that only darkness had saved Meade's army from being wiped out by the aggressive Rebels.

By evening, Jeb Stuart, who was unaware of the monumental battle unfolding at Gettysburg—twenty-five miles to the south—had arrived on the outskirts of Carlisle. He likely had been looking forward to seeing this post that he had visited in 1859 and the place where his wife, Flora, had lived as a child when her father was commandant. His cavalry had traveled almost forty miles since that morning on a march said to be more arduous than the one from Hanover to Dover, and both man and beast reflected that fact.

Lieutenant G. A. Beale later wrote that "from our great exertion, constant mental excitement, want of sleep and food, the men were overcome and so tired and stupid as almost to be ignorant of what was taking place around them." Colonel R. L. T. Beale added, "Here some of our men were busy in a search for rations, but most of them, suffering an agony for sleep, lay on the road with bridles in hand, some on rocks, and others on the wet earth, slumbering soundly."

Instead of finding easily attainable provisions that his men so direly needed, Stuart was informed that Carlisle had recently returned to Union hands. Brigadier General William F. "Baldy" Smith had cheered the local residents by retaking the town with two brigades of infantry, a detachment of cavalry, and some artillery support.

George Armstrong Custer had been assigned to Smith's staff as an aide-de-camp in 1862 at Yorktown and had at that time ascended in balloons to observe enemy movements and provide Smith with vital information. Smith had subsequently lost his command and rank (his nomination to major general had been rejected by the Senate) by publicly criticizing Major General Ambrose Burnside following the Fredericksburg debacle. Now, Baldy Smith was determined to regain his prestige as well as his old command and promised to be a determined foe.

Stuart could have chosen to bypass this moderately sized garrison, but his fatigued men and animals simply could not travel any farther without food, rest, and forage. Besides, giving quarter was not compatible with Stuart's combative style. He was intent on compelling Smith to quit the position. To that end, Stuart ordered Fitz Lee to blast the Federals into submission with artillery. Lee approached close to the barracks and commenced a highly ambitious but relatively inaccurate barrage.

Those shells that did hit their mark ignited fires that lit up the darkness but were for the most part ineffective and failed to convince the Union troops to abandon the town. When Lee paused from the bombardment to demand that the garrison surrender, a defiant Baldy Smith rejected the entreaty.

The cannons continued firing, but the weary Confederate cavalrymen were in many cases oblivious to the sound of fury. Artillerymen fell fast asleep around their cannon. One officer slept while leaning against a fence near a blasting gun, while others dozed in the saddle. A second surrender demand was greeted with the same answer from General Smith. Stuart then intensified the barrage, this time destroying the county courthouse and several empty government warehouses. John Esten Cooke said that "the light fell magnificently upon the spires of the city, presenting an exquisite spectacle."

The attack was rapidly developing into a farce for Jeb Stuart. It had become apparent that the obstinate Baldy Smith did not intend to surrender under any circumstances less than total annihilation, which would require more than merely artillery on the part of the Rebel cavalry. An angry General Stuart ordered another round of shelling, this time setting fire to the town's lumber yard and gas works and igniting several barns and at least one residence. A total of 134 shells had ripped into Carlisle Barracks yet had resulted in only a dozen or so wounded.

Then during the wee hours of July 2 an event occurred that convinced Stuart to abandon his efforts. Major Venable, who earlier had been sent to locate Jubal Early, reported back with orders from General Robert E. Lee. At least one report indicated that this courier who brought word to Stuart was James D. Watters, who would later become a district court judge in Maryland, but most confirm that it was Venable. Regardless of the messenger's identity, Stuart was informed that his services and that of his cavalry were required at Gettysburg without delay. He finally had been provided directions to find his way back to the Army of Northern Virginia. Stuart mounted his exhausted troops and lit out on a route that would pass through Heidlersburg, Hunterstown, and on to Gettysburg.

"This night march," John Esten Cooke wrote, "was the most severe I ever experienced. The long succession of sleepless nights had protrasted the strongest, and General Stuart and his staff moving without escort, passed over mile after mile asleep in the saddle." At dawn, Stuart dismounted, wrapped himself in his cape, and slept leaning against a tree. After two hours, he awoke and rode off alone to report to Robert E. Lee.

Union cavalry General Kilpatrick also received orders during the night. His commander, General Pleasonton, had paid him a visit with instructions "to move as quickly as possible toward Gettysburg."

At about 6 a.m., with Lee and Meade already in position facing each other across the field, Kil-Cavalry moved his troops down the Baltimore Pike to the York Pike. In late morning, the column swung west through New Oxford then north in the direction of Hunterstown, five miles from Gettysburg. At about 2 p.m., the 3rd Division halted at the rear of Meade's army and awaited further orders.

While Custer and his men remained formed in a column of fours, Jeb Stuart, who had ridden ahead of his cavalry, reported to Lee at Gettysburg.

The Knight of the Golden Spurs, according to some estimates, was more than sixty hours late. Lee was said to have greeted Stuart by saying, "Well, General, you are here at last."

Lee's statement cannot be properly interpreted without knowing its tone and intent, but it was in keeping with the commander's reserved character. Another reason for Lee's restraint could be attributed to the fact that the previous day had gone quite well for his army, and the prospects thus far that day were encouraging as well. Many of those present, however, suggested that Lee was piqued, perhaps even angered, by his headstrong subordinate's prolonged absence.

The meeting concluded when Lee ordered Stuart to gather whatever information he could about Union movements while guarding the Confederate left. Jeb rode off to establish his headquarters on the Heidlersburg Road about a mile from Gettysburg.

Stuart would have likely shrugged off any criticism by persuading himself that his raiding foray of the past week had been his greatest of the war. He was, however, perceptive enough to understand that his tardiness had caused a slight break in his relationship with Lee. Always the optimist, Stuart would have, in his cocky manner, vowed to carry out his present mission with his typical precision. Any doubt about his trustworthiness or competence would quickly be erased, and any criticism would be forgotten.

After a three-hour wait wilting under the hot sun, Judson Kilpatrick finally received orders in late afternoon. Longstreet had maneuvered his two divisions beyond Meade's left and attacked; the 3rd Division was told to assume a position to the right of the main force to prevent that flank from being turned. The division, with Custer and the 6th Michigan taking the lead, backtracked north to York Pike then turned east toward Hunterstown, where Brigadier General Wade Hampton and 1,750 Rebel cavalrymen had halted about a mile south.

Custer had dispatched a detachment of the 6th led by Lieutenant Charles E. Storrs forward to reconnoiter the area. At sundown, these troopers had dismounted to sneak through the woods along the Gettysburg road and eventually happened upon Hampton's rear guard, which included Hampton himself. The two sides exchanged a series of volleys that sent Hampton's men scurrying for cover.

General Hampton, however, remained in place to engage in an impromptu duel with rifleman James C. Parsons of I Company. A bullet from Parson's Spencer grazed Hampton's chest. Hampton ignored the superficial wound and was about to fire when he noticed that his adversary's rifle had fouled. In an act of chivalry, Hampton waited for Parsons to clean the bore and then calmly shot the man in the wrist. Parsons fled to seek medical attention.

The duel with the trooper was over, but Hampton now faced another threat. Without warning, Union Lieutenant Storrs dashed from the woods to strike Hampton in the back of the head with his saber. Only the general's slouch hat and thick hair saved him from a serious wound or even death. Hampton aimed his revolver point-blank at Storrs's face, but the percussion cap was faulty and failed to discharge. Storrs hastily retreated into the woods, and a disgusted Hampton retired to the rear to get patched up. While seeking medical attention, the general learned that Union cavalrymen were advancing and received orders from Stuart to head up the road to meet them.

After conferring with Lieutenant Storrs about the reconnaissance, Custer moved forward to view elements of the Confederate cavalry positioned behind rail fences and in the fields. The newly appointed general was anxious to fight and quickly estimated that there could be no more than a couple of companies, 200 or so dismounted enemy cavalrymen, to his front.

He reported this information to Kilpatrick, and it was decided that Custer would challenge the enemy force. Captain Henry E. Thompson's A Company of the 6th, perhaps fifty men strong, was formed across the road for the attack. Three other dismounted companies that would act as skirmishers were deployed to the right, the 7th Michigan to the left, and the 5th held in reserve.

When his units were in place, Custer astonished and delighted his men by riding to the front with the obvious intention of leading the charge. Generals rarely, if ever, led individual companies into battle, but this was Custer's first charge as a general and he was not about to be denied any glory associated with what he presumed would be a smashing victory. Custer drew his saber, sounded the charge, and galloped forward to lead Thompson's men directly into the rifle sights of more than 600 of Wade Hampton's troopers.

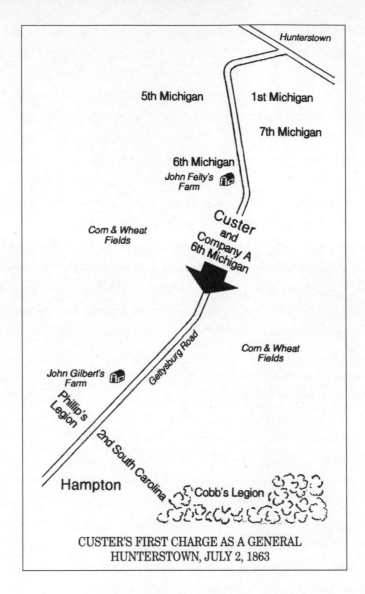

CUSTER'S FIRST CHARGE AS A GENERAL
HUNTERSTOWN, JULY 2, 1863

The result was inevitable. Company A was sliced to ribbons by volley after volley of carbine fire, some of it coming from the weapons of Union skirmishers that had been poorly deployed. Captain Thompson and more than thirty of his troopers were blasted from their saddles. Thompson's second-in-command, Lieutenant. S. A. Ballard, was also shot and subsequently captured.

Armstrong Custer narrowly escaped death or capture when his horse was shot out from under him and he became a prime target for Rebel sharpshooters. He was fortunate that Private Norvill F. Churchill of the 1st Michigan noticed the plight of his commander and rode through the fusillade to lift Custer onto his mount and gallop to the rear.

The Rebels mounted a charge, but the day was saved from total disaster when Kilpatrick ordered Pennington's and Elder's artillery batteries to open up. That timely barrage, combined with small arms fire, succeeded in relieving the pressure and pushing Hampton's men back.

The surviving Yankees high-tailed it down the road toward the relative safety of Hunterstown. Hampton's artillery dueled with the Union batteries until after dark when he chose to withdraw and return to Stuart, leaving behind twenty-two gray-clad cavalrymen. Kilpatrick reported thirty-two killed, wounded, or captured.

Custer was predictably devastated by his failure, although his conduct had for the most part impressed his brigade and was the subject of lavish praise by his commander. He had pledged when he assumed command of the Michigan Brigade that he would instill a sense of confidence in his men with his ability under fire, but that notion had been temporarily dashed. That night, Custer analyzed his actions over and over and realized that the lack of knowledge about the precise size of the enemy waiting in front of him had brought about his downfall. He vowed that he would not make that same mistake twice.

At 11 p.m., Kilpatrick moved his exhausted troops out of Hunterstown to Two Taverns, five miles southeast of Gettysburg on the Baltimore Pike. The 3rd Division cavalrymen straggled down the road, arriving at their bivouacs anywhere between 3 a.m. and dawn to catch whatever amount of sleep was possible before the next march.

The second day at Gettysburg had been another killing field for the two armies, a slaughterhouse of unimaginable proportions. Places assigned unofficial names such as the Peach Orchard, the Wheatfield, Devil's Den, Little Round Top, and Culp's Hill—the location of the final action of a day that ended with another abortive Rebel attack—would forever be inscribed on the pages of war annals as sites of some of the bloodiest engagements ever waged in this country. Most of the dirty work to this point had been conducted between opposing infantry and artillery. The cavalries on both sides, however, had now arrived in force and were itching to pick a fight with each other.

Before dawn on July 3, Jeb Stuart led four brigades of his horsemen, about 6,000 men—with 1,000 infantry men attached—northeastward along the York Pike. His destination was a position around the far right of the Union line. Lee would be renewing his attack on Culp's Hill, and he planned to later execute a bold move that would thrust a massive and powerful gray fist into the belly of the blue line. George Pickett and eleven infantry brigades were scheduled to mount a heroic frontal assault on Cemetery Ridge, the center of the Union defense.

Jeb Stuart's cavalry was without question intended to play a vital role in Lee's daring strategy. Although no definitive document from Robert E. Lee's own hand exists to verify specific orders, it would be highly unlikely, in spite of the widespread disapproval of Stuart's recent actions, that the cavalry commander would not have been briefed about the particulars of such an audacious undertaking. And there is every indication that Stuart's part in this offensive would be to wade into the Union rear in coordination with Pickett's charge that afternoon and create mass confusion as well as weaken the line by drawing away the enemy to fight the cavalry.

The exact time of this mounted attack would be determined when circumstances warranted and could be arranged by Lee dispatching a courier, but taking into consideration Stuart's subsequent actions, it was more than likely worked out to in some manner coincide with the conclusion of an artillery barrage. If Pickett's charge was to be successful, Stuart must be in precisely the right position to discover it and improve the opportunity by hitting the Union rear. This one-two punch would ultimately result in an overwhelming Confederate victory. To prepare for this mission, Stuart had consulted his topographical maps in order to select the perfect location for an offensive strike.

While Stuart rode down the York Pike, Kilpatrick received orders from General Pleasonton at 8 a.m. to move his division in support of Meade's line at Little Round Top and Big Round Top. Kilpatrick had already departed with Farnsworth's 1st Brigade by the time Armstrong Custer received orders for the movement and roused his troops.

Custer had just gotten underway when an aide from Brigadier General David Gregg, commander of the 2nd Division, brought word that Gregg wanted Custer's command to join him near the Rummel's farm about three miles north on the Hanover Road. Gregg had been charged with protecting Meade's right flank and, given the amount of enemy cavalry activity operating in the area, feared that he lacked enough men to adequately defend that position. Gregg assumed responsibility for Custer's presence without clearing the order through proper channels but did so with concern for protecting the Union rear.

Custer joined Gregg and formed his brigade in a line along the intersection of Hanover and Low Dutch Roads facing Gettysburg, partially on property owned by a farmer named John Rummel. The lesson learned the previous evening about the importance of reconnaissance convinced Custer to immediately send out patrols in every direction. The Boy General was not about to be caught unaware of enemy strength or movement on this day.

At about 10 a.m., Jeb Stuart directed his troopers off York Pike at a crossroads two and a half miles beyond Gettysburg. The horsemen rode another mile along a country road to approach a lengthy ridge that ran upward from the south, with heavy timber on the northern end. Cress Ridge, Stuart judged, was the ideal position.

The high ground of Cress Ridge fell away to a level valley and commanded views of pastoral pastureland dotted with an occasional farmhouse and separated in places by stone and stake-and-rail fences. Three hundred yards from the foot of the ridge stood a large wooden barn owned by John Rummel. Hanover Road was a mile and a quarter away, and, more importantly, the position afforded direct access to the Union line to the south. Stuart had made an effort to conceal his movement in the thick woods behind the ridge, but Hampton's and Fitz Lee's brigades happened to pass through open ground and unintentionally revealed their presence.

Custer's vigilance about dispatching patrols had been rewarded. A patrol comprised of members of the 6th Michigan had observed Stuart's cavalry. The patrol commander, Major Peter Weber, returned before midday to report that at least two brigades of Rebel cavalry and one artillery battery had been observed moving forward through the trees one mile to the west of Cress Ridge. "I have seen thousands of them over there," Weber related. "The country yonder is full of the enemy."

It did not take Jeb Stuart long to confirm the major's report. Shortly after noon, he ran out a section of Capt. W. H. Griffin's Maryland Battery and personally ordered the firing of four shots—and only four shots.

When there was no immediate response from the Federal line, Jeb dispatched a dismounted detachment of Brigadier General Albert G. Jenkins's 34th Virginia to descend Cress Ridge and occupy some outbuildings on Rummel's farm.

The reason for Stuart's impulsive artillery action at the time befuddled his adjutant, Major Henry McClellan. Later, however, McClellan speculated that the firing of the four rounds may have been a prearranged signal to let General Lee know that Stuart had successfully reached his position at the Union rear.

McClellan's assumption rings true. Stuart, the master of stealth, would not have fired the cannons and compromised his position simply to determine the location of his enemy. Jeb knew, after all, that he was at the rear of the Union line. His actions therefore can be interpreted to mean that the cavalry indeed was an integral part of a plan to strike the rear in coordination with Pickett's frontal assault. Lee was now free to carry on with his bold strategy.

Gregg held his own units in support and assigned the front to the Michigan Brigade. General Custer studied the terrain with field glasses and formulated his reply to Stuart. He ordered Pennington's battery to return fire, and deployed the 6th Michigan on the left, the 7th on the right, and the 1st in the center. The 5th was dismounted as skirmishers to the left and center. The opposing riflemen exchanged fire for some time until Union artillery fire or perhaps an order from Stuart, eventually succeeded in causing the Confederate troops and battery to withdraw. The fight at that point was reduced to long-distance sniping between the two sides.

While Gregg and Custer anxiously waited for Stuart's next ploy, the brigade commanded by Colonel John McIntosh arrived and began to relieve Custer's men at the forward positions. McIntosh's fresh troopers spread onto the field and to some extent escalated the skirmishing.

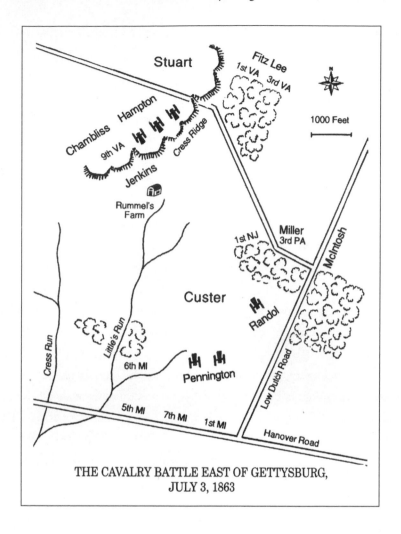

THE CAVALRY BATTLE EAST OF GETTYSBURG,
JULY 3, 1863

While Custer's men retired to the rear, a courier from General Kilpatrick reported to Gregg with orders for the Michigan Brigade to rejoin the 3rd Division. At about the same time, Gregg received orders from Pleasonton to release Custer, but he also learned from Major General Oliver O. Howard, commander of the XI Corps atop Cemetery Hill—a former classmate and friend of Jeb Stuart at West Point—that a large number of enemy cavalry earlier had been observed moving to the right.

Gregg was faced with a predicament. He was already aware of Stuart's presence but was now concerned about the strength of his enemy. He had been charged with protecting the Union rear and could use all the troops he could muster. McIntosh would at some point require reinforcements. Custer, who was of the opinion that a fight was imminent, volunteered to stay. Gregg obliged and decided to countermand both Pleasanton and Kilpatrick and keep the Michigan Wolverines with him for the time being.

At 1 p.m., the relative silence of the Cress Ridge and Rummel's farm area was interrupted by the deafening roar of an artillery bombardment originating from the direction of Seminary Ridge, some four miles distant. The ensuing barrage was so heavy that it caused the ground to shake beneath the feet of the cavalry troops. Captain James Kidd later wrote, "The tremendous volume of sound volleyed and rolled across the intervening hills like reverberating thunder in a storm."

Jeb Stuart would have been aware that the Confederates had opened fire with 150 artillery pieces in an effort to soften up the Federal line in prelude to Pickett's charge. This was his signal to ready his men for an attack on the Union rear. But first he must dispose of the blue cavalrymen that presently blocked his pathway.

Armstrong Custer, on the other hand, would have been comforted to know that Federal guns had answered the challenge with seventy-two pieces of their own fired from behind the stone walls on Cemetery Ridge. But he would not have been fooled into thinking that this was exclusively an artillery duel at Gettysburg. He was savvy enough to recognize, as were many of his men, that such an ambitious Confederate bombardment had been initiated for a specific purpose, and he would have remained alert, wary of Stuart's role in this pending offensive.

Stuart did not waste any time before attempting to remove the obstacle that stood between his cavalry and the Union rear. Shortly before 2 p.m., a skirmisher line of Virginia regiments under Brigadier General Micah Jenkins, about 1,500 men, stepped from the woods on Cress Ridge and commenced a long-range engagement with the forward line of McIntosh's regiment that ran along a fence near Rummel's spring house. At the same time, Stuart ordered Griffin to open up with his cannons.

The Rebel riflemen quickly gained the upper hand in what became a one-sided affair due to the fact that McIntosh's men were running low on ammunition. McIntosh made an effort to disengage but encountered problems getting away through the intense fire and called for assistance. Custer responded by ordering Alger's 5th Michigan to move forward on foot and deployed several companies of the 6th on their left to relieve some of the pressure on McIntosh. Stuart countered by directing his artillery at the newcomers. The shells ripped into the midst of the 5th Michigan to inflict numerous casualties. Custer moved his men back to the shelter of a fence line where they could fire from cover.

While the opposing artillery batteries engaged in a fierce duel, the dismounted Confederate cavalry broke into a charge. Alger's 5th Michigan patiently waited until the Confederates were within 120 yards before firing a furious volley. The Rebels were urged by their officers to strike before the enemy could reload. Unknown to the Confederates, however, was the fact that the Wolverines had been outfitted with Spencer carbines. The Spencer could fire seven cartridges without reloading, and the Yanks discharged four accurate and devastating volleys, which effectively stopped the onrushing Rebs in their tracks.

The tough Invincibles quickly regrouped and returned with reinforcements from Hampton's and Lee's brigades. The 5th Michigan held its ground and maintained the same fire discipline. The bluecoats, however, were dangerously low on ammunition and forced to retreat. The withdrawal of the Wolverines inspired the Confederates to press forward.

Lieutenant Colonel Vincent Witcher, commander of the 34th Virginia, described this charge: "With a wild yell the whole line dashed forward, retook the fence and swept the Federal men back." Stuart dispatched additional troopers, both on foot and mounted, to chase the retreating enemy. Relief was necessary at this point or the 5th Michigan would be overrun.

Captain Kidd noted what happened next: "Just then a column of mounted men was seen advancing from the right and rear of the Union line. Squadron succeeded squadron until an entire regiment came into view, with sabers gleaming and colors gaily fluttering in the breeze." General George Armstrong Custer had ridden to the front of the 7th Michigan and, with saber drawn, he shouted, "Come on, you Wolverines!"

The green troopers of the 7th, their average age eighteen, cheering and yelling at the top of their lungs, followed the twenty-three-year-old Custer into the open field and charged full force into the ranks of the surprised 9th and 13th Virginia regiments. Stuart's men outnumbered Custer's men, but most Rebels were on foot and commenced a hasty retreat from the intent horsemen. Custer and his Wolverines pursued their panicked enemy and rode them down while rounding up small groups of prisoners.

The aggressive Wolverines, however, were about to encounter a major stumbling block. One of the Union troopers that Custer had passed on the charge described that predicament. "To our astonishment and distress we saw that regiment, apparently without any attempt to change direction, dash itself upon a high stake and rider fence, squadron after squadron, breaking upon the struggling masses in front, like the waves of the sea upon a rocky shore until all were mixed in one confused and tangled mass."

The Union troopers had been unaware of the terrain and had topped a rise to abruptly run into a stone wall with a rail fence on top. The cavalrymen slammed into one another at this sturdy barrier, which created a chaotic mass of rebelling horses and confused riders. The retreating Confederates noticed this turmoil and turned about to fire at the trapped men from point-blank range.

While troopers from the 7th labored under heavy fire to tear down the wall, Custer and a mounted detachment veered toward Rummel's farm with the objective of attacking a Confederate battery. Stuart countered the bold attempt by Custer by ordering reinforcements, the 1st North Carolina and the Jeff Davis Legion, forward to support the 1st Virginia. These newcomers to the field waylaid Custer's move toward the battery and in a running battle forced the Yankee horsemen southward across the farm.

The 7th Michigan eventually succeeded in breaking through the stone wall but were met with another sort of wall—this one of the human variety. Johnny Reb tore into Billy Yank in a life-or-death every-man-for-himself struggle. Colonel William D. Mann reported that it was "a desperate, but unequal, hand-to-hand conflict" that grew worse for the Union by the minute.

Custer noticed that the 9th and 13th Virginia regiments were pounding toward the position from the flank and wisely ordered his battered troops to retreat. The Rebels raced forward with intentions of cutting them off. Colonel Alger was determined to ride to the rescue. While McIntosh's troopers laid down a steady base of fire, Alger mounted two squadrons of his 5th Michigan and charged into the Rebels, which allowed the besieged Wolverines to retire and restored distinct battle lines on the field.

Less than half an hour later—presumably at the same instant that Pickett and 13,000 Confederate infantrymen were streaming across the field toward the center of the Union line at Gettysburg—Stuart gathered his horsemen for one final desperate charge. If there was any conceivable hope of supporting Pickett by reaching the Union rear, Stuart must initiate his own version of Pickett's charge and force the Yankees from the pathway to his objective.

Stuart instructed Colonel John R. Chambliss to hastily organize eight regiments from Hampton's and Lee's brigades. Jeb had intended for this force to remain concealed in the timber until further orders, but his wishes were apparently misunderstood. The long gray line of mounted Southerners soon emerged from the woods on Cress Ridge and formed an impressive attack column. The appearance of the Rebel horsemen was described by one awed Union participant: "In close columns of squadrons, advancing as if in review, with sabers drawn and glistening like silver in the bright sunlight, the spectacle called forth a murmur of admiration."

Captain William Miller of the 3rd Pennsylvania added, "A grander spectacle than their advance has rarely been beheld. They marched with well-aligned fronts and steady reins. Their polished saber-blades dazzled in the sun. Shell and shrapnel met the advancing Confederates, tore through their ranks. Closing the gaps as though nothing had happened, on they came." The Southern cavalry started at a trot, picked up speed to a cantor, then galloped directly toward the center of the Union line.

The 7th and 5th Michigan were in the process of re-forming, and the 6th was protecting Pennington's artillery battery, which was furiously firing at the approaching horsemen. Custer had only one option left. Colonel Charles H. Town's greatly outnumbered 1st Michigan regiment would have to ride out and meet this overwhelming threat. The 1st was a veteran, experienced unit, but with the odds greatly stacked against them, one officer summed up the feelings of his comrades by exclaiming, "Great heavens! We will all be swallowed up!"

Colonel Town, who was ill and tired and rode strapped to the saddle, had never in his career shied away from a fight, no matter the odds. If he was to die, there was no better manner to his chivalrous way of thinking than during the execution of a heroic charge. He obediently ordered his troops forward with sabers drawn and prepared to face the enemy on what could only be called a suicide mission.

At that moment, Brigadier General George Armstrong Custer, his long, yellow curls flowing behind him, galloped up to Colonel Town, saluted, and politely indicated that he would assume command. The Boy General, much to the surprise and admiration of his troops, had decided to lead the 1st Michigan on this dangerous charge. Custer rode to the front where every eye could see him, unsheathed his heavy blade, and trotted forward with his customary bravado.

By this time, Chambliss's gray-clad horsemen had progressed halfway to their objective across the open field. Custer, hearing the cheers and yells of his inspired men behind him, confidently urged his mount forward to close the distance between the two cavalries. Perhaps glancing now and then at the faces of the awestruck spectators he passed along his lines, Custer carefully maneuvered around fences and other obstacles and aimed his regiment directly at the head of the onrushing Confederate force. Pennington's battery had been blasting canister shot into the oncoming Confederates but now ceased firing for fear of shelling their own men.

When the Rebels had advanced to within about one hundred yards away, Custer, from a position four lengths ahead of his troops, kicked his horse into a gallop and shouted, "Come on, you Wolverines!" The blue column surged forward in what Colonel Alger would later call "the most gallant charge of the war."

An eyewitness with McIntosh's brigade described the dramatic scene: "The two columns drew nearer and nearer, the Confederates outnumbering their opponents as three or four to one. The gait increased—first the trot, then the gallop. As the charge was ordered the speed increased, every horse on the jump, every man yelling like a demon. The columns of the Confederates blended, but the perfect alignment was maintained. As the opposing columns drew nearer and nearer, each with perfect alignment, every man gathered his horse well under him and gripped his weapon tighter."

Captain Miller recounted the meeting of the opposing cavalries from his position in reserve: "As the two columns approached each other the pace of each increased, when suddenly a crash, like the falling of timber, betokened the crisis. So sudden and violent was the collision that many of the horses were turned end over end and crushed their riders beneath them. The clashing of sabers, the demands for surrender, the firing of pistols and cries of the combatants now filled the air."

Custer reported: "For a moment, but only for a moment, that long, heavy column stood its ground; then, unable to withstand the impetuosity of our attack, it gave way to a disorderly rout, leaving vast numbers of dead in our possession. I challenge the annals of warfare to produce a more brilliant or successful charge of cavalry."

The fighting was so intense and at such close quarters that it was said that some of the killed were found in pairs of blue and gray, "pinned to each other by tightly-clenched sabers driven through their bodies." Another example of the intimacy of this battle was found by John Rummel when he later returned to his farm. In addition to thirty dead horses littering his lane, Rummel found the macabre sight of two opposing cavalrymen. "Their fingers, though stiff in death," Rummel recalled, "were so firmly imbedded in each other's flesh that they could not be removed without the aid of force."

Custer, for the second time in twenty-four hours, was rudely thrown to the ground when his horse, Roanoke was struck by a round in the foreleg and collapsed. The uninjured Boy General quickly corralled a riderless mount and leaped into the saddle to direct his troops and wreak havoc with his own deadly saber.

The sight of his comrades gradually driving back the enemy so affected and motivated Captain Miller that he said to Lieutenant William Brooke-Rawle, "I have been ordered to hold this position, but, if you will back me up in case I am court-martialed for disobedience, I will order a charge." Brooke-Rawle agreed, and the 3rd Pennsylvania Cavalry enthusiastically entered the fray. "The men fired a volley from their carbines, drew their sabers, sent up a shout, and 'sailed in,' striking the enemy's left flank about two-thirds down the column," Miller reported. Thirty-four years later, Captain Miller would be awarded the Medal of Honor for his courageous charge.

While Jeb Stuart directed the fighting from the vicinity of Rummel's barn, additional Union units—remnants of the 5th and 7th Michigan, and the 1st New Jersey—slammed into the Rebels' flanks while Custer and the 1st Michigan gouged a gaping hole through the center. The reinforcements proved too much for the Confederates to withstand and turned the tide in favor of the Federal horsemen. The Rebels, fearing that they would become surrounded, grudgingly gave ground back toward Cress Ridge.

Wade Hampton apparently had been delayed and left behind when the spectacular charge initiated the engagement. "I rode rapidly to the front to take charge of these two regiments," Hampton later explained, "and, while doing this, to my surprise, I saw the rest of my brigade and Fitz Lee's brigade charging." He finally entered the fight when he observed his troops being forced back. "In the hand-to-hand fight which ensued, as I was endeavoring to extricate the 1st North Carolina and the Jeff Davis Legion, I was wounded, and had to leave the field." The general had engaged in a saber duel with a trooper from the 1st New Jersey and suffered two new gashes in his head to accompany the one he had received the previous evening. Hampton also suffered at least one other injury—a bullet or shrapnel wound to the thigh.

The welfare of Jeb Stuart also was placed in jeopardy during the battle. According to John Easten Cooke: "We lost many good men. General Hampton was shot in the side, and nearly cut out of the saddle by a sabre stroke [to the head]. He was slowly being borne to the rear in his ambulance, bleeding from his dangerous wounds. General Stuart had a narrow escape in this charge, his pistol hung in his holster, and as he was trying to draw it, he received the fire of barrel after barrel from a Federal cavalryman within ten paces of him, but fortunately sustained no injury."

The Confederate cavalry fought back to its original position on Cress Ridge. Custer, realizing that Stuart's threat to the Union rear had been successfully thwarted, was content to permit him to withdraw without launching any pursuit. Four miles away, Pickett had charged the Union center with disastrous results for the South.

The battle at Gettysburg, for all intents and purposes, was over.

Casualty totals for both sides in the cavalry skirmish east of Gettysburg have been a matter of contention. Stuart reported losses of 181 killed, wounded, or missing, excluding his artillery batteries and Jenkins's brigade. Gregg reported the loss of 35 from his 2nd Division. Custer's Wolverines had suffered 29 killed, 123 wounded, and 67 missing, which left no doubt about which unit had stymied Jeb Stuart's horsemen in this significant encounter.

The last great cavalry saber battle of the war pitting Johnny Reb and Billy Yank against each other had ended with the Federals claiming victory and the Confederates contending that it had been a draw. One debate, however, that had originated at Brandy Station had been settled. Stuart's legendary Invincibles were no longer deemed invincible by the ecstatic Union cavalry.

This sentiment was echoed on the Confederate side of the line by William Blackford. After calling the battle "about as bloody and hot an affair as any we had yet experienced," Blackford added, "The cavalry of the enemy were steadily improving and it was all we could do sometimes to manage them."

The field east of Gettysburg was turned over to medical personnel who tended to those combatants showing any sign of life while loading the unfortunate ones into creaky caissons that carried away the bodies from the carnage.

At dusk, while the wary Union cavalry maintained a vigilant watch, Jeb Stuart abandoned Cress Ridge and withdrew his weary brigades down York Pike. Stuart displayed his own fatigue by leading his men in the wrong direction, directly toward enemy lines, until corrected by a staff officer. Stuart was good-natured about his error and resumed his march in this new direction with only a courier at his side while his staff rode on ahead. At one point, the courier rode forward as Stuart slept in his saddle. His horse failed to recognize his rider's headquarters and nearly carried Stuart into enemy cavalry pickets.

It had been an exhausting ten days for Stuart and his cavalry, but what lay ahead would perhaps be more personally demanding for the *Beau Sabreur*—the scrutiny of his actions by those seeking to place blame for this failure to defeat the enemy.

Somewhere along the Union cavalry lines, a jubilant Armstrong Custer rested in the darkness. He had accomplished everything that General Gregg had expected of him and, more importantly, everything that he had expected of himself. His miscalculation of the previous night would now be relegated to a mere footnote, likely forgotten, for he had gained redemption by meeting Jeb Stuart on equal terms and emerging draped with glory.

CHAPTER EIGHT

WITHDRAWAL
and PURSUIT

APPARENTLY, MOST HISTORIANS REMAIN IN DENIAL about the Custer-Stuart engagement east of Gettysburg. They refuse to give Custer credit for his heroism and field generalship, likely due to prejudices toward him in later years as an Indian fighter, which has been fueled by his unfair demonization in pop culture. Another reason is that they likely have not researched the engagement deeply enough to know the facts about how the battle played out, choosing instead to concentrate on the primary battlefields at Gettysburg.

It has been argued that it was General David Gregg, and not Custer, who was in charge of the engagement. But, with all due respect, it was Custer, not Gregg, who was issuing the orders on the battlefield and leading the charges when the action was hot and heavy.

In addition, scholars contend, with no evidence, that Jeb Stuart was positioned there on Cress Ridge so that he could gather up Union prisoners as they retreated from the lines in the face of Pickett's charge. This supposition makes no sense at all and makes fools of both Robert E. Lee and Jeb Stuart.

Would the master tactician, Robert E. Lee, attempt a suicidal frontal assault that was not backed up by some other strategic maneuver or diversion? Would he not have learned from the butchering of Union troops at Fredericksburg less than seven months earlier when General Ambrose Burnside executed a frontal assault into a powerful line of Confederate troops?

Of course, Lee would have known that a frontal assault across a barren pasture was absurd and would have been deadly for his troops. So, did he have another part of this mission in mind that would make this assault by Pickett successful? He did, and Jeb Stuart was the key player—and every act by Stuart when he arrived in Gettysburg proved it.

The strongest evidence comes from Jeb Stuart himself. Stuart stated *twice* in his official report that he was trying "to effect a surprise on the enemy's rear" from his position on Cress Ridge. His mission had not been to chase fleeing troops but, in a coordinated effort with Pickett, to charge into those entrenched blue-clad soldiers on the line. The only way Pickett's frontal assault could have worked was if Jeb Stuart's 6,000 troops had slammed into the Union rear and caught their enemy in a murderous cross fire. The Union line would have crumbled into chaos, and Pickett's men would not have had any organized opposition to their approach.

Had that happened, Gettysburg could have been the final major battle of the Civil War, and the Confederates could have held the upper hand. And that was how Robert E. Lee had planned his audacious attack.

There was only one problem—a twenty-three-year-old brigadier general named George Armstrong Custer leading weary but determined troops did not allow Jeb Stuart to reach and attack the Union rear. Consequently, the assault by Pickett fell apart, and the Confederates lost a golden opportunity to strike a significant blow to their enemy. It can be said that this victory by Custer in keeping Jeb Stuart's men on Cress Ridge and denying them the Union rear was the turning point of the Gettysburg battle and perhaps of the war itself.

Jeb Stuart's official report, by the way, can be read in the *Official Records of the War of the Rebellion*, volume 27, part 2, pages 697 and 698.

Meanwhile, the Confederates might have considered the battle a loss, but the campaign had in many ways been successful. An abundance of supplies had been confiscated in the North, perhaps enough to last through the winter months. Also, to the world and national observers, Robert E. Lee had demonstrated that his army could hold its own against the Union on Northern soil. Had Lee gained a decisive victory at Gettysburg, the Army of the Potomac would have simply withdrawn to Washington and the Army of Northern Virginia would have resumed the invasion. In that case, the best that Lee could have hoped for would have been an opportunity to negotiate a peace agreement.

On the night of July 3, Jeb Stuart reported to Robert E. Lee and learned about the disastrous result of Pickett's gallant charge. How he explained his failure to hit the Union rear from Cress Ridge, if he had, can only be imagined. And, likely for the first time, Stuart witnessed his stalwart commander briefly teeter near the emotional breaking point. Lee, who accepted personal blame for the defeat, had good reason to display his anguish.

The losses during this three-day affair were staggering. The South had suffered 3,903 killed, 18,735 wounded, and 5,425 missing. Lee's compassionate character would not permit him to simply shrug off the impact of this battle on his army or condemn anyone else for actions he had directed as its commander. Other officers, however, had already begun dividing loyalties and pointing fingers. And Jeb Stuart, who had been occupied with riding around the Union army when the fighting had commenced, was an easy target for vilification.

One can only imagine the reception Stuart received from the other staff officers at a meeting that was held overlooking the bloody field at Gettysburg. Sides were being taken in the debate about whether or not Stuart had disobeyed orders and, if so, to what extent his actions had affected the outcome of the three-day battle. For that reason, he must have endured at least a few accusatory glances, if not outright snubs, but would never have admitted—even in his own mind—that he had in any way contributed to this devastating defeat.

The dream of securing peace and independence for the Southern people had been dealt a crushing blow, but the war was by no means lost. Lee quickly gathered himself and tended to his soldiering responsibilities. His army remained entrenched in a defensive posture on Seminary Ridge, expecting an attack. But, as the hours passed, Lee correctly surmised that Meade was for the time being content to rest his battle-weary troops.

Lee summoned his officers to a council of war and arrived at the only logical conclusion under the circumstances—withdraw his army. The Confederate troops, who had expected to resume the fight, were disappointed by Lee's decision, which dispelled the rumor that the spirit of the rank and file had been broken.

William Blackford wrote: "The Battle of Gettysburg in its results was a great victory for the Federal cause, but Lee's army did not feel like a beaten one. There was no rout or confusion; not even a pursuit to remind us that our invasion had come to an end, and all the silly stuff we read in the Northern accounts of 'flying rebels' and 'shattered army' are pure fictions prepared for the northern market." John Esten Cooke added to that sentiment: "Nothing is more erroneous than the idea that the Southern army was 'demoralized' by the results of the bloody action of these three memorable days. Their nerve was unshaken, their confidence in Lee and themselves unimpaired."

Lee's first order of business would be the evacuation to Virginia of his wagons, supplies, and the ambulances that carried many of the wounded, including Wade Hampton. Unfortunately, a great number of the wounded would, out of necessity, be left behind with the hope that they would be treated with compassion by the enemy.

The safe passage of this wagon train with its vital stores and equipment was crucial to the survival of the Army of Northern Virginia. Therefore, the responsibility of guarding the extensive caravan could not be handed to just anyone, but General Lee was confident in his selection of an escort.

Brigadier General John Imboden had demonstrated skillful resourcefulness and the ability to act as a semi-independent command. His successful spring raid through western Virginia had cut the Baltimore & Ohio Railroad lines and captured a large amount of livestock. Imboden and his 2,100 Virginia cavalrymen most recently had been acting as the army's rear guard, which had freed up Pickett for his fateful presence at Gettysburg. Lee now summoned Imboden, who reported just after midnight.

Imboden greeted General Lee by saying, "General, this has been a hard day for you."

Lee replied, "Yes, it has been a sad, sad day to us." He then told Imboden about Pickett's heroic charge, and commented, "I never saw troops behave more magnificently." After a moment of uncomfortable silence, Lee's emotions poured forth, and he said, "Too bad! *Too bad*! OH! TOO BAD!" Lee composed himself and issued orders for Imboden's unit to act as escort for the departing wagon train.

At about the same time that Imboden received his orders, Jeb Stuart's cavalry was charged with the responsibility of screening the army's movement, with the exception of Hampton's and Fitz Lee's brigades, which would be detached to serve as escort for Imboden the following day.

While Stuart conferred with Lee, Armstrong Custer was released by General Gregg and reported back to Judson Kilpatrick's 3rd Division.

Certainly Gregg, as commander of the troops opposing Stuart, deserved some of the credit for the victory east of Gettysburg, but most of the glory was reserved for Custer, who had led the two daring cavalry charges and inspired and rallied his troops on the field by his courageous example. Perhaps more important to Custer than any official acclamation was that he had finally earned the utmost respect of his men.

The North, however, had little reason to celebrate, having suffered 3,155 killed, 14,529 wounded, and 5,365 missing. And although losses from the Michigan Brigade in its significant role had contributed to that incredible casualty toll, Custer was saddened and troubled to learn upon reporting to Kilpatrick about one detachment of the 3rd Division that had fallen in a senseless slaughter.

Hugh Judson Kilpatrick's division had been skirmishing with the Confederates at the south end of the battlefield below Gettysburg late on the previous afternoon. The Yankee horsemen faced a well-entrenched line of Texas and Georgia infantry barricaded behind a stone wall and a stake-and-rail fence. Attempts had been made to dislodge the Rebels, but the terrain, which was comprised of boulders, fences, and ditches, was unacceptable for effective cavalry maneuvers.

Regardless, Kil-Cavalry decided that, although this location held no significant strategic importance, he must take this Confederate position with an assault of his horsemen. Without Custer's brigade available, Kilpatrick had only the brigade commanded by Brigadier General Elon J. Farnsworth remaining to carry out the risky charge.

Farnsworth, who had been promoted to general on the same day as Custer, opposed the action with the opinion that such a charge would be tantamount to suicide. Captain H. C. Parsons, who led one of Farnsworth's battalions, described his commander as "courage incarnate, but full of tender regard for his men, and his protest was manly and soldierly." Kilpatrick responded by mocking Farnsworth's fortitude and virtually goading him into agreeing to lead the charge.

In an assault that was described by a Confederate eyewitness as wholesale slaughter, Farnsworth, who was shot at least five times, and sixty-six of his men were killed during the execution of this ill-conceived charge.

Kilpatrick's irrational act and its outcome would have likely chilled the blood of even Armstrong Custer, who, as evidenced by his bravery at Cress Ridge, was no stranger to charging into the cannon's mouth. The men of the 3rd Division were angered by Kilpatrick's reckless decision, which to them served as another example of their commander's disregard for lives when personal glory was at stake.

But there was no time to dwell on the past. Orders passed from Pleasonton to Kilpatrick that the 3rd Division would ride south and attempt to intercept the Confederate wagon train that was reportedly on the move.

Just after noon on Independence Day, Custer and his Wolverines were in the saddle when the heavens opened up to soak them and add further misery to the march. Captain Kidd wrote: "It seemed as if the firmament were an immense tank, the contents of which were spilled all at once. Such a drenching as we had! Even heavy gum coats and horsehide boots were hardly proof against it. It poured and poured, making every rivlet a river and of every river and mountain stream a raging flood."

The downpour had an even worse effect on the Confederate wagon train commanded by John Imboden. The panicked mules rebelled in the blinding torrent, and the canvas covering the wagons could not adequately repel the rain, which added to the suffering of the wounded occupants. When the caravan neared Cashtown in late afternoon and commenced its climb over the mountains, Imboden rode toward the front and realized that his wagons stretched for seventeen miles along the muddy pathway.

Imboden endured a personal nightmare as he traversed that lengthy line of wagons. "For four hours I hurried forward on my way to the front," he wrote, "and in all that time I was never out of hearing the groans and cries of the wounded and dying. Scarcely one in a hundred had received adequate surgical aid, owing to the demands on the hard-working surgeons from still worse cases that had been left behind. The jolting was enough to have killed strong men, if long exposed to it. From nearly every wagon as the teams trotted on, urged by whip and shout, came such cries and shrieks as these:

"'O God! why can't I die?'

"'My God! will no one have mercy and kill me?'

"'Stop! Oh! for God's sake, stop just for one minute; take me out and leave me to die on the roadside.'"

A shaken General Imboden swore that "during this one night I realized more horrors of war than I had in all the preceding two years."

Kilpatrick reached Emmitsburg at about 3 p.m. and rendezvoused as planned with Colonel Pennock Huey's brigade from Gregg's division, which brought his total strength to more than 5,000 men. By late afternoon, traveling in a southwest direction toward Frederick, scouts delivered a civilian, C. H. Buhrman, to Kilpatrick. Buhrman reported that a huge Rebel wagon train had been observed moving south along Fairfield Gap in South Mountain toward Hagerstown, Maryland. This was not Imboden's train but rather one commanded by Richard Ewell that had departed Gettysburg several hours after the wounded and supply train.

Kilpatrick viewed the capture of this wagon train as an opportunity to restore his somewhat tarnished image and pushed his troops along the soggy earth in a driving rainstorm toward Fairfield. At about 10 p.m., Custer's brigade, which led the march, arrived at a fork in the road—the northwest branch led to Fairfield Gap, the southwest to Monterey Pass—to learn that the Rebel wagons had passed onto the northern road within the past three hours. A Confederate picket comprised of detachments of Beverly Robertson's and Grumble Jones's brigades had been deployed near the fork but withdrew toward Fairfield after only token resistance when the Yankees approached.

In an effort to head off the train, Kilpatrick ordered Colonel Town and the 1st Michigan along the Fairfield Road to attack the rear of the wagon train while the main force moved toward Monterey.

A regiment of Town's battalion commanded by Lieutenant Colonel Peter Stagg approached their objective but were repulsed by Jones's brigade after destroying several wagons. The Wolverines suffered a number of casualties, including Stagg, who was injured when his horse was shot out from under him.

Kilpatrick's column also encountered opposition and was stopped in its tracks inside Monterey Pass by a company from the 1st Maryland Cavalry reinforced by elements of the 4th North Carolina and one artillery piece.

Despite being greatly outnumbered, the Rebels were aided by rainy weather, darkness, and terrain that afforded them a clear field of fire down the road from their positions behind rocks and trees. The narrow pass prevented an orderly retreat by the Yankees, and the Rebel sharpshooters effectively pinned them down with accurate fire.

Custer quickly deployed his troops near a once-popular health resort named Monterey Springs. Seven companies of the 5th Michigan were dismounted and scrambled up the slopes to form a skirmish line on both sides of the mountain road. The 6th was placed on the right, extending down to the road not far from a bridge across a stream that had supplied mineral water to the spa. The two remaining companies of the 5th remained mounted and poised to charge, while the 1st and the 7th were held in reserve.

Custer ordered the Wolverines forward in a series of attempts to mount an offensive and dislodge the Rebels, but the pitch-black darkness, nagging rain, and thick underbrush—not to mention the accurate fire of the hidden enemy—thwarted each effort. James Kidd, who more than once was sent sprawling by vines and briars, wrote: "One had to be guided by sound and not by sight."

Finally, just after midnight, Colonel Alger of the 5th Michigan returned from a reconnaissance and reported to Custer that the bridge remained intact and could be crossed. That was all the frustrated Custer needed to hear to formulate his strategy. An immediate charge was in order.

Custer accompanied Alger on the assault, and the Wolverines of the 5th Michigan rushed full tilt across the bridge into the midst of the enemy. By sheer numbers, firing their Spencer rifles at muzzle flashes, Custer's men cleared the way for the 7th Michigan to follow across the bridge. The small Confederate force understood that in the face of this resolute attack, it was now time to break contact, and they vanished into the dark countryside. During the brief fray, Custer's horse was shot—reportedly his seventh mount lost in the Gettysburg Campaign. Custer was uninjured in the fall.

The next order of business was to secure the wagon train, which was located a half mile away. Kilpatrick's men, embarrassed that only a handful of the enemy had stymied three brigades for several hours, swooped down with a vengeance on Ewell's wagons. The train, with its 400 vehicles that reportedly extended for some ten miles, was easily captured along with 1,360 prisoners, who were for the most part Gettysburg casualties. Supplies were confiscated, and most of the wagons were hacked apart or burned before Jones's brigade arrived to chase away the Yankee cavalry. Kilpatrick moved his troops, prisoners, and new-found riches to Ringgold, where at dawn a halt was ordered.

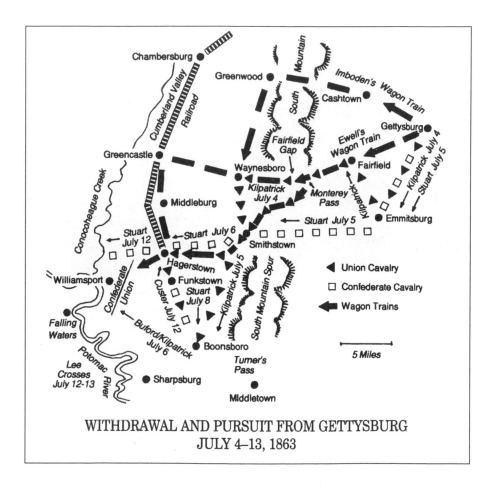

WITHDRAWAL AND PURSUIT FROM GETTYSBURG
JULY 4–13, 1863

The division, according to *New York Times* reporter E. A. Paul, was "tired, sleepy, wet, and covered with mud. Men and animals yielded to the demands of exhausted nature, and the column had not been at a halt many minutes before all fell asleep where they stood." Custer found refuge under the eaves of a chapel and slept, "his golden locks matted with the soil."

This respite from the saddle was short-lived, however, when after two hours Kilpatrick roused his weary troops. He was determined to locate and engage Stuart's cavalry, and pushed onward in the direction of Smithstown (present-day Smithsburg), fifteen miles away.

The entire Confederate army was on the move, and Jeb Stuart's men, who were guarding both of Lee's flanks, had no better time of it in the downpour and barely passable roads than did the Union cavalry. It was dawn on July 5, several hours after Kilpatrick had passed through, before Stuart, in the company of the brigades led by Colonel Chambliss and Colonel Milton J. Ferguson (commanding the wounded Albert Jenkins's brigade), reached Emmitsburg, the point nearest to the enemy. Stuart made the decision to remain in Emmitsburg long enough to plan strategy and interrogate the sixty prisoners that he had captured on his advance into town.

One of those Union prisoners, a signal officer named Louis R. Fortesque, provided an interesting description in his diary of Stuart: "To those who have never had the misfortune of an introduction under such unfavorable conditions, his [Stuart's] appearance might have awakened adulatory criticism, particularly by believers in his theory of southern rights. But to us his self-assumption and bombastic exaggeration of dress simply invited contempt. In stature he was six feet, and weighed about one-hundred and ninety pounds. A complexion somewhat ruddy from exposure, with light brown hair, worn rather long, and full flowing beards. His regulation gray uniform was profusely decorated with gold braid, and was topped with a broad-brimmed felt hat, pinned up at the side with a star from which drooped an extravagantly large ostrich feather. On his left breast was a shield, about two inches in width, which held a chain attached to the handle of a small stiletto, the blade being passed through the button holes of his coat."

Stuart decided to detour around Kilpatrick, and with that in mind, he departed Emmitsburg at midmorning. He led his horsemen south to Cooperstown (present-day Creagerstown) and then turned west while descending the Catoctin Mountains to arrive at a fork in the road in which both branches would eventually lead toward South Mountain. Colonel Ferguson was dispatched along the lower, more direct route toward Smithstown, while Stuart led Chambliss on the northern passage.

Stuart approached the outskirts of Smithstown and was surprised to discover that Kilpatrick was lying in wait with skirmishers deployed on each side of the road and artillery positioned on three hills. Colonel Huey and Colonel Nathaniel P. Richmond (now commanding Farnsworth's brigade) had been assigned the front; Custer's Wolverines remained in the rear.

Federal guns pounded Stuart's advance units, and he was incapable of immediately counterattacking inasmuch as his own artillery was far behind and inaccessible for the time being. Stuart quickly dismounted his troops to return fire, dispatched a courier to bring up the artillery, and summoned Ferguson, who was engaged with Richmond, to reinforce Chambliss.

The Union cavalry held a major advantage and threatened to trap Chambliss in the pass even with assistance from Ferguson. Stuart, however, was afforded a lucky break when Kilpatrick, who was informed of Ferguson's movement, committed a tactical blunder. Instead of pressing his advantage, Kilpatrick inexplicably disengaged his troops and ordered them to ride for Boonsboro, twenty miles to the south.

The 3rd Division commander later wrote in his report that he had broken off contact in order "to save my prisoners, animals, and wagons." Perhaps Kil-Cavalry had suffered a momentary bout of faintheartedness at the prospect of fighting Stuart's Invincibles. But, to be fair, Kilpatrick may possibly have been uninformed about Stuart's true strength and, although uncharacteristic for a man with a reputation for sending his men headlong into the face of danger, on this occasion chose to error on the side of prudence. Kilpatrick's troops reached Boonsboro at 10 p.m. and bivouacked for a well-deserved rest.

Meanwhile, Stuart dutifully reported the movements of the Union cavalry to General Lee, then led his column toward Leitersburg to rendezvous with Beverly Robertson. Stuart, who had been informed that Kilpatrick was in Boonsboro, had his four brigades in the saddle by daylight heading southward toward Hagerstown and the Potomac.

Along the way, Grumble Jones, who had been feared lost or captured, rejoined the column and reported that Imboden's wagon train had reached Williamsport but could not immediately ford the Potomac River due to flooding caused by the recent rain.

Stuart realized that Hagerstown, only six miles from Imboden's caravan, would be a strategic location in the eyes of the enemy. He dispatched Jones's brigade out the Boonsboro Road a few miles toward Funkstown in order to protect Hagerstown from an attack from the east. Two small brigades commanded by Chambliss and Robertson proceeded on a direct route to Hagerstown.

Kilpatrick had caught wind of Stuart's movement and was preparing to mount a pursuit when John Buford arrived in Boonsboro. Buford had been on the trail of Imboden's wagon train and was armed with the information that his quarry was presently stalled at Williamsport, thirteen miles to the northwest. The capture of this supply train could conceivably cripple the Army of Northern Virginia beyond recovery. It was decided that Buford, supported by Custer's Wolverines and personally accompanied by Kilpatrick, would attempt to surround the train at Williamsport, while the other column would ride for Hagerstown and engage Stuart and prevent his cavalry from assisting Imboden.

Colonel Richmond led the Union advance into Hagerstown and encountered Chambliss and Robertson approaching from the northeast. The Confederates initially gained the upper hand. Fighting street to street, they pushed Richmond's disorganized troops backward. Reinforcements were sent in to bolster the attack and eventually succeeded in driving Chambliss's undersized unit out of town.

Stuart was aware that Kilpatrick's ultimate objective would be Imboden's wagon train at Williamsport, and he must at all costs hold Hagerstown. Chambliss was ordered to charge directly down the road while Ferguson and two of Robertson's regiments would attempt to strike the enemy's flank.

While the blue and the gray horsemen dueled on the streets of Hagerstown, Buford had approached Williamsport at about 1:30 p.m. to discover a well-fortified enemy. General Imboden had deployed his two brigades of cavalry, two regiments of infantry, twenty-four pieces of light artillery, and even the teamsters armed with the weapons of the wounded into a tight perimeter at the base of a hill below town to protect his immobile caravan.

Ambulances had been unloaded and the wounded moved into nearby houses, and makeshift rafts had begun ferrying supplies across the swollen river. Imboden had prepared to hold the position until the remainder of Stuart's cavalry and Lee's infantry could arrive to reinforce the position and drive off any enemy.

Imboden greeted Buford with a barrage of small arms fire and artillery designed to impress upon the Yanks that they would pay dearly should they advance. Skirmishers were sent forward in various spots along the line to bluff an attack and keep Buford confused with respect to the size and position of his troops. Buford retaliated with a series of assaults, which were for the most part easily repulsed.

At one point, Kilpatrick dispatched Custer and the 5th Michigan to advance through town on a saber charge but had second thoughts and rescinded the order. Alger's riflemen were then dismounted and sent forward but were met with heavy resistance and, as one cavalryman described, "with shells bursting over our heads," could not get close enough to be effective.

Back at Hagerstown, Stuart was supported by the head of Lee's infantry column and an artillery brigade from Ewell's Corps, which supplied enough firepower to push the Union cavalrymen into a fighting retreat. The final blow was administered when the head of Longstreet's Corps arrived to reinforce Stuart. Colonel Richmond halted once to counterattack but was quickly routed by the 5th North Carolina and 11th Virginia. Now this strategic position was in sole possession of the Army of Northern Virginia. By evicting the enemy from Hagerstown, Stuart was now free to concentrate on the threat by Buford and Kilpatrick to Williamsport.

With darkness descending and Jeb Stuart and Fitz Lee approaching, General Buford made the decision to withdraw. Custer and his Wolverines accompanied Buford's 1st Division into camp at Jones's Crossroads, while Kilpatrick and Huey retired to Boonsboro. General Imboden summed up the sentiments on the Confederate side of the line at the sight of the retreating Yankees when he wrote: "The news was sent along our whole line, and was received with a wild and exultant yell. We knew then that the field was won."

The heroic actions by Jeb Stuart and his horsemen had saved the day for the Confederates. The loss of the supply wagon—gathering supplies, after all, had been the initial purpose of the campaign—would have been disastrous.

The reports written by both Buford and Kilpatrick grudgingly acknowledge their failure to seize this opportunity to possibly crush the Confederacy. Buford wrote: "The expedition had for its objective the destruction of the enemy's trains, supposed to be at Williamsport. This, I regret to say, was not accomplished. The enemy was too strong for me, but he was severely punished for his obstinacy. His casualties were more than quadruple to mine." Buford might have overestimated the losses suffered by his obstinate enemy. Federal casualties in the engagement amounted to about 400; the Southerners reported 254.

Custer and his men remained in a rain-drenched camp to rest throughout the day on July 7, while Stuart deployed his troopers in strategic locations to enable General Lee to freely inspect approaches to the river that would afford a safe crossing for his army back into Virginia. Lee, whose army was now concentrated around Williamsport and Hagerstown, was in no hurry to test the flooded river. He spent his time consulting with his subordinates and discussing the merits of various potential crossing areas designated on maps drawn by his engineers before he would make a final decision.

The opposing cavalries engaged in a heated skirmish on July 8 when the wily Stuart, who intended to aggressively cover the presence of his army, executed a ploy designed to make his enemy think that he was heading for the South Mountain passes beyond Boonsboro. General Pleasonton had issued orders for his cavalry to protect these mountain gaps in order to enable passage by Meade's infantry, which was on the far side of the mountain moving south. And Stuart intended to keep the cavalry confused with respect to specific movements and locations.

Stuart led four brigades (Lee, Jones, Chambliss, and Baker) down the Hagerstown Pike from Funkstown and met Union forces at about 5 a.m. near Jones's Crossroads and Boonsboro. The battle commenced when Stuart ordered McGregor's artillery battery to open up on Buford's right flank. This action was followed by an attack by Grumble Jones's dismounted brigade, who were on foot due to the soft, saturated earth, which made it difficult for mounted troops to maneuver. Colonel Ferguson's brigade arrived from the northwest and was dispatched by Stuart to strike the Union left flank. The combination of smoking cannons and bold skirmishers was successful. Buford's men were compelled to withdraw up the mountain into Turner's Pass.

Kilpatrick responded by stabilizing the center of Buford's line with Custer's brigade and the left flank with Richmond. The batteries commanded by Elder and Pennington, which were positioned on the hills behind Boonsboro, began having an effect on holding back the aggressive Confederate skirmishers. The horsemen of Custer and Richmond, supported by Colonel William Gamble's infantry, shored up defenses and in time gained the upper hand. Custer and his Wolverines forced the enemy back to Beaver Creek, three miles away.

The intense fighting continued throughout the afternoon, with casualties mounting on both sides, including Colonel Russell Alger of the 5th Michigan, who was severely wounded when struck with a minnie ball in the left thigh. The capable Alger would not return to action until September.

As five o'clock approached, Jeb Stuart was aware that he had accomplished his mission. Upon learning that his men were running low on ammunition, he ordered a gradual pull back in a northerly direction on the old National Road toward Funkstown. The Federal troops pursued, but Stuart deployed a strong line of defense four miles away below Funkstown, which effectively brought an end to hostilities.

Buford and Kilpatrick reasoned that their original role had been to guard the mountain passes, and that endeavor had been achieved by chasing away Stuart. They were now content to return south with their jubilant albeit battle-weary troops, who to a man were certain that another victory had been won that day. One ecstatic wolverine wrote: "This is the eighth fight we have had with the Rebs and have whipped them everry [sic] time."

It would appear that both sides were satisfied with their performance. Jeb Stuart, however, had more of a reason to celebrate. His valiant efforts had once again thwarted any possibility of the enemy inflicting a serious, or even fatal, blow to the Confederacy by striking Lee's army and supply train at Williamsport.

The effort of keeping his enemy at bay coupled with the earlier exhausting ride to Gettysburg and fighting at Rummel's farm was apparently exacting a serious physical and mental toll on the Confederate cavalry commander.

Adjutant Henry McClellan recounted an incident that occurred likely that evening after the hard day of incessant battle.

At about 9 p.m., Stuart and his staff officers arrived in Hagerstown at a house occupied by a young lady whose father was a Southern sympathizer. The countryside had been depleted of provisions, and the men were extremely hungry. This lady generously offered to prepare supper for them, which was gratefully accepted. Stuart, who had not eaten in twenty-four hours, had fallen asleep on a sofa in the parlor and refused to answer the call to supper. McClellan gently led the general to the table, but Stuart merely picked at his food.

Their concerned hostess noticed Stuart's apathy and asked, "General, perhaps you would relish a hard-boiled egg?"

"Yes," Stuart replied, "I'll take *four or five*."

The eggs were served, but Stuart broke and ate only one of them, and then absently left the table. It was apparent to everyone that their commander was completely oblivious to his surroundings and actions.

This uncharacteristic behavior greatly troubled McClellan, who, in an effort to arouse and cheer up Stuart, suggested that they sing "Jine the Cavalry." With McClellan at the piano, Stuart heartily joined in the singing of his favorite song.

The music served to snap Stuart from his lethargy. And when told about his discourtesy to the young lady who had tried so hard to please him, he was mortified and profusely apologized.

General George Meade, who by that time had moved his army to within eight miles west of South Mountain, had issued orders for Pleasonton's cavalry to harass the enemy all they wanted but to avoid a major engagement. That reluctance to crush the Army of Northern Virginia, which was virtually trapped with its back to the river, did not particularly sit well with President Lincoln, Secretary of War Edwin Stanton, or Chief of Staff Major General Henry Halleck. But, taking into consideration the consolidated Confederate position, which extended in an almost uninterrupted line for eight miles and contained a six-foot-wide parapet dotted with frequent gun emplacements, Meade's decision in hindsight was appropriate.

Meade's cautiousness afforded Armstrong Custer and his Wolverines a couple of lazy days spent resting and refitting. The Union cavalrymen and horses had endured an extensive stretch of continuous battle in elements that would test even the hardiest person.

The morale of the troops, however, was soaring, as evidenced by George R. Barse, who wrote: "Although much worn down by fatigue and need of rest, the cry is, 'No rest until the rebels are driven from the State.' We can whip them, and must do so, cost what it will." This welcome respite provided ample time to clean and repair mud-covered clothing and equipment, care for the horses, and reflect on the victory at Gettysburg and perhaps speculate about the victories that surely lay ahead.

General Robert E. Lee had selected a crossing point for his army at the village of Falling Waters, four miles below Williamsport, and his engineers toiled to construct pontoon bridges at that location. Jeb Stuart and his horsemen were kept busy in the saddle protecting the stranded army from the enemy, which would prove to be a constant chore.

At about 8 a.m. on July 10, Buford's foot soldiers waded Beaver Creek and advanced down the road from Boonsboro toward a line of Stuart's dismounted cavalry. The Federal attack pushed the Rebels north to Funkstown toward a Confederate infantry position above Antietam Creek. The engagement continued until about 3:00 p.m., when Buford's men ran out of ammunition and chose to withdraw and bivouac about four miles away. While directing the vicious fighting, Stuart had a horse shot out from under him but otherwise emerged unscathed.

Early on July 12, with Meade's infantry arriving to darken the hills around them, Custer and his Wolverines were roused from their inactivity. Custer's brigade, in advance of the 3rd Division, charged "screaming and yelling" into Hagerstown unopposed to grab fifty prisoners and occupy the town. Detachments of the 1st, 5th, and 7th Michigan advanced toward Williamsport but ran into Rebel entrenchments and wisely decided to wait for reinforcements from Meade's infantrymen. The foot soldiers, who had not fought in the ten days since Gettysburg, compared to Custer's men who had seen battle every couple of days, soon appeared and enabled the cavalrymen to fall back.

This raid by the Union cavalrymen compelled Stuart to withdraw his line back to Conococheague Creek on the National Road where Lee's army had established heavily fortified positions. That night, according to Adjutant

McClellan, Stuart once again displayed the effects of his sleep deprivation and stress of command.

Stuart was dictating dispatches directing cavalry movements for that night and the following morning to McClellan as they rode, accompanied by one courier, along a turnpike near Hagerstown. McClellan required light, so they stopped at a toll house. While McClellan worked, Stuart fell asleep at the table.

When the dispatches were completed, Stuart was awakened by the adjutant to review them, as was the custom. In the dispatch to the artillery, Stuart took out a pencil, erased the names of two places, and inexplicably substituted the towns of "Shepherdstown" and "Aldie" in their place. "This was manifestly absurd," McClellan wrote, "and I saw at once that he was unconscious of what he was doing. I aroused him with some difficulty. These incidents seem to bear on the disputed question, whether the mind can act and yet be unconscious of its action." McClellan did not, however, offer an opinion about whether or not these foggy episodes had diminished Stuart's ability to effectively command the cavalry.

At about this same time, Stuart wrote a letter to his wife that, due to the exaggeration of its contents, could conceivably hint at his detached state of mind. "I had a grand time in Pennsylvania," he wrote, "and we return without defeat, to recuperate and reinforce, when, no doubt the role will be re-enacted. I shelled Carlisle and burned the barracks. I crossed near Dranesville and went close to Georgetown and Washington, cutting four important railroads, joining our army in time for the battle of Gettysburg, with 900 wagons and splendid teams. My cavalry is the finest body of men on the planet. General Lee's maneuvering the Yankees out of Virginia is the grandest piece of strategy ever heard of."

Upon closer examination, however, the letter expresses the upbeat attitude customarily demonstrated by Stuart in his regular correspondence to Flora and does not reflect the ramblings of a man who had completely lost touch with reality. He may have suffered temporary lapses in concentration due to lack of sleep and fatigue, but Jeb Stuart, as he had throughout the war to this point, was firmly in command of himself and his men when duty called. And he would be required to stave off sleep and exhaustion a while longer. There would be no rest for Stuart until he had shielded the army from the enemy while they crossed the Potomac and were deep onto home soil. And that moment was drawing close.

On July 13, the same Saturday that George Armstrong Custer's Wolverines had charged into Hagerstown, General Meade convened a council of war to relate his intention to thrust his massive army against Confederate fortifications at Williamsport in order to follow up on his success at Gettysburg. The majority of his infantry generals at the meeting, however, argued in opposition to an immediate attack. Meade, in another controversial decision, deferred to their wishes. The assault would be postponed. Instead, reconnaissance patrols would be dispatched in the morning to gather additional intelligence regarding the specific positions of his enemy.

By that time, the water had receded to a level low enough to chance a crossing, and the Rebel engineers and sappers had completed their work placing the pontoons across the river. General Lee had hoped that his enemy would test the strength of his entrenched army. But, upon learning that the Federals had commenced digging fortifications, which indicated that an attack was not imminent, Lee decided that he could wait no longer to cross. He remarked, "They have but little courage."

At 4:15 p.m., Jeb Stuart was summoned and issued his orders by Lee: "I know it to be a difficult as well as delicate operation to cover the army and then withdraw your command with safety, but I rely upon your good judgement, energy, and boldness to accomplish it, and trust that you may be as successful as you have been on former occasions."

Stuart's cavalrymen would assume the positions of 50,000 foot soldiers in an attempt to deceive the enemy into thinking that the trenches along the nearly eight-mile line remained occupied. After the entire army had crossed, Stuart and his men would ride to safety.

On that dark, rainy night, with thunder rolling and lightning cracking, the Confederate army made its move. Longstreet's corps and Hill's corps began crossing at Falling Waters while Ewell's corps forded at Williamsport.

William Blackford reported: "I witnessed the passage of Ewell's corps and it was a strange and interesting sight. On either bank fires illuminated the scene, the water reached the armpits of the men and was very swift. By the bright lurid light the long line of heads and shoulders and the dim sparkling of their musket barrels could be traced across the watery space, dwindling away almost to a thread before it reached the further shore."

In writing about the mules as they pulled the wagons across the deep and treacherous current, Blackford said: "As the water rose over their backs they began rearing and springing vertically upward, and as they went deep and deeper the less would be seen of them before they made the spring which would bring their bodies out of the water; then nothing would be seen but their ears above the water, until by a violent effort the poor brutes would spring aloft; and indeed after the waters had closed over them, occasionally one would appear in one last plunge high above the surface."

By first light, despite losing a small number of men and wagons that had been swept away, Lee's army was well on its way to completing its mission with near flawlessness.

At about 3:00 a.m., the first word of an enemy movement reached General Kilpatrick's ears. Scouts informed him that Confederate pickets had retired from the works below Hagerstown. General Buford's reconnaissance reported at the same time that Confederate positions farther to the east were empty, and the enemy had been observed crossing the river. Both divisions advanced slowly forward. Buford indicated that he would attempt to maneuver between the river and Lee's rear guard, apparently expecting Kilpatrick to follow suit with his cavalry and assist by distracting the enemy.

Instead of coordinating his efforts with Buford, Kilpatrick headed south, with Custer and the 5th Michigan in the lead, and at about 6 a.m. arrived at Williamsport. Custer's troopers discovered only a few stragglers from Ewell's corps at that location and chased those panicked men into the river with the support of Pennington's guns. Perhaps as many as fifty Rebels drowned, and twenty-five wagons with their mule teams were swept away in the raging torrent.

Local residents informed Kilpatrick that a large force of Confederate troops was presently crossing the river four miles downstream at Falling Waters. The 5th Michigan remained at Williamsport to mop up while Custer and his three other Michigan regiments hastened toward Falling Waters.

By now, most of the Confederate army as well as Stuart's cavalry had reached Virginia. Only two divisions of Henry Heth's and William Pender's infantry remained behind on the north bank at Falling Waters.

Two miles from their objective, Custer and an advance detachment of the 6th Michigan encountered the Rebel rear guard and drove them steadily south. At about 7:30 a.m., the Wolverines halted in a woodlot a mile and a half from the river, and from that point could view the enemy crossing point. The imposing breastworks and trenches had been constructed on a crescent-shaped knoll and were manned by artillery and veteran troops of the 13th Alabama and the 1st, 7th, and 14th Tennessee.

Custer, who at the present had only two companies at his disposal, thought it prudent to probe the position with dismounted skirmishers while waiting for the main force to arrive. Companies B and F under Major Peter Weber were ordered forward on foot for that purpose. Major Weber, who was known as "the best officer in the regiment," had confided to Captain James Kidd that he desired one more chance to make a saber charge. Kilpatrick arrived on the scene and afforded Weber that opportunity. The 3rd Division commander countermanded Custer's order and directed Weber to mount about 100 men and charge the thousands of enemy that occupied the hill.

Major Weber must have been aware that this situation was strikingly similar to Elon Farnsworth's earlier ill-fated charge on the last day at Gettysburg. Regardless, he offered no objection, and obediently mounted his men and lighted out at a trot across the open field and up the hill at a gallop.

The advance of the Union horsemen was observed by General Heth and his staff as soon as it had emerged from the woods. But the consensus of opinion was that it must be the rear guard of Stuart's cavalry. No detachment of Federals this small would dare attack a Confederate infantry division. And it was believed that the cavalry, which, incidentally, had earlier crossed by mistake, was bringing up the rear.

The identity of Weber's cavalry unit remained a mystery to the Rebels until it was in their midst, unfurling a "Stars and Stripes" guidon and unleashing a murderous saber attack. The relaxed Confederates had stacked their weapons, and now resorted to using fence rails, axes, and rifles as clubs to fend off the surprise assault.

James Kidd, who was wounded in the foot by a bullet while in the rear of the charge, wrote about what happened next: "Weber, cutting right and left with his saber, and cheering on his men, pierced the first line, but there could be but one result. Recovering from their surprise the Confederate infantry rallied, and seizing their arms, made short work of their daring assailants."

The Confederate infantry blasted Weber's men with a point-blank volley. Weber and his executive officer, Lieutenant Charles E. Bolza, were cut from their saddles, along with at least thirty other Wolverines who were killed, wounded, or captured. Captain David G. Royce of the 6th Michigan was also killed when his dismounted squadron supported the initial charge. One notable casualty for the Confederates was General J. Johnston Pettigrew, who had participated in Pickett's charge. Pettigrew was shot and killed when thrown from his mortally wounded horse.

General Custer dismounted what remained of the 6th and, along with the 1st and 7th, led a series of charges. After a couple of hours of fierce fighting, this resulted in the capture of about 500 prisoners, three battle flags, and a cannon, as the Rebels poured across the pontoon bridge to escape. Private Victor E. Comte of the 5th Michigan, who had been chosen as personal escort to Custer and was at his side throughout the engagement, later wrote home: "I saw him [Custer] plunge his saber into the belly of a rebel who was trying to kill him. You can guess how bravely soldiers fight for such a general."

Confederate General Henry Heth, who had fired the opening shots at Gettysburg, now cut the ropes behind him on the pontoon bridges at Falling Waters to effectively end the campaign.

That night, the 3rd Cavalry Division bivouacked near Boonsboro. In the morning, Kilpatrick requested and was granted a medical leave of absence until August 4. In place of Kil-Cavalry, Pleasonton chose twenty-three-year-old Brigadier General George Armstrong Custer to command the division. Now that the dust—or rather the mud—of the Gettysburg Campaign had settled, Custer was on the verge of becoming a national hero for his exploits during this significant campaign.

Across the Potomac in Virginia, Jeb Stuart might have commendably accomplished his mission of screening Lee's army on its withdrawal, but the reaction of his contemporaries as well as the Southern public toward him would be less than enthusiastic. In fact, Stuart was about to endure a withering attack that would engender long-lasting effects on his reputation.

CHAPTER NINE

THE BRISTOE CAMPAIGN

CIVIL WAR OFFICERS WERE EXPECTED TO MOTIVATE and inspire their troops under fire by example—bravery was contagious. George Armstrong Custer, however, elevated that responsibility to a higher level. Custer had proven during the Gettysburg Campaign that, contrary to those who had questioned Pleasonton's judgment in promoting the twenty-three-year-old to brigadier general, he was quite capable of commanding a brigade. In addition to that, he had gained the admiration of his men with his propensity for leading charges rather than simply directing movements from a safe position in the rear. This one distinct trait had instilled within his troops a confidence that if Custer, a general, had the nerve to charge into the blazing guns of the enemy, then there was reason to believe that if they followed, victory would be within their grasp.

Edwin Havens of the 7th Michigan described Custer in a letter dated July 9, 1863: "Gen. Custerd [sic]. He is a glorious fellow, full of energy, quick to plan and bold to execute, and with us has never failed in any attempt he has yet made." Another proud Wolverine praised: "Our boy-general never says, 'Go in, men!' HE says, with that whoop and yell of his, 'Come on, boys!' and in we go, you bet." Captain S. H. Ballard of the 6th Michigan remembered that "The command perfectly idolized Custer. The old Michigan Brigade adored its brigadier, and all felt as if he weighed about a ton." He added: "When Custer made a charge, he was the first sabre that struck for he was always ahead." Another said that Custer "was not afraid to fight like a private soldier . . . and that he was ever in front and would never ask them to go where he would not lead." Lieutenant James Christiancy wrote to Custer's future father-in-law, Daniel Bacon: "Through all that sharp and heavy firing the General gave his orders as though conducting a parade or review, so cool and indifferent that he inspired us all with something of his coolness and courage."

The Michigan Brigade was so impressed that they had, in their opinion, whipped Jeb Stuart at Gettysburg that they began to emulate their commander by adopting Custer's trademark scarlet neckties, which he wore to make himself conspicuous to his troops during a battle. An artist for *Frank Leslie's Illustrated Newspaper* noted this gaudy feature of Custer's uniform and described the necktie as "an emblem of bravado and challenge to combat—with the motion of the toreador flouting the Crimson cloth to infuriate and lure the bull to doom."

That regard by his troops and the press for Custer's actions during the Gettysburg Campaign was echoed by his superior officers. General Kilpatrick wrote in his official report: "To General Custer all praise is due." Alfred Pleasonton stated in his report that Custer and Wesley Merritt "have increased the confidence entertained in their ability and gallantry to lead troops on the field of battle." The War Department rewarded Custer with a promotion to brevet major in the Regular Army, which dated from July 3, 1863.

George Armstrong Custer, the obscure aide-de-camp who astonishingly had been promoted to brigadier general in command of a brigade, had suddenly captured the eye of the nation. The press had a fresh story, and a star had been born at Gettysburg that promised to rise higher with each ensuing engagement.

Another star that had brightly shone over Southern skies throughout the war, however, was rapidly becoming obscured by clouds of vilification. Blame for the humiliating defeat at Gettysburg had become a subject of widespread gossip and debate within the Confederate army and the public at large, and Jeb Stuart found himself at the center of the controversy.

The issue that has tarnished Stuart's reputation over the years has not focused on his failure to reach the Union rear in coordination with Pickett's charge but rather on the conduct of his earlier reconnaissance mission and the timing of his arrival at Gettysburg.

Charles M. Blackford, the brother of William, wrote that "General Stuart is much criticized for his part in our late campaign. In his anxiety to 'do some great thing' General Stuart carried his men beyond the range of usefulness and Lee was not thereafter kept fully informed as to the enemy's movements as he should have been, or as he would have been had Stuart been nearer at hand."

A reporter for the *Mobile Daily Advertiser and Register* wrote: "There are many wild reports in circulation today regarding Gen. J. E. B. Stuart, the Chief of Cavalry in Virginia. It is said that he will be deposed, and that Gen. Hood will be put in his place. For some time back many serious charges have been made against Stuart, reflecting severely upon him. His vanity seems to have controlled all his actions, and the cavalry was used frequently to gratify his personal pride and to the detriment of the service.

"At the Battle of Gettysburg he was not to be found, and Gen. Lee could not get enough cavalry together to carry out his plans. But that inordinate personal pride—that weak-minded vanity, so subject to flattery and praise, ruin entirely his character as an officer."

The roster of those officers who had harsh words for Stuart's alleged malfeasance that contributed to the loss at Gettysburg included James Longstreet, Henry Heth, Edward P. Alexander, Walter Taylor, and C. M. Wilcox. There was one officer, however, whose reaction was particularly blunt and condemning of Stuart. Chief of Staff Colonel Charles Marshall, the officer who had prepared the orders issued for that questionable ride by Stuart around the Yankees, recommended that the cavalry commander should stand a court-martial.

Stuart did not help his cause when defending his actions in his official report, which was an astounding 14,300 words in length. He recounted his success in "spreading terror to the very gates of the [Union] capital," and in a sense chided Lee by professing that enough cavalry had been left behind that, "properly handled, such a command should have done everything requisite." Jubal Early as well as A. P. Hill and James Longstreet came under Stuart's scrutiny for their alleged blunders for not finding him sooner or for advancing without better coordination with his cavalry.

The report, in many respects, was a fictional account of Stuart's true mission. At the time Stuart delivered his report, he made an attempt to convince Colonel Marshall to admit that the conduct of the cavalry had been justified. Marshall retorted that Stuart should have obeyed orders, and, predictably, an argument followed with neither man backing down.

The last word—at least for the time being—belonged to Marshall. After reading Stuart's report, he wrote a second report over the signature of Robert E. Lee, which said in part: "The movements of the army preceding the battle of Gettysburg had been much embarrassed by the absence of the cavalry. As soon as it was known that the enemy had crossed into Maryland, orders were sent to the brigades of Robertson and Jones, which had been left to guard the passes of the Blue Ridge, to rejoin the army without delay, and it was expected that General Stuart, with the remainder of the command would soon arrive. In the exercise of discretion given him when Longstreet and Hill marched into Maryland, General Stuart determined to pass around the rear of the Federal Army with three brigades and cross the Potomac between it and Washington, believing that he would be able, by that route, to place himself on our right flank in time to keep us properly advised of the enemy's movements."

Marshall toughened his previous stance by adding that perhaps Stuart should have been shot. Lee later modified the report to exclude that severe and prejudiced opinion. He did note, however, that "the march toward Gettysburg was conducted more slowly than it would have been had the movements of the Federal army been known," and he did not delete the statement that his army's operations were "much embarrassed by the absence of the cavalry."

The question of whether or not Stuart disobeyed orders has been debated by battle participants and noted historians since that July day in 1863 when the battle of Gettysburg became a bitter disappointment for the South. Stuart has borne the brunt of the accusations likely because in death he was a convenient scapegoat to those contemporaries who fixed blame for the defeat on him in order to perhaps camouflage their own inadequacies during that battle.

Did Jeb Stuart disobey orders on his reconnaissance prior to the battle and therefore contribute to the Confederate defeat? Not if the spirit of Lee's orders are interpreted with minimal common sense and with the realization that the battle was initiated by two opposing units that happened to stumble upon each other out of the blue. It is conceivable that Stuart could have found himself in this same predicament had a major battle occurred while he was riding around McClellan in 1862 or while on any of his subsequent raids. On this mission, as with the others, he had simply followed orders, which gave him great leeway with respect to a timetable for his return.

Perhaps Edward Coddington, in his excellent work *The Gettysburg Campaign: A Study in Command*, summed up Stuart's actions best when he wrote: "While Stuart's vainglorious ride around the Union army was a gross misuse of horseflesh and manpower, it neither stripped Lee of cavalry nor deprived him of all opportunities to learn Hooker's whereabouts. There are no indications that Lee ordered the troopers still available to him to look for the enemy at the obvious places."

For those researchers or casual readers who wish to delve into this controversy in depth, no finer source exists than Mark Nesbitt's *Saber and Scapegoat: J. E. B. Stuart and the Gettysburg Controversy*. Mr. Nesbitt has presented a careful analysis of virtually every available source and concludes that Stuart has been a victim of false accusations that have been perpetuated over the years.

Stuart's denial of any wrongdoing also was reflected in letters to his wife that contained passages complaining about lies spread by jealous enemies and factual errors published by newspapers in Richmond. Outwardly, his apparent contempt for detractors and customary self importance remained on display for all to observe—as evidenced by his arrival in Martinsburg, Virginia, during the withdrawal from Pennsylvania.

Charles M. Blackford witnessed the passing of the Army of Northern Virginia through that town. Lee and his three corps commanders—Longstreet, Hill, and Ewell—rode along in a somber fashion befitting the mood after Gettysburg. Stuart, on the other hand, arrived in town with his typical flair of pounding hooves, announced by two buglers "blowing most furiously." The *Beau Sabreur* was not about to let anyone perceive that his spirit could be broken by rumors and innuendos that, in his mind, were totally baseless.

While Jeb Stuart was fending off criticism, Armstrong Custer's spirits were flying high. He welcomed the opportunity to command a division, albeit temporarily. His troops were kept busy on patrol throughout the summer but engaged in only a series of minor skirmishes, which resulted in few casualties.

The lone conflict with potential to be of any consequence occurred on July 24 when Custer's command of 1,200 men had penetrated fifty miles into enemy-held territory. An informant told Custer that General Ambrose Hill's Corps was moving toward Culpeper. Custer was aware that if he could reach Culpeper before Hill, he could create a wedge between Hill and Longstreet. Should that be accomplished, it would enable Meade to send up reinforcements and attack each Confederate corps separately, which would greatly enhance the prospects of victory.

Custer's report, dated August 28, 1863, summarizes this skirmish: "My advance guard came upon the skirmishers of the enemy when within a half mile of the road leading from Gaines' Cross-Roads to Culpeper, at a point called Battle Mountain. The force in my front proved to be the corps of A. P. Hill. I attacked with both cavalry and artillery, compelling the enemy to halt his column and form line of battle.

"Having done this much, and knowing the overwhelming force the enemy was bringing to bear against me, I prepared to withdraw my command. An unlooked-for delay occurring in relieving my skirmishers, the enemy succeeded in pushing two brigades of infantry to my left and rear. By this movement the Fifth and Sixth Michigan Cavalry (Colonel Gray) and two guns of Battery M, under command of Lieutenant Woodruff, were entirely cut off, but, by a display of great courage by both officers and men, Colonel Gray succeeded in extricating his command from this perilous position with but slight loss."

Custer lost thirty men killed, wounded, or missing, reporting "that [losses] of the enemy was known to be much greater," and withdrew to Amissville. He informed Pleasonton of the opportunity to strike a major blow to the Confederate army, but Meade refused to send reinforcements, and on July 31, Custer was ordered to withdraw across the Rappahannock.

On August 4, Custer relinquished command of the 3rd Division to Kilpatrick, who had returned from leave, and resumed his duty with the Michigan Brigade. With time on his hands, he turned his attention to refitting the men, gathering horses, and assembling a staff.

Among those chosen to serve Custer were Captain Jacob Greene, a flute-playing friend from Monroe, Michigan, who would serve as adjutant or chief of staff. Greene, whom Custer met while on leave, was the suitor of Nettie Humphrey, who had been acting as the go-between for Custer and Libbie ever since Judge Bacon had forbidden a relationship. Custer also added two other Monroe residents—George Yates, who would die with Custer at the Little Bighorn, and James Christiancy, the son of Judge Isaac Christiancy. Bugler Joseph Fought was summoned, and a waif named Johnny Cisco, who washed clothes, waited tables, cared for the horses, and slept with Custer's dog, attached himself to the general. The staff was complete when a seventeen-year-old runaway slave named Eliza Denison Brown "jined up with the Ginnel."

Jeb Stuart also utilized this summer lull to care for his men and horses and push for enactment of his pet project. He had urged Lee since May to reorganize the cavalry and had submitted recommendations that the commanding general now decided to entertain. There was perhaps an element of self-interest to Stuart's plan. He presently commanded a division composed of six brigades. This new approach would require three divisions with an option for a fourth. If Lee enacted the plan as designed, Stuart would be in charge of a cavalry corps, and, by an act of the Confederate Congress on September 18, 1862, "each army corps shall be commanded by a lieutenant general."

Jeb Stuart was of the opinion, perhaps rightfully, that he deserved a promotion to lieutenant general. After all, his horsemen had been instrumental in so many successes up to that point, and he was as capable and dedicated an officer as any of the corps commanders. In two letters written in August, he told Flora that his promotion was "still in suspense" and later stated, "Rumor is quite rife that I have been actually appointed Lt. Gen'l. I think it might be so." Perhaps Stuart viewed the reshuffling and his promotion as an affirmation that Lee retained confidence in his abilities despite rumors that continued to swirl behind his back.

To be fair, Stuart also desired to reward other officers—Hampton, Fitz Lee, and Rooney Lee, in particular—who would command the new divisions with a promotion to major general. Other positions required qualified officers as well. Hampton was temporarily out of commission due to the wounds suffered at Gettysburg; Rooney Lee had been captured by a raiding party in late June; Beverly Robertson, who had been a disappointment to Stuart, had requested another assignment; and Albert Jenkins also had been captured.

On September 9, Lee unveiled his intentions, and the cavalry was rearranged into two divisions—the 1st Division commanded by newly appointed Major General Wade Hampton the 2nd Division by newly appointed Major General Fitzhugh Lee. Brigade commanders, all brigadier generals, in Hampton's division would be William E. "Grumble" Jones, Lawrence S. Baker (newly appointed), and M. C. Butler (newly appointed). Fitz Lee's brigade commanders, all brigadier generals, would be Rooney Lee, Lunsford L. Lomax (newly appointed), and Williams C. Wickham (newly appointed).

Although the cavalry technically had been organized as a corps, Jeb Stuart, much to his disappointment, had been passed over for promotion. Official recognition of a corps of cavalry had not been announced by army headquarters, and it is doubtful that Lee had even suggested a promotion for Stuart to President Davis. This omission by Lee was not intended as a personal affront directed at Stuart but rather most likely reflected Lee's belief that a cavalry command was not equal in responsibility to that of an infantry corps.

In addition to Stuart, two other officers who had been passed over for promotion were quite dissatisfied. Both Tom Munford and Tom Rosser had expected to play a major role in the reorganized cavalry, but apparently Lee and the War Department had not agreed.

Colonel Thomas T. Munford of the 2nd Virginia, the VMI graduate from Lynchburg, was one of the senior colonels in the army and had participated in every campaign after First Manassas, or Bull Run, where he had led a spectacular charge. Munford had been criticized for arriving late at Brandy Station but had redeemed himself during the Gettysburg Campaign. Stuart and other influential friends asked Lee to reconsider promoting Munford, but to no avail.

Perhaps more disappointed than Tom Munford was Colonel Thomas L. Rosser, a close friend and classmate at West Point of George Armstrong Custer. Rosser had also distinguished himself with his bravery and had recovered from serious wounds sustained during the Peninsula Campaign. Stuart attempted to mollify Rosser by assuring him that he would be the next one promoted to brigadier general and provided Rosser with a letter to that effect. Rosser, however, believed that he had been betrayed by Stuart.

His venom spilled forth in letters to his wife, Betty: "Stuart has been false to *me* as he has ever been to his country and to his *wife*. I will never give him an opportunity of deceiving me again."

Unknown to Tom Rosser was that it had not been Stuart who had betrayed him. The War Department had judged that Rosser's regiment had declined in efficiency and that he personally had been affected by the separation from his wife of three months, which had affected his morale and driven him to drink.

Meanwhile, Stuart became embroiled in a feud with Grumble Jones, who had made no secret of his dislike for his commander. The final straw apparently was the fact that Stuart had slighted Jones during the Gettysburg Campaign by assigning the brigadier to guard Virginia mountain passes under the direction of Beverly Robertson. Lee made an effort to patch up this rift between the two strong-willed men, but the result was that Stuart had Jones arrested for disrespect to a superior officer. Jones swore that he would never again serve under Stuart and was relieved of duty until he could be brought before a court-martial.

To compound Stuart's military woes, his personal life required attention. One of his sisters passed away, and his wife, who was eight months pregnant, became ill and pleaded with him to visit her in Lynchburg. The *Beau Sabreur*'s iron constitution was being put to the test, and he would find no relief from the enemy.

The newly reorganized Confederate cavalry barely had time to become accustomed to riding together before they had to fight together. Meade's army remained above the Rappahannock, Lee's stayed below the Rapidan, and Stuart's cavalry patrolled the middle ground. Public and political pressure in the North called for Meade to push onward toward Richmond. Meade had learned that Lee had detached thousands of troops to the western theater and ordered Pleasonton to cross the Rappahannock and conduct a reconnaissance to confirm this information. The Union cavalry set out on September 12 to probe Lee's positions in Northern Virginia.

At 6 a. m. on September 13, Kilpatrick's cavalry splashed across the upper Rappahannock at Kelly's Ford and rendezvoused with Buford and Gregg at Brandy Station. The combined units—10,000 men strong—resumed the march down the Orange & Alexandria Railroad and finally halted on high ground about three-fourths of a mile north of Stuart's headquarters at Culpeper Court House.

This time, Stuart was not caught unaware of the Union advance due to an informant who had visited his headquarters during the previous night. Dr. Hudgin, a surgeon with the 9th Virginia, had been home on leave following the death of his wife, who, according to Henry McClellan, "had recently died from fright caused by the conduct of some of Kilpatrick's men." Hudgin had observed the enemy movements and reported that information to Stuart. This intelligence afforded the cavalry commander ample opportunity to prepare.

Without knowing the size of his enemy, Stuart immediately dispatched the wagons and disabled horses toward Rapidan Station. He then deployed Brigadier General Lunsford Lomax, commanding Grumble Jones's brigade, supported by three artillery pieces around the vicinity of Culpeper—hardly a large enough force to contend with three Yankee divisions.

Lomax was in position when at about 1 p.m. Buford and Gregg attacked. The Union troops were met with a ferocious barrage that stopped them in their tracks. Pleasonton then ordered Kilpatrick to enter the fray. Colonel Henry E. Davies and the 2nd New York charged the artillery battery while the dismounted 6th Michigan laid down a base of fire. Davies's troops drove Lomax's brigade through town, taking numerous prisoners, capturing two of the guns, and dealing severely with those who resisted.

Custer had been deployed at the extreme left of a semicircle on the Union line with directions, if possible, to pass around the Confederate flank and strike from the rear. At the height of the fighting, Custer noticed a Rebel railroad train loaded with supplies chugging into town. He mounted a battalion of the 1st Michigan and 1st Vermont at once and charged after this prize.

His troops were compelled to cross a swollen creek and pass through a marsh in order to reach Culpeper, and they quickly became bogged down in the murky water and thick mud. While the troopers struggled through the morass, Pennington was ordered to open up with his artillery in an effort to stop the train. Custer rallied what troops he could muster from the swamp and led a charge. But by that time, the train crew had reversed the engine and outraced the pursuit. Custer did, however, capture the remaining Rebel cannon and chased the rest of the enemy troops out of town.

At this point, Jeb Stuart, who was content to allow Lomax to command the field, sent forward additional artillery to support the Virginians who had regrouped on Greenwood Hill, southwest of Culpeper. The Confederates lobbed canister shot with deadly accuracy at the attacking 5th New York Cavalry.

Custer reacted instantly to this threat and rallied elements of the 1st Vermont and 7th Michigan on a charge toward this enemy gun emplacement. The Virginians turned their attention to those Federal horsemen and sent shells bursting into their midst—one cannonball exploding precariously near Custer. Pieces of shrapnel struck and killed his white stallion, while another shard tore through his boot to strike his foot. His command continued up the hill to capture the enemy battery as Custer proceeded to rise from the ground and assess the seriousness of his injury—amazingly, his lone wound of the war.

Accounts exist that indicate Custer simply shrugged off his injury, mounted a loose horse, and rejoined his men to resume the charge through the streets of Culpeper to rout the Rebels, including Stuart, who was forced to abandon his dinner to flee. Although that would be a fitting addition to the Custer legend, it is more likely that the wounded Boy General was helped from the field while his men carried on to seize the artillery. Also, the evidence suggests that Stuart at that point in time would have been seeking an escape route for his harried troops and would not have by any means been sitting down to a leisurely dinner within reach of his enemy.

Custer's wound was attended to by a surgeon. The Boy General was said to have then ridden up to Pleasonton and exclaimed, "How are you, fifteen-days' leave-of-absence? They have spoiled my boots but they didn't gain much there, for I stole them from a Reb." Pleasonton evidently enjoyed Custer's humor and granted his brigade commander a twenty-day furlough.

Stuart had no choice but to withdraw from the overwhelming force of Yankees. He reached Rapidan Court House after nightfall, leaving behind three artillery pieces. Tom Rosser wrote his wife: "This I think is the finishing stroke to Stuart's declining reputation."

On September 16, Brigadier General George Armstrong Custer, hometown boy made good, returned to Monroe, Michigan. The local celebrity was much in demand, particularly from the young ladies. But Armstrong only had eyes for Libbie Bacon. He was confused, however, about the mixed signals that Libbie had relayed through Nettie Humphrey's letters and set out to "attack," as Libbie would later call it, this girl of his dreams. Custer executed a frontal assault that Jeb Stuart could not have withstood—calling on Libbie, strolling with her, and sitting beside her in church. It was soon apparent that Libbie Bacon was madly in love with Armstrong Custer.

While Custer romanced Libbie, Jeb Stuart contended with the relentless Union cavalry. On September 22, Buford's cavalry advanced on a reconnaissance from Madison Court House toward Liberty Mills on the Rapidan, and Stuart attacked him at Jack's Shop. Both mounted and dismounted charges by the Southern horsemen resulted in a standstill. Meanwhile, Kilpatrick's cavalry intended to rendezvous with Buford and advanced to a position that trapped Stuart between the two Federal forces.

Stuart deployed his artillery battery atop a little hill with orders to fire at both Union divisions. Two detachments of his troopers charged the Yankees in both directions as well. This bold tactic permitted Stuart to break contact and withdraw across the Rapidan to take refuge with Wilcox's infantry. Stuart had a horse shot out from under him during the fray and was congratulated by Lee for "arresting" the enemy. Tom Rosser quipped to his wife that Stuart "as usual, was whipped."

On September 28, Armstrong Custer escorted Libbie Bacon to a masquerade ball given in his honor. He attended dressed as Louis XVI and she as a gypsy girl, complete with tambourine. Later that night, Custer proposed marriage, and Libbie readily accepted. The only drawback was that she insisted that the engagement not be announced until Custer had asked for and received her father's blessing. That proposition would test the mettle of the young cavalry officer.

The saga of Jeb Stuart and Grumble Jones came to a conclusion when the court found Jones guilty of disrespect, and he was exiled to command the cavalry in Southwest Virginia. Stuart recommended that Tom Rosser be promoted to brigadier general to replace Jones, and Lee endorsed the request. Rosser, who presently played the role of Stuart's main critic, would be commissioned on October 10.

On October 5, with Libbie, Judge Bacon, and other friends seeing him off, Custer boarded the train for his return to duty. The gallant field general who had time and again confronted his enemy with abandon had not been able to bring himself to ask for Libbie's hand from Judge Bacon. He did, however, promise to write him about a matter that concerned them both. "Very well," the judge responded, and Custer bid them farewell. Custer reported to his unit camped southwest of Culpeper Court House on October 8 and received three cheers from the troopers as the band played "Hail to the Chief."

As Custer returned to the adulation of his men, General Robert E. Lee was in the process of implementing his latest strategy. Lee had never abandoned his ambitious plan to maneuver his army between Meade and Washington, and now he amassed his troops with intentions to march west around Meade's right flank. Jeb Stuart's responsibility would be to protect and conceal the right of Lee's army during the turning movement. Fitz Lee would remain at Racoon Ford on the Rapidan, and Stuart would assume personal command of wounded Wade Hampton's division.

On the night of October 9, Stuart bivouacked at Madison Court House while his patrols probed Federal lines as a diversion. Back at Lynchburg, Stuart's wife, Flora, had given birth that day to a daughter, who would later be named Virginia Pelham by her father in honor of his beloved state and his favorite artillery officer, the late Major John Pelham.

Meade was unaware of the extent of Lee's plan and chose to wait until further intelligence could be gathered before challenging his enemy. Custer, whose men were prepared to move at a moment's notice, found the time to write a letter to Nettie Humphrey. "I arrived last evening and was welcomed in a style both flattering and gratifying," he told her. "I feel that here, surrounded by my little band of heroes, I am loved and respected. Often I think of the vast responsibility resting on me, of the many households depending on my discretion and judgment—and to think that I am just leaving my boyhood makes the responsibility appear greater. That is not due to egotism, self-conceit. I try to make no unjust pretensions. I assume nothing I know not to be true. It requires no extensive knowledge to inform me what is my duty to my country, my command ... 'First be sure you're right, then go ahead!' I ask myself, 'Is that right?' Satisfied that it is so, I let nothing swerve me from my purpose." The charming and thoughtful suitor of Libbie Bacon enclosed some flowers for his fiancée that had been picked in front of headquarters near the Rapidan.

Custer's letter writing was interrupted when his pickets along the north bank of Robertson's River were attacked, and a portion of the line was forced back upon the reserves. At the same time, heavy enemy columns moving toward Madison Court House had been sighted by scouts. Custer advised Meade about this Rebel movement, and the commanding general decided to dispatch two divisions of cavalry—Kilpatrick and Buford—across the Rapidan on a reconnaissance to determine precise enemy positions.

On the morning of the 10th, Jeb Stuart sent Colonel O. R. Funsten, commanding Jones's former brigade, as advance guard toward Woodville on the Sperryville Pike, and led his remaining troops toward James City. Stuart drove enemy pickets at Russell's Ford back to Bethsaida Church, where the 120th New York Infantry waited. Gordon's brigade drew the attention of the New Yorkers from the front while Stuart led his detachment through the woods to the right and rear. The 1st South Carolina was ordered to charge and quickly routed the whole line, capturing eighty-seven prisoners in the process. Stuart then led his troops to James City, a two-and-a-half-mile ride.

At 1 p.m., Custer received orders to advance to James City; he arrived two hours later to discover Stuart already in possession of the town. Custer ordered Pennington to open up and shell the enemy position in the woods at the edge of the village while Alger and one battalion of the 5th Michigan charged the artillery battery. Stuart met the advance of the Wolverines with sharpshooters from the 1st South Carolina, and, in Custer's words, the charge "failed for want of sufficient support."

Stuart abandoned that particular artillery position for another that was out of range but declined to attack. John Esten Cooke explained Stuart's strategy: "Stuart's orders were to keep the enemy off the infantry flanks, and this could be best accomplished by remaining quiet. So, every demonstration was made; lines of sharpshooters were advanced, our artillery opened, and—no attack was made."

The opposing cavalries traded sporadic fire throughout the remainder of the day, but for the most part were content to observe each other from parallel positions of high ground with James City located in the valley between.

Kilpatrick received urgent orders at about 3 a.m. to move his command across the Rappahannock toward Culpeper Court House to cover the withdrawal of the infantry. By seven o'clock, the Union cavalry was in the saddle, with Custer's brigade on the eastern flank.

Stuart noticed this withdrawal, gathered his troops, and hurried down the Sperryville Pike toward Culpeper. Cooke observed: "It is hard to say whether this great soldier was better in falling back or in advancing. When he retired he was the soul of stubborn obstinacy. When he advanced he was all fire, dash, and impetus. He was now following up a retreating enemy, and he did not allow the grass to grow under his feet."

Kilpatrick's division had passed through Culpeper, oblivious to the fact that Meade had already removed the infantry from the vicinity, virtually abandoning the cavalry in enemy-held territory. The horsemen were finally informed of Meade's action and raced toward the Rappahannock before being caught in an exposed position without infantry available for support.

Custer's brigade rode at the end of the column, and the first word of the potential consequences of this predicament came from a young woman in Culpeper who informed the rear guard, "You will catch it if you don't hurry." Custer had departed town, following the tracks of the Orange & Alexandria Railroad, when the rear guard was struck by Stuart's cavalry. Kilpatrick was some distance ahead, and Custer would be on his own if the enemy chose to attack in force.

Jeb Stuart, riding with his advance, the 12th Virginia, had ordered the charge. His men bravely responded but encountered a wide ditch and a stone wall, which effectively aborted the advance.

Custer reacted to Stuart's initial charge by deploying his troops on the ridges north of Culpeper and preparing for an attack.

Stuart at this time learned that the Union infantry had crossed the Rappahannock and decided not to strike Custer's position. Instead, he devised a plan designed to trap the enemy cavalry between his division and that of Fitz Lee's division, which was presently located north of Culpeper. Stuart left behind a detachment to harass Custer, withdrew the remainder of his troops, and led them along the back roads toward Brandy Station.

When it became evident that an assault by Stuart was not forthcoming, Custer resumed his desperate ride toward the Rappahannock to rejoin Kilpatrick, Buford, and Pleasonton.

Custer had ventured only a short distance when Stuart's horsemen once again commenced nipping at the heels of the column. At the same time, Custer noticed a strong gray column—Fitz Lee's division—on his outer flank racing to intercept his line of march. Rather than halt and deploy, Custer pushed his men in the direction of Brandy Station—riding directly into Jeb Stuart's trap.

Lieutenant George Briggs, the adjutant riding with Colonel William D. Mann's 7th Michigan, described the action with the rear guard: "To unflinchingly face and hold in check the advancing enemy until the receding column of your comrades is out of sight; to then break to the rear a short distance and again face about to meet an on-coming and confident foe, is a duty that only brave and well disciplined troops can properly perform. Breaking to the rear only to repeatedly face about in a new position, which must be held as long as safety will permit, is one of the most trying services that a soldier is called upon to perform."

Kilpatrick, however, was not entirely fooled by Stuart's ploy and ordered Buford's 2nd New York into the fray. Custer's men rode to save themselves from being cut off, while Fitz Lee encountered Buford's New Yorkers at the railroad tracks on the outskirts of Brandy Station and forced them into a fighting retreat across Racoon Creek. Lee, expecting that Buford would make a stand at Brandy Station, chased his enemy in that direction. Tom Rosser, officially named in command of the Laurel Brigade that day, detached the 1st Maryland and 15th Virginia from Fitz Lee and spurred ahead in an effort to maneuver in front of Custer at the river.

Stuart, with Hampton's division, pressed forward and encountered a battalion of the 5th New York that had been separated from the main column.

He ordered the 12th Virginia and 4th and 5th North Carolina to charge. The Union troops held their ground by blockading the road with drawn pistols. Stuart then dispatched the 7th Virginia into the Union flank, killing and capturing many of them.

Stuart's vise was closing when, unexpectedly, he came under heavy artillery shelling—originating, much to his surprise, from the direction of Fitz Lee's guns. Stuart's advance had been so rapid that his horse artillery could not keep up, and he therefore had no way of notifying Lee of his arrival. Lee had mistaken Stuart's command for enemy cavalry. Now, the only manner in which to reveal their identity was to attack the Yankees. The 12th Virginia was formed and prepared to charge into the scattered enemy.

When Custer arrived at the depot, Rosser was in a position at his front, which cut him off from the river. Custer reported: "The heavy masses of the rebel cavalry could be seen covering the heights in front of my advance (where it is remembered that my rear guard was hotly engaged with a superior force), a heavy column was enveloping each flank, and my advance confronted by more than double my own number. The peril of my situation can be estimated."

Jeb Stuart had successfully surrounded Custer's command. The only question was whether or not the *Beau Sabreur* could coordinate his various detachments effectively enough to deliver the killing blow before the Wolverines could escape.

Custer ordered Pennington's battery to blast their way through the impasse, but the Yankee guns were soon quieted by heavier Rebel shelling. At that point, Generals Pleasonton and Kilpatrick surprisingly braved the ride through the enemy to confer with Custer. There were few options. When Custer proposed "to cut through the force in my front, and thus open a way for the entire command to the river," Pleasonton approved.

Custer wasted little time mounting the 5th Michigan on his right in a column of battalions and the 1st on his left in a column of squadrons. The 6th and 7th would guard the flank where Stuart's horsemen were poised. The Boy General then scanned the enemy position with binoculars in an attempt to discern a weak point. Satisfied that he had located a likely spot, Custer rode to the front of his men and ordered, "Draw sabers!"

Custer "informed them that we were surrounded, and all we had to do was open a way with our sabers. They showed their determination and purpose by giving three hearty cheers." The enthusiasm of the command was heightened when Custer ordered the band to play "Yankee Doodle." Custer issued the order to move forward. "I never expect to see a prettier sight," he later wrote to Annette Humphrey. "I frequently turned in my saddle to see the glittering sabres advance in the sunlight."

Custer shouted, "Charge!" The buglers echoed the call, and the Wolverines bolted toward the ranks of the Southerners. Captain William Glazier described the scene: "Custer, the daring, terrible demon that he is in battle ... dashed madly forward in the charge, while his yellow locks floated like pennants in the breeze. Fired to an almost divine potency, and with a majestic madness, this band of heroic troopers shook the air with their battle cry."

Within forty rods of Stuart's cavalry, Custer's opposition wilted way— but within moments wheeled around and charged his flank and rear. Confederate Tom Rosser explained his actions: "I withdrew my regiment, and advised the other colonels to fall back so as to avoid the heavy blow in our rear. These troops were moving at a full gallop; they were not charging upon us, for we stood in line off to one side, and for a moment I looked on in amazement at the performance. I soon concluded that they were being pursued, and charged them in flank."

Jeb Stuart supported his horsemen with a vicious artillery barrage. Custer was blown from his horse by a bursting shell, quickly remounted another, which was slain by a bullet, and resumed the charge atop a third mount.

The two cavalries charged and countercharged throughout the afternoon and into the evening. The Federals tried to fight their way through Confederates who were just as determined to stop them. Stuart placed Lomax's and Chambliss's brigades on the right to pour a cross fire into the Union flank, while the main force attacked the front. At one point, Kilpatrick's wagons and ambulances were threatened, but the 6th and 7th Michigan thwarted Stuart's men long enough for most of the train to escape.

Brandy Station, in the words of Henry McClellan, was once again the scene of a "sanguinary cavalry battle. [The Union cavalrymen] fought bravely, even desperately. Several times [our] dismounted men, while eagerly pressing forward, were surrounded by the enemy's cavalry, and either fought their way out with their carbines and revolvers or were rescued by charges of their mounted brigades. Five times did the 5th, 6th, and 15th Virginia Cavalry make distinct sabre charges." Rosser added, "Never in my life did I reap such a rich harvest in horses and prisoners."

Custer successfully punched a hole through his enemy wide enough to allow the cavalry to commence withdrawing across the river. He later wrote to Annette Humphrey: "Oh, could you but have seen some of the charges that were made! While thinking of them I cannot but exclaim 'Glorious War!'"

By that time, Fitz Lee realized what was happening and joined Stuart. The beleaguered Yankees, supported by artillery, had managed to occupy Fleetwood Hill. A series of counterattacks failed to dislodge this resolute enemy, and Stuart eventually declined to send his troops against such a strong position.

Colonel P. M. B. Young arrived with his Georgian brigade just before nightfall. Young deployed his men as sharpshooters and commenced a determined barrage, which deceived the Federals into believing that infantry support had arrived. As darkness descended, Confederate campfires were built along a two-mile line, and the brass band played "Bonnie Blue Flag" and "Dixie" while the Union cavalrymen quietly slipped away in the night. By about ten o'clock, every able-bodied Yankee had reached the relative safety of the far side of the river but had left over 500 of their comrades behind as Jeb Stuart's prisoners.

Meade resumed his retreat, and Lee ordered Stuart to follow and gather information. On October 13, Stuart headed toward Catlett's Station on the Orange & Alexandria Railroad with three brigades, seven pieces of artillery, and five ordinance wagons. Lomax's brigade was dispatched to Auburn to guard the rear while Stuart continued on to Catlett's Station with Funsten and Gordon. William Blackford was sent ahead to scout and soon sent a note to Stuart reporting that he had happened upon Meade's rear.

Stuart was elated and came forward to join Blackford. This was an opportunity for Lee to strike the enemy while it was strung out on the march. Major Reid Venable was chosen to convey this information to Lee but reached Auburn to discover that two corps of Union infantry had driven away Lomax and were approaching Stuart's rear. Venable sent back a courier to inform Stuart of this turn of events. The Union troops were ignorant of the fact, but Jeb Stuart understood that the enemy was between his cavalry and Lee, and he was in a most precarious position.

Stuart mounted his brigades and rode back toward Auburn while weighing his options. It was doubtful that he could simply slip past the Federals, and there would be a heavy price to pay in casualties should he decide to fight his way through. By this time, Stuart had attracted the attention of his enemy, which was now positioned at his front and rear.

Just before dark, "with the inspiration of his genius," Stuart spied a small, wooded valley north of Auburn. He led his troops into this secluded spot, stationed pickets on the road with orders to not return enemy fire under any circumstances, and passed the word that each horse and mule be muzzled and absolute silence be maintained. Stuart and his men then hunkered down to "outwatch the stars" as the Union infantry marched past them.

McClellan wrote: "So close were we to the marching columns of the enemy that we could distinctly hear the orders of the officers as they closed up the column. We could even hear the voices of the men in conversation." Stuart dispatched six couriers requesting help from Lee during the anxious night and captured several enemy messengers.

At daylight, Stuart observed that most of the Union forces had passed, and only the rear guard remained in sight. They had halted within 150 yards of the Rebels and were preparing breakfast. Stuart deployed his seven guns on a ridge and mounted his men. Lee had responded to his messages, and the sound of firing could be heard originating from the west. Stuart ordered his gunners to fire on the unsuspecting rear guard. His shelling not only rained down on the Yankees but stopped the advance of Ewell's troops, which were about to swoop down on their mutual enemy.

The Union troops regrouped and formed a line of battle. Stuart sent Colonel Ruffin's 1st North Carolina on a mounted charge, which quickly routed the skirmishers. Stuart then wisely withdrew his command to the rear of the enemy's position. Instead of trapping the Union troops between his cavalry and Lee's infantry, Stuart had to console himself with the knowledge that he had escaped what could have escalated into a perilous situation.

While Stuart rode off in pursuit of the enemy withdrawal, Lieutenant General A. P. Hill met Union forces at Bristoe Station with disastrous results for the Army of Northern Virginia. Hill's poor generalship caused the slaughter of two Confederate brigades and permitted Meade to solidify his lines around Centreville. Lee decided to pull back to the Rappahannock.

On October 18, Meade ordered Kilpatrick to confirm reports that Lee was withdrawing. At three o'clock that afternoon, the 3rd Division crossed Bull Run and moved down the Warrenton Turnpike. Stuart was covering Lee's withdrawal, and his horsemen offered only token resistance at Gainesville before retiring when the 1st Vermont advanced. Kilpatrick's troops bivouacked at Gainesville for the night, while Stuart deployed Hampton's division, which remained under his personal command, into a strong defensive position just three miles to the west at Buckland Mills.

At daybreak on the cold, rainy morning of October 19, Custer's brigade, with Major Kidd's 6th Michigan in the advance, moved down the Pike from Gainesville to Buckland and encountered only light skirmishing. Shortly before noon, however, the Wolverines approached Broad Run and came under intense small arms and artillery fire from Stuart's three brigades located on the southern bank. Custer quickly dismounted the 5th, 6th, and 7th Michigan and placed them on both sides of the Warrenton Turnpike. The mounted 1st Michigan and 1st Vermont were held in reserve. Custer understood that an assault under the circumstances would not be prudent and dispatched the 7th downstream in an attempt to cross the creek below the Rebel right flank.

Jeb Stuart was aware of Custer's intentions to try and turn his flank. While contemplating a tactic to counter this threat, a courier from Fitz Lee arrived. Lee's division, he informed Jeb, was approaching from the east. Lee suggested that Stuart withdraw toward Warrenton and lure the Yankees into pursuit, which would permit his division to strike from the flank while Stuart could turn around and hit them from the front. Fitz would fire a cannon shot to indicate when he was in position. Stuart gladly accepted the plan and commenced pulling back.

Custer waited for the 7th Michigan to engage the Rebels on the flank, then sent Colonel Alger and the 5th on a charge across the creek. Reporter E. A. Paul wrote: "The conflict, though comparatively brief here, was sharp, the enemy contending manfully for every foot of ground." The Confederates began to withdraw in the face of this assault. Custer was of the opinion that he had forced Jeb Stuart's horsemen from their position and halted after a mile or so of pursuit to allow his hungry men to prepare dinner.

Kilpatrick arrived with Davies's brigade and ordered Custer to mount up his troops. Custer protested that his men had not eaten since the previous evening, and Kilpatrick agreed that they should eat. Custer warned Kilpatrick that something was amiss, that his lone brigade should not have so easily dislodged an entrenched enemy division. In addition, his scouts had observed great numbers of Confederate infantry on both flanks, and he advised his commander to be wary and proceed with caution. Kilpatrick scoffed at his subordinate's concern and ordered Custer to follow the last brigade that passed. Kilpatrick then rode off with Davies, vowing to overtake Stuart's retreating troops.

Stuart had hidden his division behind ridges at Chestnut Hill, two and a half miles northeast of Warrenton, and watched as Kilpatrick and Davies rode toward them along the turnpike. The Union Cavalry was within 200 yards of Stuart's position when Fitz Lee announced his presence with cannon fire. The Southerners attacked Kilpatrick's column from the front and flank, and the blue-clad cavalry had little choice but to flee for their lives.

At about 3 p.m., Custer had just gotten underway when his Wolverines came under attack by a line of foot soldiers. Fitz Lee, one of Custer's instructors at West Point, had sent Colonel Thomas Owen's Virginia brigade up from Auburn as an advance unit to strike Kilpatrick's rear. Lee's entire division had followed, and Custer quickly discovered that with Davies in retreat, he had been left on his own. He posted the dismounted 5th, 6th, and 7th in the woods, with the mounted 1st Vermont and 1st Michigan in reserve, and ordered Battery M to open up.

Lee countered with his own artillery and an overwhelming number of troopers. The Rebels charged time and again, but the Wolverines made a series of valiant stands against this seemingly endless flood of aggressors.

Finally, Custer wisely realized that he was in peril of being trapped between Lee and Stuart. He had no other choice but to order his men to withdraw across Broad Run and ride away to save themselves from certain annihilation.

Confederate Major P. P. Johnston, who was commanding a section of the artillery, reported: "The battle was of the most obstinate character, Fitz Lee exerting himself to the utmost to push the enemy, and Custer seeming to have no thought of retiring. Suddenly, a cloud of dust arose on the road toward Warrenton, and as suddenly everything in our front gave way. The mounted cavalry was ordered forward, and I saw no more of the enemy."

Custer led his Wolverines toward Gainesville, where they found safety behind the pickets of the VI Corps. He would later call the episode "the most disastrous [day] this Division ever passed through." To add to Custer's anger and humiliation, his baggage and correspondence had been captured. William Blackford noted: "Some of the letters to a fair, but frail, friend of Custer's were published in the Richmond papers and afforded some spicy reading, though most of the spicy parts did not appear."

Stuart chased the Federals for five miles and along the way captured about 250 prisoners and eight to ten ambulances. Stuart jokingly termed this hasty retreat by the Union cavalry the "Buckland Races," and boasted that he was "justified in declaring the rout of the enemy at Buckland the most signal and complete that any cavalry has suffered during the war."

The Knight of the Golden Spurs and his Invincibles had regained, at least for the time being, a dominance over the enemy that had been a matter of contention in recent days.

CHAPTER TEN

THE WINTER
of 1863–64

"UNDER VERY DISTRESSING CIRCUMSTANCES," George Armstrong Custer wrote to Nettie Humphrey on October 20 from Gainesville, "I turn to you and her [Libbie Bacon] for consolation . . . Yesterday was not a gala day for me. I was not responsible, but I cannot but regret the loss of so many brave men . . . all the more painful that it was not necessary."

With those words, Custer for the first time displayed criticism of Kilpatrick. The loss of 214 Wolverines killed, wounded, or captured in the previous ten days, combined with the previous day's debacle, compelled him to break his silence in correspondence if not in private to confidants. Kil-Cavalry had ignored Custer's warning about a potential trap at Buckland, and only Custer's foresight had averted a worse disaster for his own men. The battered Michigan Brigade would require an extended recuperation, clothing to replace their "rags," and the replacement of hundreds of mounts lost in the fighting.

The bright spot in Custer's life remained his relationship with Libbie, yet one major hurdle remained—the letter to Judge Bacon. He had finally composed what he considered the most important letter of his life, which arrived at the Bacon residence on October 21. "I had hoped for a personal interview," Custer told the judge, but obligations had prevented that while he had been in Monroe on furlough. Custer asked the judge for Libbie's hand in marriage, then attempted to promote his worthiness and explain away any concerns by saying, "It is true that I have often committed errors of judgement, but as I grew older I learned the necessity of propriety. I am aware of your fear of intemperance, but surely my conduct for the past two years—during which I have not violated the solemn promise I made my sister, with God to witness, should dispel that fear. You may have thought my conduct trifling after my visits to Libbie ceased, last winter. It was to prevent gossip . . . I left home when but sixteen, and have been surrounded with temptation, but I have always had a purpose in life."

The letter was received by Judge Bacon and his family with mixed emotions and evoked much debate from the various members. The judge replied to Custer that his decision on the matter would require "weeks or even months before I can feel to give you a definite answer." Following a lengthy discussion with Libbie one evening that lasted until the fire had burned down to embers, however, the judge lifted his ban on her corresponding with Custer. Her father's "great soul," as Libbie put it, had opened the door for her marriage to Autie.

"My more than friend—at last—Am I glad to write you some of the thoughts I cannot control?" Libbie opened her first letter to Armstrong. "I have enjoyed your letters to Nettie, but am delighted to possess some of my own." She related her family's guarded blessing to their proposed union and admitted to her own apprehension. "Ah, dear man, if I am worth having am I not worth waiting for? The very thought of marriage makes me tremble. Girls have so much fun. Marriage means trouble . . . If you tease me I will go into a convent for a year."

Custer immediately sought a furlough in order to travel to Monroe and claim his bride-to-be. General Pleasonton agreed, but with one stipulation— Custer must first go out and capture Jeb Stuart. Armstrong consoled himself by spending the evening singing songs around the campfire with Jacob Greene and James Christiancy, who both had just returned from Monroe. With guitar and violin accompaniment, they sang "Then You'll Remember Me," the song that Libbie had promised to sing for him when they were reunited. That same night, Libbie entered in her journal: "I love you Armstrong Custer. I love *you*. I love my love and my love loves me—and I am happy."

The Bristoe Campaign had been a solid performance for General Jeb Stuart and his horsemen. Stuart had conducted daily operations like a maestro fully in command of his orchestra. His cavalry had flawlessly carried out its mission of preventing the Union cavalry from interfering with Lee's infantry movements. Stuart had collected nearly 1,400 prisoners and inflicted

390 casualties. The one instance when Stuart had found himself surrounded served to add another chapter to the adventurous and romantic legend of the gallant Southern cavalier. General Lee praised Stuart for his actions during the final days by writing: "I congratulate you and your officers and men on this handsome success. The plan was well conceived and skillfully executed."

The campaign, in Stuart's estimation, deserved a fitting ceremonial closure with a commemorative grand review. On November 5, Stuart assembled his cavalrymen—appropriately at Brandy Station, the scene of his finest grand review five months earlier—and once again demonstrated for the appreciative audience the grandeur of his cavalry. General Lee, whose rheumatism was acting up, attended the event, as well as Virginia governor John Letcher and his wife.

The rank and file troops, however, were less than thrilled about participating in the review. One disgruntled trooper wrote: "Gen. Stuart purposed holding another of his 'spread eagle' grand reviews, which did no good except to give Yankee spies an opportunity to count the exact number of cavalry attached to the Army of Northern Virginia, and to display the foppishness of Stuart, who rode along his war-torn lines with a multitude of bouquets, which fair hands had presented to him, fastened in his hat and coat."

When the celebrating had concluded, Stuart turned his attention to the subject of readiness. He wrote in his official report: "The matter of greatest concern to me during this short and eventful campaign was the subject of forage for the horses. Operating in a country worn out in peace, but now more desolate in war, it is remarkable how the horses were able to keep up. But our brave men, actuated by a spirit which prompted them to divide the last crust with their favorite steeds, have not been wanting in the noble attributes of patient endurance as well as heroic daring."

Not only was Stuart worried about the subsistence and supply of horses, but the public had become aware of this problem when a letter to the editor of the *Richmond Examiner* estimated that the Gettysburg Campaign had cost the Confederates as many as 1,500 dead horses. This shortage of horse flesh had compelled many cavalrymen to suffer the indignity of drilling with the infantry.

The government paid each cavalryman forty cents per day to furnish their own mount. The health and welfare of this animal became the responsibility of the individual—feed and shoeing were provided by the government—and only if his horse was killed in action would the owner be compensated for its fair value. If the horse was captured, or simply wore out, or was disabled in any other manner but combat, the cavalryman must acquire another mount or be transferred out of the cavalry to a different branch of the service, usually the infantry.

Another disadvantage of the system was that a cavalryman who had lost his horse would be sent home to procure a replacement, which would generally require him to be absent for thirty to sixty days. Stuart's command numbered 9,530 men on September 10, but three weeks later only 8,376 were available for duty. The difference—1,154 men—were likely out scouring the countryside, attempting to locate remounts. Stuart had personally lost six horses to combat wounds or disease in the past six months.

According to Henry McClellan: "Many a gallant fellow whose horse had been irrecoverably lamed for the want of a shoe, or ridden to death at the command of his officer, or abandoned in the enemy's country that his owner might escape capture, impoverished himself and his family in order that he might keep his place in the ranks of his comrades and neighbors." McClellan suggested that this predicament could have been avoided had the government simply purchased horses at the beginning of the war and continued replenishing losses.

Stuart's horsemen were not alone in their lack of adequate cavalry mounts. Custer and his Wolverines had lost a huge number of horses, and the replacements furnished by the government, in Custer's judgment, were less than satisfactory. Custer took up the matter with Pleasonton, who forwarded his subordinate's letter to Major General George Stoneman. The chief of cavalry took a dim view of Custer's complaint and wrote back his assurance that the Wolverines had been sufficiently remounted—with the opinion that "Custer's brigade are great horse killers."

Custer may have fretted over the quality of mounts for his troops, but his mind never ventured far from his intention of marrying Libbie Bacon as soon as possible, despite her protestations of scheduling a wedding anytime in the near future. On November 22, he wrote: "I am sorry I cannot accede to almost the first *written* request my little Gypsie has made, but such unfortunately is the case. You bid me maintain strict silence upon a certain subject until next winter and then we are to discuss the subject of your becoming Mrs. ------ and arrive at a conclusion the following winter. This like all other bargains requires two to complete it. Now had you presented a single, good reason why the course you make out should be adopted, I might have yielded assent, but you have not done so." Custer was not bashful about revealing his true intentions and had initiated a frontal assault on Libbie worthy of his reputation as a bold and daring cavalry officer.

Letters of contrary opinion were also a part of Jeb Stuart's life during November. Two Richmond newspapers printed a debate with respect to Stuart's fitness for command. The *Whig* published a letter under the pseudonym "Investigator" that questioned nearly every aspect of Stuart's cavalry—from an alleged lack of bugles to Stuart's incompetence as evidenced by his ride around the Union army in 1862 and the Chambersburg Raid, which, according to the writer, had accomplished absolutely nothing of benefit and had been costly and needlessly reckless.

The tirade by "Investigator" was immediately challenged by "W. W. G." in the *Richmond Enquirer*. This anonymous writer personally attacked "Investigator" as an "ignorant and bitter enemy of the cavalry of this army and its commander." The charges against Stuart were part of a "covert plot" and were labeled "lies" in a campaign designed "to blacken his pure fame." "Investigator" shot back that he held no personal enmity toward Stuart and claimed that "The real enemies of Gen. Stuart . . . are overzealous friends."

The debate, for the time being, was settled when one of Stuart's friends, writing under the pseudonym "C. Effingham, Esq.," published a poem, "The Ballad of Sir James," in the *Southern Illustrated News*. The rhythmic narrative recounted Stuart's early exploits in the war and was later adapted by William Blackford to conform to the tune of a song called "The Pirate's Glee."

Blackford renamed the song "The Cavalier's Glee," and added verses of his own composition:

> Spur on! Spur on! We love the bounding
> Of barbs that bear us to the fray;
> "The charge" our bugles now are sounding,

And our bold Stuart leads the way.
The path of honor lies before us,
Our hated foemen gather fast;
At home bright eyes are sparkling for us—
We will defend them to the last.

The tune was a favorite around Stuart's headquarters during that winter and became widely known and sung throughout the cavalry.

On November 26, General Meade, prodded by Washington to undertake an offensive before winter, crossed the Rappahannock in a maneuver designed to turn Lee's right flank and force the Confederates toward Richmond. Meade's 85,000 troops undertook this movement against Lee's 48,000 in what would be called the Mine Run Campaign.

Armstrong Custer had once again assumed command of the 3rd Division when Kilpatrick departed two days earlier on furlough after learning that his wife had passed away. Custer's mission would be to act as a diversionary force upriver from the Federal crossing site. Davies's brigade was deployed at Raccoon Ford; Colonel Town, commanding the Wolverines in place of Custer, was sent to Morton's Ford; and Major James Kidd led the 6th Michigan upstream toward Somerville Ford.

Once these units were in position, Custer ordered Pennington to open up with artillery while the troops feinted crossing the Rappahannock at four points. The Rebels answered with at least thirty-six guns of their own and revealed that the trenches were occupied by infantry. "I have been entirely successful in deceiving the enemy to-day as to my intention to effect a crossing," Custer reported to Meade late that afternoon. "I have compelled him to maintain a strong line of battle, extending without break from Morton's to above Raccoon. The enemy was massing his infantry and strengthening his artillery ... He evidently expects us to attempt a passage at those points to-morrow morning." As night approached, Custer added to the ruse by ordering that a long line of campfires be built and having his band serenade the Confederates from several different places along the river.

The following morning, however, the fortifications across the waterway were found to be empty. The enemy had vacated upon learning about Meade's actual movements. Colonel Town was sent to investigate and happened upon a small force of cavalry, which he chased, and captured thirty-two prisoners while losing only one man.

Meade's slow advance permitted Lee to position his army in strong defensive fortifications along the west bank of Mine Run. During the wait for Meade's attack, Jeb Stuart maintained his headquarters a few hundred yards from Lee at the center of the infantry front. His cavalry occupied the flanks and, other than a few reconnaissance patrols, remained for the most part on the defensive.

One such patrol was on November 27, when Jeb Stuart and Brigadier General Tom Rosser—now in command of Grumble Jones's former brigade—attacked an ordnance train at the Federal rear and captured a number of prisoners. Stuart had commanded one of Wade Hampton's brigades although Hampton had returned to duty, an act that, should it become a habit, was bound to eventually create friction between the two major generals. In addition, Stuart had for all intents and purposes abandoned his other five brigades without leadership while he had roamed the countryside.

Stuart, whose function in the reorganization was to supervise overall cavalry operations, had perhaps demonstrated that he was not entirely comfortable with delegating authority when his impulse was to command on the battlefield. He explained that he had taken over Hampton's brigade only because the division commander was late in arriving, and his intervention was tactically necessary. On November 29, however, Stuart once again commandeered Rosser's brigade. Hampton had received no orders and was not even aware that his men had departed. Hampton later wrote in his official report: "In the absence of all orders and without any intimation of the direction or destination of Rosser's brigade, which had been taken by General Stuart, I followed the line of march of this brigade."

Tom Rosser, however, benefited greatly from these forays with Stuart. He had reversed the earlier assessment by the War Department of his lack of qualification for command with glowing reports from Stuart, Hampton, and Lee. Lee's endorsement read in part: "General Rosser in this as in other cases has well performed his duty."

When an assault by the Union had not materialized by November 30, Lee seriously considered attacking Meade. That night, Lee held a council of war to discuss the matter. Lee and Stuart favored an immediate assault; Ewell and Hill were opposed. Lee decided to make a personal reconnaissance the following day.

In the meantime, Meade thought better of a frontal assault on Lee's position and, on December 1, wisely retired across the Rapidan. A disappointed Lee wrote: "After awaiting his advance until Tuesday evening, preparations were made to attack him on Wednesday morning. This was prevented by his retreat." Both armies prepared to settle into winter quarters with the Rappahannock and Rapidan as barriers between them.

Custer and his Wolverines settled into the 3rd Cavalry winter quarters, located in the vicinity of Stevensburg. The Boy General had been relentless with his frontal assault to convince Libbie to marry him as soon as possible. On December 12, Autie received a letter from Judge Bacon that raised his hopes that matrimony would be a part of his near future.

"My Young Friend," Bacon began, and addressed the matter of marriage: "You cannot at your age realize the feelings of a parent when called upon to give up and give away an only offspring," the judge wrote. "I feel that I have kept you in suspense quite too long, and yet when you consider my affection and desire for her happiness you will pardon me for this unreasonable delay." Bacon acknowledged that he had no right to stand in the way of his daughter's wishes, and although he might have preferred if Custer had been "a professor of the Christian religion," affirmed that "you are the object of my choice."

Five days later, Custer opened a letter from Libbie that compelled him to exclaim, "I am so supremely happy that I can scarcely write, my thoughts go wandering from one subject to another so rapidly that it is with difficulty that I return [to] one long enough to transfer it to paper. Am I not dreaming? Surely such unalloyed pleasure never before was enjoyed by mortal man." Libbie Bacon had surrendered to his aggressive advance and agreed to marry him that winter.

Jeb Stuart had established his headquarters—"Wigwam"—for the winter at Orange Court House. Flora stayed in a room at an earby house with an outside entrance to accommodate Jeb's comings and goings, and his three-and-a-half-year-old son, Jimmy, was a frequent visitor to the camp. Stuart journeyed to Richmond on New Year's Eve, and the following day attended a reception for President Jefferson Davis. While in the capital, he conferred with his brother, William Alexander, who was managing the family business in Jeb's absence.

While Libbie Bacon prepared for a February wedding—the exact date dependent upon Armstrong's ability to gain a furlough—Custer was informed by Pleasonton of a rumor that dampened a portion of his happiness. Pleasonton, who betrayed his own shock, had heard that Custer's official confirmation as brigadier general was being opposed by Republican senator Jacob M. Howard of Michigan, who was a member of the Military Affairs Committee. Howard had questioned Custer's youth and the fact that the Ohio native was not a "Michigan Man." More than likely, however, the real reason was that Custer was a "McClellan Man," who presumably was out to sabotage the policies of the present administration. Pleasonton told Custer that "it would be a lasting disgrace on the part of the government to allow such injustice," and advised Custer to exert whatever influence he could muster to fight this action by Howard and other unnamed political enemies.

Custer speculated that Governor Austin Blair and the former commander of the Michigan Brigade, Joseph Copeland, were "at the bottom of this attempt." He took action that night by writing to senators Jacob Howard and Zachariah Chandler, and Congressman F. W. Kellogg, requesting that they "look after my interests." In a letter to Isaac Christiancy, Custer wrote: "I have addressed this letter to you with the hope that you could and would bring influence to bear with both Howard and Chandler which would carry their votes in my favor. If my confirmation was placed in the hands of the army I would not expect a single opposing vote."

Christiancy replied with assurance that he would contact the senators on Custer's behalf. He added his opinion that Custer, as the son of a Democrat, a former member of McClellan's staff, and now a general in the army, was subject to the bitter political infighting that ruled Washington. The views of a general about such matters as the Emancipation Proclamation could be as influential as his exploits in combat.

At the same time, Custer received a reply from Senator Howard, which requested answers to questions about whether or not the Boy General was indeed a "McClellan Man" or a "Copperhead." Copperheads, of course, were those Democrats who were more conciliatory toward the South— Peace Democrats—who represented primarily Midwestern states, which included their leader, Clement L. Vallandigham of Ohio, Custer's native state. They wore a copper penny as an identification badge, hence the name. The Copperheads, a strong and vocal minority in Congress, accused the Republicans, who were mostly from the Northeast, of provoking the war for their own interests, and asserted that military means would fail to restore the Union. And George B. McClellan, whom Custer was known to worship, was being touted as their presidential candidate to oppose Lincoln in the next year's election.

Custer was pleased about the opportunity to state his case rather than being labeled by others without recourse. He wrote to Senator Howard and established his position as a loyal supporter for the policies of his commander in chief, Abraham Lincoln. The president, Custer affirmed, "cannot issue any decree or order which will not receive my unqualified *support* . . . All his acts, proclamations and decisions embraced in his war policy have received not only my support, but my most hardy, earnest and cordial *approval*."

Custer addressed his position on the Emancipation Proclamation by declaring that his friends "can testify that I have insisted that so long as a single slave was held in bondage, I for one, was opposed to peace on any terms . . . I would *offer* no compromise except that which is offered at the point of the bayonet."

Custer privately had blamed Lincoln and Secretary of War Stanton for the dismissal of George McClellan as commander of the Army of the Potomac and had at that time shared the general's opinion regarding the conduct of the war. The beliefs stated to Howard in this most important letter, however, can be judged sincere rather than simply a contrived, hypocritical performance presented in order to gain confirmation of his promotion. Custer was no longer a wandering aide-de-camp but a brigadier general whose leadership had been tested under fire, and that in itself had a way of maturing and altering youthful impressions. To add further credence to the issue,

Custer had previously pledged his loyalty to the Lincoln administration in a letter to Judge Bacon—and his future father-in-law was known to despise Lincoln.

Howard and his Republican colleagues were satisfied that Custer was a loyal "Lincoln Man," and the Senate readily confirmed his nomination to brigadier general. Custer was relieved that he had escaped becoming a victim of politics and expressed his feelings to Judge Bacon: "The subject has caused me no little anxiety, but now my fears are at rest. I would have written you at once when I learned of the efforts made to injure me, but did not wish to trouble Libbie. You would be surprised at the pertinacity with which certain men labor to defame me. I have paid but little attention to them, trusting to time to vindicate me. And I do not fear the result." Custer would take pains in the future to curry favor with the power elite in Washington rather than rely merely on his battlefield prowess.

While Armstrong Custer was occupied with politics and preparations for marriage, Jeb Stuart indulged himself in writing poetry, acting out the role of the South's gallant knight, and dallying with pretty girls. Stuart made the social rounds, attending various parties and balls, and gained the reputation as "the gayest of the gay."

At a charade party held at the home of former Secretary of War George Wythe Randolph, Stuart openly flirted with two cousins from Baltimore who were known as Richmond's most popular belles. He was overheard at another party telling a group of women that they "should not judge his taste by his wife. She was extremely homely." After returning to Orange Court House from Charlottesville, Stuart composed a poem:

> While Mars with his stentorian voice
> Chimes in with discordant noise,
> Sweet woman in angelic guise
> Gives hope and bids us fear despise.
> The Maid of Saragossa still
> Breathes in our cause her dauntless will
> Beyond Potomac's rockbound shore
> Her touch bids southern cannon roar.

This poem was added to a volume of poetry praising the traditional virtues of women.

James Ewell Brown Stuart, date unknown. (The Museum of the Confederacy)

Apparently rumors circulating about his interest in young ladies had reached Flora's ears. Stuart responded: "As to being laughed at about your husband's fondness for Society and the ladies. All I can say is that you are better off in that than you would be if I were fonder of some other things, that excite no remark in others. The society of ladies will never injure your husband and ought to receive your encouragement. My correspondence with the ladies is that kind of correspondence which pertains to the position I hold, and which never could obtain with me were I a subordinate officer, such no doubt as you hear insinuations from."

Although Stuart, by virtue of his position and reputation, received the attention of adoring ladies, there exists no concrete evidence to confirm that he ever plucked any forbidden fruits from the tempting orchard of women through which he strolled. He may have lost his heart a time or two in flirtatious interludes, but it would be doubtful if he compromised his honor or vows of matrimony.

Women in his eyes would have been regarded from a romantic point of view rather than objects of a physical relationship. The only hint of true controversy was presented in a fit of anger by Tom Rosser in a letter to his wife after being passed over for promotion, and such accusations can hardly be taken seriously. Stuart embraced all that was chivalrous and assumed the responsibility to play the role of the gallant knight of yore who placed women on a pedestal and was indeed inspired by their attention.

Perhaps John Esten Cooke offers the best appraisal of this issue when explaining the "young lady" element of Stuart's life. Cooke was in position as a member of Stuart's staff—and possessed the eyes and ears of a writer—to observe or at least hear about the particulars of Stuart's trifling. He also was Flora's cousin and would not have treated Stuart as reverently in print had Stuart been a rogue. "Never have I seen a purer, more knightly, or more charming gallantry than his," Cooke wrote. "He was here, as in all his life, the Christian gentleman. He was charmed, and charmed in return. Ladies were his warmest admirers—for they saw that under his laughing exterior was an earnest nature and a warm heart. The romance of his hard career, the adventurous character of the man, his mirth, wit, gallantry, enthusiasm, and the unconcealed pleasure which he showed in their society, made him their prime favorite. They flocked around him, gave him flowers. Stuart was married, a great public character, had fought in defence of these young ladies upon a hundred battlefields, and was going to die for them."

Stuart's courtly persona was evidenced when he participated in a game of charades at a party, where the rules required the actors and actresses to present a scene depicting the chosen word. Jeb was involved with acting out the word "pilgrimage." His role came in the finale after other pilgrims had entered the stage and knelt to lay offerings at a shrine with a cross above it. Another actor recounted: "The band struck up 'See! the conquering hero comes.' Forth strode grand 'Jeb' Stuart, in full uniform, his stainless sword unsheathed, his noble face luminous with inward fire. Ignoring the audience and its welcome, he advanced, his eyes fixed on the shrine until he laid the blade, so famous, upon it." Women in nun costumes entered "to bless the sword laid there as votive offering to country: no breath now breaking the hush upon the audience." Other religious pilgrims touched and bowed before this sword and chanted in a tribute that perhaps captured the essence of Stuart's symbolic fame to the Southern people.

Stuart also spent much of the winter seeking a house to buy for his family. His military houschold, however, underwent a change when William Blackford received a promotion to major and departed to join a newly formed corps of engineer troops. Blackford had served with Stuart since the first year of the war, and they parted with some measure of sadness. "To say that I part with you with regret is a poor expression of what I feel," Stuart wrote. "We do not part, as those who part to meet *no more*—often on the battlefield, at the bivouac, or the bower—I trust we shall meet again, with no tears shed, be glad in the sunshine of victory, till peace shall encircle with her rainbow the Independent Confederate States." Stuart suffered another great personal loss when banjo player Sam Sweeney died of smallpox, thus silencing the man who had cheered many a lonely campfire.

Family matters were also foremost in the mind of George Armstrong Custer at this point in time. The wedding date with Libbie had been set for February 9, and he had secured a furlough. On January 27, Custer, Jacob Greene, George Yates, and James Christiancy boarded a train and, with a stopover in Washington, made the three-day trip to Monroe, Michigan.

The Custer family, who with Autie's financial assistance had moved from Ohio to Monroe, welcomed the cavalrymen with a party. Private Tom Custer of the 21st Ohio Infantry had also obtained a furlough, and the two brothers were reunited for the first time since Autie had visited home in 1859.

A series of teas and receptions feted the couple in the days preceding the ceremony, and the wedding gifts were displayed in the Bacon parlor. The 1st Vermont Cavalry had sent a silver dinner service, engraved with "Custer"; the 7th Michigan, a seven-piece silver tea set; Judge Bacon presented his daughter with a Bible; Mrs. Bacon gave Libbie a white parasol covered with black lace; and Armstrong bestowed upon his bride-to-be a gold watch engraved with the initials "E. B. C." Dozens of other well-wishers had responded with items such as napkin rings with gold linings, a knit breakfast shawl, a lavishly bound copy of Elizabeth Browning poems titled *Whispers to a Bride*, and a mosaic chess stand made of Grand Rapids marble.

At 8 p.m. on February 9, 1864, George Armstrong Custer and Elizabeth Clift Bacon were united in marriage at the First Presbyterian Church (which still stands) in a storybook wedding with a standing-room only congregation of witnesses. Reverend Erasmus J. Boyd, who served as principal at the Young Ladies' Seminary and Collegiate Institute where Libbie had attended primary school, performed the ceremony, assisted by Reverend D. C. Mattoon.

Custer, with hair cut short and wearing his dress uniform, chose his adjutant Jacob Greene as best man. Libbie wore a traditional gown, described by her cousin, Rebecca Richmond, as "a rich white rep silk with deep points and extensive trail, bertha of point lace; veil floated back from a bunch of orange blossoms fixed above the brow." Libbie was given away by her father, who later boasted, "It was said to be the most splendid wedding ever seen in the State."

The wedding party was whisked away in sleighs with bells jingling for a reception in the Bacon parlor that was attended by more than 300 guests. The judge provided a generous buffet of delicacies that featured tubs of ice cream. According to Rebecca Richmond, "The occasion was delightful, hilarious and social." She had never met Custer, and found him to be "a trump," a "right bower . . . he isn't one bit foppish or conceited. He does not put on airs. He is a simple, frank, manly fellow. And he fairly idolized Libbie. I am sure he will make her a true, noble husband. As for Libbie, she is the same gay, irrepressible spirit we found her a year ago. They cannot but be happy."

At midnight, the bridal party—four couples—boarded a train and arrived in Cleveland at 9 a.m. the following morning. After an afternoon reception and an evening party hosted by friends, Armstrong and Libbie traveled to Buffalo, then on to Rochester, where they attended a performance of *Uncle Tom's Cabin*. The honeymoon continued by calling on Libbie's upstate New

York relatives, a trip down the Hudson River to visit West Point, on to New York City, and finally to Washington, DC, where they dined with Michigan members of congress and other dignitaries.

The Custer's honeymoon came to an abrupt end when Autie was ordered back to duty for the purpose of being a pawn in a grand scheme concocted by Hugh Judson Kilpatrick.

Kilpatrick had learned that Richmond was presently guarded by only about 3,000 old and worn-out militia men and proposed that he could lead a force of 4,000 past Lee's right flank and free the 15,000 Union prisoners held in the Confederate capital. Cavalry commander Alfred Pleasonton objected to the plan, but Kilpatrick went over his head and gained the backing of President Lincoln and Secretary of War Stanton, which was all that was required to earn Meade's approval.

Colonel Ulric Dahlgren, the twenty-one-year-old son of Admiral John Dahlgren, volunteered to accompany Kilpatrick. Dahlgren, who had lost a leg at Gettysburg and had been fitted with an artificial limb, was heartily welcomed. Armstrong Custer would not participate in this raid of Richmond; rather, he would command a diversionary force of 1,500 with orders to draw away any interference from Jeb Stuart's cavalry.

Custer departed headquarters on February 28 to rendezvous at Madison Court House with his unit, which would consist of the 1st and 5th New York, the 6th Ohio, the 6th Pennsylvania, and a battery of artillery. Support would be provided by the VI Corps commanded by Major General John Sedgwick.

At daylight on the following morning, Custer's decoy force crossed the Rapidan at Bank's Ford, where the 6th Pennsylvania chased away Rebel pickets, and arrived three hours later at Stanardsville. Another enemy outpost was scattered, and curious townspeople watched the blue column pass through town. Custer had given orders to capture all adult men, which came as quite a shock to those in Stanardsville who became prisoners. The procession encountered another group of Rebs north of the Rivanna River, and the 6th Pennsylvania again pushed them away.

About a half mile across the river, three miles from Charlottesville, Custer ran into four batteries of Jeb Stuart's artillery, commanded by Captain Marcellus N. Moorman, resting in winter quarters. Captain Joseph P. Ash and a sixty-man detachment from the 5th New York were sent to scout the position, and subsequently charged. Ash routed the Southerners, inflicted two casualties, and captured six caissons, nine mules or horses, and two forges, but the artillery pieces were removed to safety. The camp was burned, destroying the personal effects of the Confederate artillerymen. Custer brought up the main body but withdrew after receiving an erroneous report of the approach of enemy infantry. The raiders burned the Rio Bridge and stores of corn and meal at nearby Rio Mills, then, at about 9 p.m., halted to rest the horses and allow the men time to eat.

Jeb Stuart had been completely unaware of Custer's raiders until receiving information that afternoon about the enemy approaching Charlottesville. He gathered Brigadier General Williams C. Wickham's brigade and set out in that direction. The distant sound of firing could be heard, but Stuart was informed that the enemy had withdrawn. He decided to turn his march northward with intentions of intercepting Custer's return at Stanardsville.

Custer dispatched Colonel William Stedman of the 6th Ohio ahead with 500 men as an advance guard and resumed his march with the main force. Heavy rain and sleet plagued both columns, and Custer decided to bivouac for the night. Colonel Stedman, "through a misunderstanding," became separated from Custer and, unaware of the whereabouts of the main column, decided to continue on toward the Rapidan. Artist Alfred Waud of *Harper's Weekly* had accompanied Custer and commented about enduring the night under such miserable conditions. "The night was rainy, and all had to lie upon the ground and get wet through. It was difficult to get fires to burn, and the rain began to freeze upon the limbs of the trees, so that by morning everything appeared to be cased in crystal."

Stuart's troops also suffered through the freezing night but reached their destination at about daylight to learn that one detachment had already passed on toward Madison Court House. Jeb would lie in wait for Custer's arrival. Henry McClellan wrote: "For two or three hours his men sat on their horses or on the ground, exhausted, wet, and shivering. They had no food, and no fires can be built. Under such circumstances men cannot fight."

Custer roused his troops into the saddle at daylight on March 1 and rode through Stanardsville toward the Rapidan, destroying everything in their path. The raiders then headed along the road leading toward Madison Court House. About two miles outside of town, scouts informed Custer that Stuart's cavalry had been sighted across a fork in the road that led to nearby fords—Bank's Mills on the Rapidan and Burton's on the Rappahannock.

Jeb Stuart, aware of Custer's approach, chose not to wait for the main body of Union cavalrymen. He personally led a charge with elements of the 1st and 5th Virginia into Custer's advance guard, composed of one squadron of the Regulars with the 5th US Cavalry. The Federals were for the moment forced back, but they counterattacked with the rest of the regiment, which scattered Stuart's men into a hasty retreat. In the process, about twenty Rebels were captured. Custer ordered his artillery to lob shells at the fleeing enemy and sent his entire command forward in pursuit.

Stuart concentrated his troops at Burton's Ford and prepared for an assault. Custer, however, for once was not looking for a fight. He had accomplished his mission of diverting Stuart and decided to face his command about and withdraw. By the time Stuart realized his enemy's intentions, the Yankees were out of reach. The 500 cavalrymen that Jeb had dispatched to chase Custer watched as the rear guard of blue cavalrymen crossed the river to safety.

Stedman's "lost" detachment joined the main force en route, and the frozen, weary Union horsemen arrived back at Madison Court House at about 6 p.m. Custer reported marching 150 miles in forty-eight hours, and capturing over fifty prisoners, about 500 horses, and a Virginia state flag, without suffering any casualties. In addition to destroying a substantial amount of supplies, a bridge, six artillery caissons, and three large mills, Custer also returned with about 100 runaway slaves.

Meade called Custer's raid "perfectly successful," and Pleasonton's assistant adjutant general sent a note that read: "The major-general commanding desires me to express his entire satisfaction at the result of your expedition, and the gratification he has felt at the prompt manner in which the duties assigned to you have been performed." Custer gained further tribute when the cover of the March 19 issue of *Harper's Weekly* featured one of his classic charges, and a week later drawings of his raid were depicted. Custer's lauded diversionary action, however, could not assure that Kilpatrick would be capable of duplicating that success.

In truth, the Kilpatrick-Dahlgren raid on Richmond was an embarrassing total failure. Kilpatrick, leading one column of 3,000 cavalrymen against only 500 defenders with six pieces of artillery, lost his nerve on the outskirts of Richmond and pulled back to the safety of Union lines on the lower peninsula. A second column under Ulrich Dahlgren was ambushed, and every one of its 100 men was either killed or captured. Dahlgren, who was killed, was found to be carrying documents instructing his raiders to burn the city and kill President Davis. The contents of Dahlgren's papers incensed the Southerners and inspired within them a renewed fighting spirit.

This folly by Kilpatrick, who was described by one staff member at army headquarters as "a frothy braggart without brains," cost the Union 340 men killed, wounded, or captured, and over 500 horses lost. To Custer's great distress, 176 of those casualties were members of the Michigan Brigade.

Major James Kidd, who had led a detachment of the 6th Michigan during the raid, observed: "It was a fatal mistake to leave Custer behind . . . In a movement requiring perfect poise, the rarest judgement and the most undoubted courage, Kilpatrick could illy spare his gifted and daring subordinate . . . With him the expedition as devised might well have been successful; without him it was foredoomed to failure."

On March 2, Custer returned to his winter headquarters at Clover Hill near Stevensburg, a farmhouse he shared with Libbie, which was the former residence of John S. Barbour, the president of the Orange & Alexandria Railroad. The lower floor served as brigade offices; the upper floor was family quarters that Libbie had done her best to decorate until "it looked very homey."

While waiting for Armstrong, Libbie had been well cared for by Chief of Staff Jacob Greene and Eliza, who had assumed "sole control" of the household chores with assistance from Johnny Cisco. Her introduction to military life, especially as the wife of a general, was an eye-opening experience. "All the new life was in the way of surprise," she later wrote. "If I had been transported to Mars it could not have been greater." She was most impressed by the respect afforded her husband by "so many observances that go to enhance that dignity that hinges around a King."

With minimal duties for Custer to perform, he and Libbie were free to spend their days getting to know each other, dining with other generals, and taking the occasional carriage ride, escorted by a handful of troopers. On March 14, the couple was involved in a carriage accident when the team bolted. Libbie was unharmed, but Armstrong suffered a concussion when he was thrown from the carriage. To add to the pain of his head injury, Custer was about to become entangled in an espionage investigation.

Jeb Stuart, it would seem, was not alone when it came to contending with rumors about involvement with female camp followers. A young lady who had been accused of espionage claimed that in the summer of 1863 she had been with the Union cavalry "as the friend and companion of Genl. Custer." Anna E. "Annie" Jones testified that General Kilpatrick had become jealous of her relationship with Custer and, in retaliation, alleged that she was a Confederate spy. She was subsequently arrested and incarcerated in Washington for three months. Pleasonton requested that both Kilpatrick and Custer explain their relationships with the woman.

Allegations of womanizing were the last thing that the newlywed Custer needed at the moment, but in keeping with his style on the battlefield, he faced them head-on. Kilpatrick refused to respond, but Custer prepared an official statement, which was submitted on March 22. He admitted that the woman in question had visited his camp on two occasions—the second time arriving in an ambulance furnished by Major General Gouverneur Warren. "Her whole object and purpose in being with the army," Custer speculated, "seemed to be to distinguish herself by some deed or daring . . . In this respect alone, she seemed to be insane . . . So far as her statement in relation to Gen. Kilpatrick and myself goes, it is simply not true. I do not believe," he added, "that she is or ever was a spy."

Not surprisingly, evidence does not exist to substantiate or debunk the allegations directed at Custer or Kilpatrick by Miss Jones. Whether either man engaged in a relationship with her would be mere conjecture, a minor footnote of inconsequential nature that apparently was not worthy of documenting by those who shared campfires with the two generals. Perhaps desperation compelled the accused spy to prove her credibility in defense of the espionage charges by implicating these officers. Regardless, Annie Jones eventually received a parole and vanished from the public record.

Custer, who was still recuperating from his concussion, and his wife resumed their extended honeymoon with a twenty-day furlough that began on March 24. They boarded a train to Washington where they would dine with congressmen and other dignitaries and meet President Lincoln. One of the officers on that train was a man whom Libbie described in a letter to her parents: "Sandy hair and mustache; eyes greenish-blue. Short, and Mother, not 'tasty' but very ordinary-looking. No show-off but quite unassuming, talked all the time and was funny."

This particular general happened to be Ulysses S. "Sam" Grant, who had been summoned east to become general-in-chief of the army. Meade remained in command of the Army of the Potomac, but Grant, the hero of Shiloh, Vicksburg, and Chattanooga, had been handed authority no other military man had wielded since George Washington and would command Meade. One of Grant's first decisions was to relieve Major General Alfred Pleasonton as commander of the Cavalry Corps and replace him with a thirty-three-year-old West Pointer named Philip H. Sheridan.

Major General Sheridan had commanded an infantry division in the western theater and had caught Grant's eye at Chattanooga while leading a brilliant charge up Missionary Ridge. In appearance, Sheridan did not by any means portray the prototype image of a cavalryman. He was "a small, broad-shouldered, squat man, with black hair and a square head." Lincoln wryly described him as "a brown, chunky little chap, with a long body, short legs, not enough neck to hang him, and such long arms that if his ankles itch he can scratch them without stooping." But what the Irishman lacked in physical presence was offset by his demeanor on the field of battle. "In action," one officer noted, "or when specially interested in any subject, his eyes fairly blazed and the whole man seemed to expand mentally and phys-ically. His influence on his men was like an electric shock." These traits endeared him to the troops, who affectionately called him "Little Phil."

Sheridan wasted no time reshaping the Union cavalry corps to suit his own taste in fighting men. The first move came when Wesley Merritt, who was thought by most observers to be in line as Buford's successor, was passed over for command of the 1st Division in favor of Brigadier General Alfred T. A. Torbert, a thirty-three-year-old West Pointer from Delaware.

Surprisingly, Torbert, who had led a brigade in the VI Corps, had no experience in the cavalry. He had been, however, a schoolmate of Phil Sheridan.

Command of the 2nd Division remained in the capable hands of General David Gregg, but Judson Kilpatrick was relieved of his command and assigned to the western theater. Custer believed that he was a worthy successor and had been told as much by Kilpatrick. Instead, command of the 3rd Division was given to Brigadier General James H. Wilson. Wilson, who had been a classmate of Wesley Merritt at West Point, was an engineer officer and had never served in the cavalry. But the twenty-six-year-old had one major advantage over other qualified candidates. He had formed a friendship with U. S. Grant in the West, and it was Grant who had personally hand-picked him for the command.

There was one problem in this chain of command, however. Wilson had received his promotion to brigadier general on October 30, 1863, which made him junior in rank to Custer, Merritt, and Henry Davies. Regulations stated that Wilson could not command senior officers. To remedy the situation, Custer's brigade—the 1st, 5th, 6th, and 7th Michigan—was transferred to the senior one-star position in the cavalry—the 1st Brigade of Torbert's 1st Division. Henry Davies's brigade was assigned to Gregg's 2nd Division. Custer was pleased with the new assignment and with Torbert, whom he called "an old and intimate friend of mine and a very worthy gentleman."

Despite Custer's father-son relationship with Pleasonton, whose removal must have saddened him, he professed an agreeable initial opinion of Phil Sheridan. This view was the result of a "get acquainted" meeting between Little Phil and Custer on the evening of April 15. "I remained at Genl. Sheridan's headquarters last night and to-day until nearly 4 o'clock," Custer wrote to Libbie. "[He] impresses me very favorably." He also mentioned his new cavalry commander to his sister: "Gen Sheridan from what I learn and see is an able and good commander and I like him very much."

Grant was anxious to test the resolve of Lee's Army of Northern Virginia, and "Little Phil Sheridan was equally as eager to pit his horsemen against Jeb Stuart." And now that the winter cold had given way to spring, it was time to heat up the action on the field of battle.

CHAPTER ELEVEN

THE WILDERNESS CAMPAIGN

PHIL SHERIDAN HAD AMBITIOUS PLANS for his 12,500-man cavalry and sought a meeting to present them to Meade. He envisioned his horsemen as an independent unit with the freedom "to march where we pleased, for the purpose of breaking down General Lee's communications and destroying the resources from which his army was supplied." Sheridan also proposed that he draw Jeb Stuart's cavalry away from the protection of the infantry, where he could destroy it. Meade denied Sheridan's requests and insisted that the cavalry perform the traditional role of subservience to the infantry and screen and protect its movements. The decision did not set well with Sheridan, but the temperamental Irishman had no choice but to bow to Meade's wishes—for the time being, at least.

Grant was anxious to take the offensive and devised a strategy that called for his army to cross the Rapidan and Rappahannock rivers at various points—up the St. James, south of Richmond; up the Shenandoah to threaten the South's vital granary; and a march by Sherman on Atlanta. The main body would pass through the Wilderness toward Richmond, a movement that would assuredly draw the Army of Northern Virginia from winter quarters to engage the superior Union force. It would then become a war of attrition, with the numerical odds favoring Grant's army.

At daylight on May 4, the Union cavalry departed winter quarters in the vicinity of Culpeper-Stevensburg and rode south. Custer was disappointed to learn that his Wolverines had been assigned Torbert's rear—to guard the supply train—while the 2nd and 3rd Divisions led the infantry into the dense, second growth timber known as the Wilderness. Grant had intended to pass beyond Lee's right flank and traverse this brambly arboreous maze, where Fighting Joe Hooker had been defeated the previous year, before engaging the Confederates under conditions that would obstruct his artillery and impede cavalry movements.

Jeb Stuart was informed by his scouts during the night that from all indications, Grant was preparing to advance. Further reconnaissance confirmed that the Union army was indeed crossing the rivers. Stuart ordered that the Wigwam winter quarters be struck and that everyone ready themselves for active operations. After the noon meal on May 4, he dispatched a courier to intercept Flora and Jimmy, who were on their way from their temporary residence at Beaver Dam Station, and notify them to cancel the trip. Jeb then headed for Lee's headquarters, taking a cross-country shortcut that required his horse to jump numerous fences en route.

Stuart declined an invitation to dine with Lee at the bustling headquarters and, following a brief meeting, departed with his complement of couriers down the Orange-Fredericksburg Plank Road for a personal reconnaissance of the Wilderness. Volunteer aide Alexander Boteler, who was a Virginia congressman, described this forbidding region: "Not only do over-arching trees on either hand hem in the road and hide the sky, making it at high noon there seem more like twilight gray, but there is also on both sides a tangled mass of undergrowth apparently interminable and so densely intricate that it would be difficult for a dog to get through."

Stuart and his entourage cautiously rode for some miles down Plank Road. Suddenly, his advance was fired upon from the side of the road. Another volley and an attempted charge were quickly checked by return fire. Now that the enemy had been located, Stuart calmly reversed course in the growing darkness and headed back toward friendly lines. He had the intelligence he had sought.

The lead element of Hill's Corps had assumed a position on both sides of Plank Road near where it crossed Mine Run. As Stuart approached, a column of Hampton's division appeared from the darkness heading to the right flank. Stuart halted in the middle of the road to observe the movement and was immediately recognized by his troops. The rank and file cavalrymen honored their commander with a vocal ovation as they trotted by in a column of fours.

Congressman Boteler was greatly impressed with this impromptu display of adoration. "An artist could hardly find a finer subject for his pencil," he wrote in his diary, "though a picture of it, however perfect in its handling and details, would necessarily fall far short of reality in representing a scene so full of animation and excitement. Stuart himself a little in advance of us with his plumed hat in his hand, looked like an equestrian statue—both man and horse being as motionless as marble—his fine soldierly figure fully revealed in the light of the camp fires that were blazing brightly on both sides of the road as far as the eye could reach and lighting up the foreground splendidly. The cavalry came up in columns of fours, saluting the General with a shout as they wheeled off at a gallop, toward their designated positions while the infantry, catching inspiration from their cheers, mingled their loud hurrahs with theirs in one grand chorus of twice ten thousand voices. It was really a grand spectacle to see these gallant horsemen coming toward us out of the gloom of night into the glare of the fires, making the welkin ring with their wild war cries and the earth to tremble beneath their horses [sic] hoofs."

Stuart and his staff made camp at Verdiersville, spurning the filthy, dilapidated buildings to sleep on the ground beneath the trees. After such a rousing reception by his cavalrymen, it would not be surprising if Jeb and his band of merry men sang a few verses of "Jine the Cavalry" and other songs around the campfire before turning in for the night.

At about 3 a.m. on May 5, Armstrong Custer's brigade with the cumbersome wagon train were on the move in the direction of Ely's Ford, trailing by some miles the main army. The column arrived at its destination by midmorning, and the tedious task of crossing to the south bank was executed. The cracking of distant firing from the west could be distinctly heard as the wagon train rolled along, finally reaching Chancellorsville at noon and camping about a mile beyond on the slope of a plateau overlooking the Wilderness.

The nearby thick woods produced an eerie, confounding acoustic effect, which compelled staff member George B. Sanford to remark: "The sound of musketry exceeded in intensity anything to which I have ever listened before or since." Custer could only anxiously gaze into that dark wall of timber, listen to the roar of gunfire, and imagine the battle that was unfolding without him.

Jeb Stuart had risen early and personally guided Hill's infantry down Plank Road to the location where he had encountered resistance on the previous night. Stuart then rode off to witness Tom Rosser's brigade confront Wilson's cavalry and drive them back toward the vicinity of Todd's Tavern. Grant's intention to clear the confines of the Wilderness before Lee could react had failed. Rosser's initial engagement had triggered a firestorm of conflict that escalated into a full-scale, continuous skirmish between the two armies that for the most part took place along roads and around the few clearings. It was virtually impossible to maintain military formations within the tangled undergrowth, which caused mass confusion on both sides and neutralized the numerical superiority of Grant's force.

Jeb Stuart departed Rosser's contentious engagement and paid a visit to General Lee, who had set up a temporary command post off Plank Road in a small field hidden by dense foliage. Jeb joined a conference that Lee was conducting with Generals Pendleton and Hill and other staff members. Within moments, this meeting was abruptly interrupted by the unexpected appearance of a small group of the enemy who had emerged from the woods within point-blank range. Lee hurriedly leaped onto his horse and galloped to safety, Hill ran on foot into the woods, and the others scattered for their lives. The Union intruders, who had mistakenly wandered ahead of their lines, were just as surprised as the Confederate officers and vanished in the woods just as quickly as they had appeared. The Confederacy had escaped what could have been a disastrous day had just one volley been fired by the Federals.

The line of battle extended for six miles through the Wilderness. Stuart endured an uncomfortable afternoon directing his men in support of Hill as the infantry fought their way through thorny thickets while under constant fire from the enemy. The cavalrymen and their commander emerged from this prickly jungle late in the afternoon with ripped uniforms and faces scratched and bleeding.

By evening, when Stuart bivouacked near a place called Parker's Store, the day's fierce, bloody fighting had produced a stalemate between the two armies. Stuart and his men had just settled down when a courier dashed into camp to inform them that the surrounding woods were full of Yankees. An artillery piece was readied, and Stuart with his thirty men waited for an attack. When none came, he mounted his troopers and cautiously advanced into the timber. Before long, the source of this threat was exposed when a frightened Union infantryman of German descent charged out of the bushes. This unfortunate man earlier had become separated from his unit and had hidden in the woods throughout the day with the hope of locating his comrades after dark. Instead, he had become Jeb Stuart's prisoner.

Custer's ears had been filled with the sounds of distant fury all day, and now, as nighttime silence settled around the Wilderness, the orders that he had been waiting for finally arrived. The Wolverines would move out at 2 a.m. and reinforce David Gregg's division, which was positioned south of Todd's Tavern. Wilson's division had been bested all day by Stuart's cavalry and had been saved from total disaster only by the timely arrival of Gregg. Custer had been relieved of the frustrating duty of dragging along the supply train at the rear and was elated that he would have the opportunity to participate in tomorrow's struggle for control of the Wilderness.

Several days before embarking on this operation, Custer had written Libbie (from Camp Libbie, Virginia), and professed his most intimate preparations when a battle was imminent. "On the eve of every battle in which I have been engaged," he wrote, "I have never omitted to pray inwardly, devoutly. Never have I failed to commend myself to God's keeping, asking Him to forgive my past sins, and to watch over me while in danger . . . and to receive me if I fell, while caring for those near and dear to me. After having done so all anxiety for myself, here or hereafter, is dispelled. I feel that my destiny is in the hands of the Almighty. This belief, more than any other fact or reason, makes me brave and fearless as I am."

Custer arrived before daylight and deployed his troops at the intersection of Furnace Road and Brock Pike. Pickets from the 1st and 6th Michigan were posted around a 500-yard-wide field, which was cut in half by a sloping ravine, while the remainder of the men were hidden in the woods. Custer received an order from Gregg to move down Brock Pike with two brigades and harass Longstreet, who was moving on the left flank. But before the order could be executed, the 35th Virginia Cavalry, one of the regiments in Tom Rosser's brigade, burst from the trees to assail Custer's picket line, their Rebel yells splitting the stillness.

Custer immediately sprang into action. As Rosser's men streamed from the trees to drive back the Federal pickets, Custer rode to the front of his brigade and ordered the band to play "Yankee Doodle," which signaled to every Wolverine to form for a charge. Custer rode to the front, drew his saber, extended it toward the enemy, and shouted, "Forward, by divisions!"

Major James Kidd described the charge: "The two regiments [the 1st and 6th] charged with a yell through the thick underbrush out into open ground, just as the rebel troopers emerged from the woods on the opposite side. Both commands kept on in full career until they reached the edge of the ravine, when they stopped, the rebels apparently surprised by our sudden appearance and audacity, Custer well content with checking . . . the vicious advance."

Rosser rolled out a section of artillery and reinforced his attack with another brigade that threatened the right flank. Custer countered by deploying the 5th Michigan to meet that rush and moved the 7th beside the 1st. Rosser launched a series of frontal assaults, bolstered by part of Fitz Lee's division, but the Wolverines held firm. Gregg sent up eight artillery pieces, which Custer quickly brought into play and silenced the enemy's guns. Finally, Colonel Thomas Devin's brigade arrived, and Custer struck the Confederate left with the 5th and 6th Michigan as the 17th Pennsylvania and the 1st and 7th Michigan charged from the ravine.

Custer reported: "The enemy, after contesting the ground obstinately, was driven from the field in great disorder, leaving his dead and many of his wounded upon the ground. We also captured a considerable number of prisoners, who informed us that we had been engaged with Fitzhugh Lee's division of cavalry. Orders having been received not to pursue the enemy beyond this point, we remained on the field until near night."

Since daylight, Jeb Stuart had been patrolling Plank Road, directing his men's efforts in support of Longstreet. At about noon, Stuart assisted Brigadier General Edward Porter Alexander, who was seeking positions for Longstreet's artillery. The entourage traveled along the picket line and eventually came upon a clearing some 200 yards distant. Stuart suspected that the woods on the opposite side was occupied by the enemy and ordered one of his couriers to ride forward in an attempt to draw fire. The appearance of the courier was instantly greeted by a volley from sharpshooters hidden in the trees. He quickly wheeled his horse and returned to Stuart. The courier was uninjured, but his horse had been clipped on the muzzle by a bullet and proceeded to unceremoniously snort blood onto Jeb Stuart.

The day ended with Stuart halting a retreat caused by a furious Federal charge by placing his staff officers across Plank Road to restore order to the lines. At nightfall, neither side had asserted domination over the other, but the South had gained one strategic advantage by securing the area around Todd's Tavern.

The Confederates, however, did suffer one significant loss that can be attributed to the difficulty of fighting in such dense foliage. Reminiscent of the blunder that took the life of Stonewall Jackson, General Longstreet was mistaken for the enemy by his own men, who fired a volley at him from point-blank range. Longstreet was struck by a bullet that entered near his throat and passed into his right shoulder. He was carried from the field with a serious wound that would incapacitate him for some months.

An earlier incident that day demonstrated the aggressive nature of Robert E. Lee. At one point in the battle, Lee happened upon a brigade of Texans who were preparing to charge the enemy. He impulsively decided to lead this charge, but the Texans refused to move until Lee removed himself to a place of safety. The bridle of his horse was grabbed by some of the men, with calls for "Lee to the rear!" The commanding general grudgingly complied, and it became Longstreet's duty to tactfully inform Lee that he was much too valuable to be leading charges.

On the morning of May 7, neither side resumed the infantry battle, but Custer and his Wolverines pushed two miles down Brock Pike to connect with Gregg. Custer encountered Fitz Lee's brigade three-fourths of a mile beyond the crossroads of the Pike and Furnace Road and engaged in a fierce fight. With assistance from Gregg, the combined force successfully drove the Confederates out of the area. The Wolverines settled in on Gregg's right flank and were not challenged for the remainder of the day.

Stuart received a note from Fitz Lee at about 1:30 p.m. that informed him of the earlier withdrawal from Todd's Tavern. It was feared that the enemy would now be targeting New Spotsylvania Court House, and indeed Wilson's 3rd Division, supported by infantry, had advanced toward that crucial road juncture.

By evening, Fitz Lee was tangling with Wilson's troops, while Stuart guided the approach of infantry reinforcements. The Union cavalrymen had managed to push Rosser's brigade from Spotsylvania, but Sheridan suddenly recalled Wilson to Fredericksburg, and any pursuit was abandoned. The opposing infantries were involved in a heated battle until the Union troops withdrew, and quiet once again settled over the Wilderness.

That night, Stuart dispatched a telegram to Flora assuring her that he was "safe and well," and offered the overly optimistic view: "We have beaten the enemy badly but he is not yet in full retreat."

The battle to occupy Spotsylvania resumed on the following day, May 8. Jeb Stuart was kept busy directing the deployment of Longstreet's infantry—now commanded by Richard H. Anderson—and placed his dismounted cavalry on the left of the line for a period of about three hours until reinforcements arrived. Stuart remained exposed to enemy fire, as McClellan put it, "with more than his usual disregard of danger, and in spite of the repeated and earnest remonstrances of several of the infantry officers."

During this time, not more than a few miles away from the scene of this action, Stuart's name was being bandied about in a heated discussion between Generals Sheridan and Meade.

Meade had made a habit of issuing orders for the cavalry without bothering to consult or inform Sheridan. This incessant meddling had provoked Little Phil's fiery Irish temper, which boiled over during a confrontation between the two strong-willed men.

"Meade was very much irritated," Sheridan later wrote, "and I was none the less so. One word led to another until, finally, I told him that I could whip Stuart if he would only let me, but since he insisted on giving the cavalry directions without consulting or even notifying me, he could henceforth command the Cavalry Corps himself—I would not give it another order."

Sheridan added, "If I am permitted to cut loose from this army I'll draw Stuart after me, and whip him, too."

Meade reported this incidence of insubordination by Sheridan to Grant, likely with the prospect of being backed up in his handling of the cavalry and its commander—and possibly filing charges against him. Instead, Grant replied, "Did Sheridan say that? Then let him go out and do it."

Meade might not have agreed with Grant, but he dutifully issued orders for Sheridan "to proceed against the enemy's cavalry." For the first time in the war, the Union cavalry had been cut loose from the infantry and was authorized to operate as an independent unit.

Sheridan, without delay, gathered his three division commanders—with Wesley Merritt temporarily replacing Torbert, who was sidelined by an abscess at the base of his spine—to relate his plans and expectations. The cavalry would prepare to depart in the morning and would at that time assume a route around Lee's flank in the direction of Richmond, a movement that would assuredly draw Stuart and his horsemen in hot pursuit. "We are going out to fight Stuart's cavalry in consequence of a suggestion from me," Sheridan told them. "We will give him a fair, square fight; we are strong, and I know we can beat him, and in view of my recent representations to General Meade I shall expect nothing but success." Each one present understood that the only hope the Union cavalry had of ever reaching Richmond would be over the dead body of Jeb Stuart.

At daylight on May 9, Sheridan's cavalry—seven brigades, six batteries, and a wagon train, 10,000 men strong—saddled up and rode out in a column of fours that stretched for thirteen miles and required four hours to pass any given point. Custer's Michigan Brigade led the impressive procession that proceeded east of the infantry battle raging at Spotsylvania and then south on the Telegraph Road. Sheridan moved them at an easy pace that would conserve both man and horse in the event of an engagement, and, perhaps more importantly, would make them quite conspicuous to Jeb Stuart's scouts.

This bold move by the Union cavalry to pass around the farthest of Stuart's outposts was immediately detected by Williams Wickham's brigade. Wickham dispatched a courier to inform Stuart, then dashed off in pursuit. The Confederate cavalry reached the Union rear guard, the 6th Ohio

Cavalry, and engaged in a running battle. The 6th Ohio was quickly reinforced by the 1st New Jersey and made a determined stand near Mitchell's Shop, which succeeding in temporarily fighting off the Rebels. By this time, Stuart had mounted three brigades—Fitz Lee, Lomax, and Gordon, about 4,500 men—and took up the chase.

Sheridan turned his column and took the route toward Beaver Dam Station on the Virginia Central Railroad. With so many troops on the move, this would indicate to Stuart that Beaver Dam was not his enemy's final destination but that the march would proceed toward Richmond. Stuart must interpose his cavalry between Sheridan and the capital. Another factor, however, likely affected Jeb Stuart. His family had established a residence in Beaver Dam Station and were now placed in imminent danger.

Sheridan did not intend to ignore the railroad town. Shortly before sunset, Custer's Wolverines approached Beaver Dam Station to observe a detachment of the enemy escorting about 400 Union prisoners, captured in the Wilderness battle, toward the railroad depot for transport to Richmond. One battalion of the 1st Michigan charged the Rebels and succeeded in liberating the prisoners as well as capturing a number of the enemy. The freed soldiers included one colonel, two lieutenant colonels, and many other officers, who were most grateful to their rescuers.

That fortuitous timing was further evidenced when the piercing shriek of locomotive whistles reached their ears from the direction of the depot. The impatient engineers were waiting for delivery of their human cargo but were also there to restock Lee's advance supply base.

Custer's 1st and 6th Michigan dashed into town and easily seized two locomotives and three trains laden with several million dollars' worth of supplies that had been destined for the Confederate army. Custer reported that the boxcars were full of "bacon (200,000 pounds), flour, meal, sugar, molasses, liquor (confiscated by provost guards), and medical stores; also several hundred stand of arms, a large number of hospital tents." In all, supplies composing 1,500,000 rations had been waylaid.

Custer distributed all the rations that his men could carry, then burned what remained. He also ordered the 100 railroad cars and depot put to the torch, disabled the locomotives by firing artillery shells through the boilers, tore up the tracks in the vicinity, and cut ten miles of telegraph line. The Wolverines then departed to bivouac south of the South Anna River.

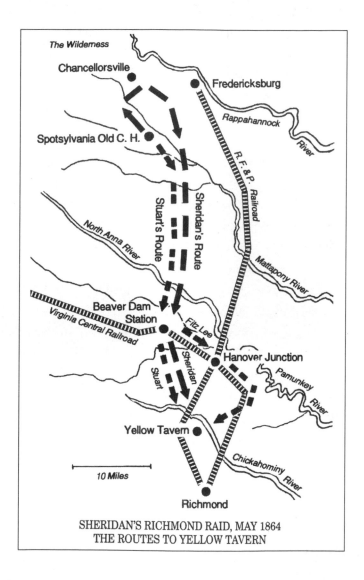

SHERIDAN'S RICHMOND RAID, MAY 1864
THE ROUTES TO YELLOW TAVERN

Jeb Stuart rode through the night, crossed the North Anna at Davenport's Bridge, and reached Beaver Dam Station on the morning of May 10. He must have approached with some anxiousness, which heightened as he viewed the destruction that Custer's troops had left in their wake. Flora and the children were staying at Beaver Dam, the town's namesake plantation owned by Colonel Edmund Fontaine, located a mile and a half outside of town. To his profound relief, his family had not been harmed. Without taking the time to dismount, Jeb visited briefly in private with Flora, affectionately kissed her goodbye, and then rode off with Reid Venable.

Stuart was strangely somber upon departing and rode for some distance in contemplation before speaking. In a step out of character, he confided to Venable that he never expected to outlive the war, and further, that he did not want to survive if the South was defeated.

Sheridan had roused his men early on May 10 and angled toward Hanover Junction on a pace more leisurely than on the previous day. Several miles before reaching that depot, the column crossed the South Anna River and headed northeastward toward Ashland Station. Sheridan's troops would cover eighteen miles to Ground-Squirrel Bridge before resting for the night.

Stuart, however, could not afford to tarry in his pursuit of the Union cavalry. It would be far more advantageous to fight with his back to the home front than it would be if Sheridan succeeded in threatening Richmond before Stuart could interpose his cavalry between the enemy and the capital. He dispatched Gordon's brigade to nip at Sheridan's heels and led the three other brigades—Fitz Lee, Lomax, and Wickham—on an alternate route in an effort to get ahead of the Yankees.

Stuart reached Hanover Junction after dark. At the request of Fitz Lee, he reluctantly agreed to rest the weary men. Adjutant Henry McClellan was directed to remain awake and ascertain that Lee's troops were back in the saddle by 1 a.m. Stuart rode ahead to Taylorsville, two and a half miles south, where he and Venable slept for several hours.

At the same hour that Fitz Lee resumed the march, Sheridan had his cavalrymen, with Merritt's division in front, on the march down Mountain Road toward its junction with Telegraph Road. Sheridan was confident that this was the area where Jeb Stuart would make his stand.

Stuart led his cavalrymen down the Telegraph Road through familiar country. On the left side of the road they passed the Winston Farm, the place where Jeb had camped twenty-three months earlier on the night before his ride around the Army of the Potomac. Stuart came upon the road that led to Ashland—the area where he had met Jackson at the beginning of the Seven Days Campaign. He learned that a squadron of the 2nd Virginia had earlier driven part of the 1st Massachusetts out of town, but not before the enemy had destroyed a train and a storehouse of supplies.

McClellan reported that as they rode along, Stuart "conversed on many matters of personal interest. He was more quiet than usual, softer, and more communicative."

At 10 a.m., after nine hours of steady riding, Stuart and his troopers arrived at the intersection of Telegraph and Old Mountain Roads. These two roads merged into Brook Turnpike, which led to Richmond, only six miles beyond. The place was known as the Yellow Tavern, named for a nearby abandoned, ramshackle inn whose bright color had by now faded to gray.

Stuart had succeeded in placing his men ahead of the Union cavalry's drive toward Richmond and mulled his defensive options. He could assume a position directly in front of Sheridan's approach or remain on the flank where he could attack his enemy as they rode toward the capital. With the numerical odds stacked against him by at least three to one—10,000 Yanks as opposed to 3,000 Rebs—he decided that it would be more prudent to strike the enemy's flanks rather than attempt to absorb a frontal assault.

With that in mind, Jeb dispatched Henry McClellan to Richmond to inform General Braxton Bragg, who commanded the city's defense force, about his disposition. The eventual strategy would depend on Bragg's ability to defend the capital. Stuart, however, was unaware that Sheridan's primary objective was not Richmond but to destroy once and for all the legend of invincibility possessed by the Confederate cavalry and its bold commander.

Without knowing Sheridan's intentions or how many troops were at Bragg's disposal, and with Gordon's brigade at the enemy's rear, Stuart finally compromised between his two defensive options. He deployed Wickham's brigade along a ridge line on the right, parallel to Telegraph Road, facing south-southwest. Lomax was placed on the left along another ridge at right angles to the road. Stuart's dismounted cavalrymen maintained an excellent defensive position, supported by several artillery pieces, but nonetheless were greatly outnumbered.

Within an hour, the Union cavalry had advanced to the vicinity of the Yellow Tavern and observed the line of gray-clad defenders. One detachment was dispatched across country to seize the Brook Turnpike and effectively cut off Stuart from Richmond. Merritt sent Gibbs and Devin to feel out Stuart's lines, while Custer's Wolverines waited in reserve. The Federals were met with intense fire from the woods where Lomax's right connected with Wickham's left. This threat compelled the entire Confederate line to open up, and the Federals answered in kind. Full-scale combat, much of it hand-to-hand at close quarters, ensued as the Union forces attempted to assert its will upon the unyielding opponent.

Custer's brigade was finally ordered to the front, and at once came under blistering fire from the woods directly ahead. The Boy General ordered the 5th and 6th Michigan forward to silence the Rebel riflemen. Before the 6th could dismount, an eager Colonel Alger had led his 5th ahead on foot into an open field that stretched for some 400 yards to a ridge where Lomax's men waited. Alger's troops immediately came under a vicious cross fire as scores of Southerners materialized from the timber to draw a bead on the exposed Yankees. In the words of Sergeant E. L. Tripp: "We were trying to return the fire, shooting in three directions."

Custer galloped up in clear view of enemy sharpshooters and shouted to Alger's men: "Lie down, men—lie down! We'll fix them!" He ordered Major Kidd's 6th Michigan to contend with the flank and, joining that unit with the 5th, formed a skirmisher line and moved steadily forward.

Custer's brazen maneuver, not to mention the firepower produced by the seven-shot Spencer repeaters, drove the surprised Virginians up the slope to their original position. The Wolverines remained in a swale and exchanged fire with the enemy for about two hours while Custer went off to reconnoiter and consult with Merritt.

Stuart was not concerned for the moment with the fact that his enemy had gained a position between his troops and Richmond. More significant, was holding the flank on Telegraph Road, and his troops had responded to the initial Union challenge with unflinching determination. He was most impressed with the grit displayed by the 5th Virginia, whose position was crucial to the overall defense of the line. This unit was commanded by Colonel Henry C. Pate, an officer whom Stuart had assisted in freeing from John Brown years ago in Kansas. That good relationship, however, had deteriorated into a bitter feud when Stuart had sided with Tom Rosser rather than Pate in a dispute that had led to Pate standing a court-martial.

Now, during the heat of the battle, Stuart rode over to Colonel Pate and told him how much he was needed, asking him to hold off the enemy at all costs. Pate regarded Stuart, then firmly said, "I will do it." Stuart thanked him for his resoluteness. After a moment, the colonel extended his hand, and Stuart warmly accepted this gesture of conciliation.

Stuart returned to his headquarters and resumed the direction of his men as Sheridan's cavalry pressed the issue. Casualties on both sides mounted as the Yankees probed every inch of the line in an effort to detect any vulnerability. One of the areas most contended was the position of Colonel Pate's 5th Virginia, which time and again repelled the earnest assailment. Although the Virginians had thus far successfully held their ground, word reached Stuart that their commander, Henry Pate, had been killed in the process.

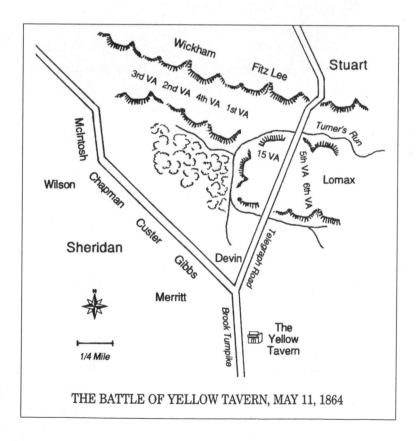

THE BATTLE OF YELLOW TAVERN, MAY 11, 1864

At about 2 p.m., Henry McClellan returned from Richmond. Due to the presence of the enemy, the adjutant had been obliged to detour across fields adjacent to Brook Turnpike in order to avoid capture. McClellan's message from General Bragg, however, greatly relieved Stuart's concern for the security of the capital. Richmond was defended by 4,000 irregular troops supported by artillery, and three brigades from Petersburg were presently on their way to bolster the fortifications. Bragg was confident that his force could withstand an enemy assault.

During a lull in the fighting, Stuart relaxed near one of the batteries on the right of his line and conversed for more than an hour with McClellan, Venable, and other staff members. He expressed his intention to maintain his present position and speculated that if reinforced by infantry coming up from Richmond, he could assume the offensive and cripple the Yankee cavalry. "I cannot see how they can escape," he observed.

Perhaps that was wishful thinking, but it was certainly in keeping with Jeb Stuart's usual optimism. Apparently, Jeb had not as yet arrived at the realization that Sheridan's true mission was annihilation of the Confederate cavalry. Stuart, in Sheridan's position, without question would have deployed a rear guard to occupy his enemy and then made a mad dash for the capital with his main force. For that reason, Stuart was of the opinion that the worst was over and that Sheridan would at some point break contact and head south.

The idea of withdrawing when his quarry was at bay never entered Sheridan's mind. In fact, Little Phil was in the process of finalizing a plan designed to strike the entire length of the Confederate line with one massive assault. This concentrated thrust would deny Stuart the opportunity to shore up his defenses in any one place by moving reinforcements from another.

But at about four o'clock, before Sheridan could launch the attack, Stuart opened up with an artillery barrage from the south end of his line that wreaked havoc on Custer's horse-holders and the ranks of the 1st and 7th Michigan.

"From a personal examination of the ground," Custer wrote in his official report, "I discovered that a successful charge might be made upon the battery of the enemy by keeping well to the right." Custer informed Merritt that he had detected a weakness that he could exploit with a mounted charge. Merritt approved, saying, "Go in, General. I will give you all the support in my power." Custer rode off to form his command as Sheridan joined Merritt and was briefed about the plan. "Bully for Custer!" Sheridan exclaimed. "I'll wait and see it."

Custer formed Lieutenant Colonel Peter Stagg's veteran 1st Michigan in a mounted column of squadrons out of sight in the trees and ordered Alger's 5th Michigan and Kidd's 6th Michigan to move forward on foot as a diversion to confuse the enemy. He was concerned about his left and borrowed—with Sheridan's permission, over the objections of the brigade commander—the 1st Vermont from Wilson's 3rd Division to guard that flank.

Lieutenant Asa B. Isham of the 7th Michigan, who earlier had been nicked by a shell fragment from the offending Rebel battery, described the appearance of his comrades: "My attention was diverted by what appeared to be a tornado sweeping in the rear. It was the 1st Michigan Cavalry, in a column of squadrons, moving at the trot. It wheeled upon my flank as a pivot with beautiful precision, and it came to a halt a little in advance of me, squarely in front and in full view of the Rebel guns. This splendid body of horsemen was halted but for a moment, when General Custer reined in at the head of it with an order to 'charge,' and away it went toward the guns. It was swallowed up in dust and smoke, a volume of exulting shouts smote the air, the earth shook and it was evident that a besom of destruction was sweeping over the face of nature."

One member of Merritt's staff remembered: "His [Custer's] headquarters flag—of the gayest colors—was flying in advance of the moving mass of glittering blades. The shrill blast of one hundred bugles and the familiar air of 'Yankee Doodle' rang out upon the battlefield while ... brave men of the Michigan brigade rode boot to boot into what seemed the very jaws of death."

The Confederate battery intensified its shell and canister barrage directed at both the diversionary force and the riders as they entered the clearing. To make matters worse, the terrain that Custer and the 1st Michigan would be required to traverse was rife with obstacles. The horsemen anxiously awaited while five fences were opened to permit passage, and they temporarily broke formation to cross a narrow bridge that only three at a time could pass over. Advancing to within 200 yards of the battery on the bluff, the troopers dug their spurs into their horse's flanks and charged with what Custer termed "a yell that spread terror before them."

The Rebel battery was obliged to contend with the carbine and cannon fire from the advancing 5th and 6th Michigan, which enabled the charging horsemen to gain momentum and sweep into the position before any effective resistance against them could be mounted. The Confederate gunners were overwhelmed. Many of them fell under the sabers of the Wolverines, while two cannon, two limbers of ammunition, and a large number of prisoners were captured.

Jeb Stuart mounted and hurried with his staff to the scene of this breach in his line to encourage Lomax's regiments, which had fallen back about 400 yards to a ravine and re-formed at right angles with Wickham to halt the Yankee advance for the time being. Stuart sat in the saddle exposed to the enemy fire as he directed his men. Reid Venable was concerned for Jeb's safety and remarked that men behind trees and other cover were being hit, so perhaps Stuart should be more cautious. The *Beau Sabreur*, who had managed to elude enemy bullets during countless battles, laughingly replied, "I don't reckon there is any danger!"

General Sheridan was elated by Custer's actions and jubilantly ordered Merritt to "send a staff officer to General Custer and give him my compliments. The conduct of himself and his brigade deserves the most honorable mention."

But Armstrong Custer's job was far from finished. The 1st Michigan was exhausted and required reinforcement to dislodge the Rebels who had withdrawn to the ravine. He dispatched the mounted 7th Michigan toward the enemy line, but the terrain impeded progress, and the troopers became bunched up and easy targets for Rebel sharpshooters.

Jeb Stuart decided that the best defense was an offensive. To that end, he ordered Venable to prepare Lomax's brigade for a counterattack. Meanwhile, Jeb rode to the left flank to join the 1st Virginia just as a combined force of blue-clad cavalrymen assailed that position. To relieve the pressure on the 1st Michigan, Custer had assembled every available man from his four brigades of Wolverines and, reinforced by the 1st Vermont, threw them all at once against the tenuous Confederate position. Stuart calmly advised:

"Steady, men, steady; give it to them." He emptied his pistol at the onrushing Union troopers, but his line virtually dissolved from the might of Custer's charge. Stuart shouted for them to rally, but the retreat was in full stride.

Nearby, forty-four-year-old Private John A. Huff of Company E, 5th Michigan, a veteran of the 2nd US Sharpshooters, steadied his .44-caliber Colt pistol upon a fence rail. He peered through the sights to observe an officer wearing a plumed hat who sat astride his horse, only ten to fifteen yards distant, while firing his own pistol in the midst of the confusion. Huff took careful aim and squeezed the trigger.

Jeb Stuart was about to shout a command when a sudden, stabbing pain in his right side knocked him off balance. He reeled in the saddle, his head dropping, his hat tumbling to the ground, but remained astride his horse. Concerned troopers noticed and rushed to Stuart's side to inquire about the seriousness of his wound. "Go tell General [Fitzhugh] Lee and Doctor Fontaine to come here," Jeb rasped.

Captain Gus W. Dorsey, who commanded Company K, understood the danger of an incapacitated Jeb Stuart lingering in the line of fire. He led Jeb's horse toward the rear, but the animal resisted and became unmanageable. Stuart was incapable of controlling his mount and asked Dorsey to help him down. Although fearing that the enemy would appear at any moment, Dorsey grudgingly obliged. The fierce battle still raged, and Stuart ordered Dorsey to gather his men and engage the enemy, but the captain refused to leave until Stuart was safely aboard another horse and headed for the rear.

Private Fred Pitts soon arrived with his horse, and Jeb was helped into the saddle. At about this time, a greatly distressed Fitz Lee, upon hearing the news, had raced along the entire length of the line to reach Stuart. Lee was the senior officer on the field now that Stuart was out of action, and was told by his commander, "Go ahead, Fitz, old fellow. I know you will do what is right!"

Dorsey, Pitts, and others helped balance Stuart atop this mount and led him beyond the limits of another Union charge. All the while, Stuart implored that his men must repel the enemy and protect Richmond from Sheridan. An ambulance was provided, and Jeb was placed in the bed. Major

Venable ordered the vehicle moved to the lowland near the bridge, which would assure that they were completely out of range.

During this short jaunt, Stuart noticed numbers of his cavalrymen running away in a disorganized retreat. An angry Jeb Stuart shouted as loudly as possible in his condition, "Go back, go back and do your duty, as I have done mine, and our country will be safe. Go back, go back! I had rather die than be whipped!"

Dr. John B. Fontaine and a staff member, Lieutenant W. Q. Hullihen, turned Stuart over on his side to allow the doctor to examine the wound.

"Honey-bun," Stuart addressed Hullihen by his pet name, "how do I look in the face?"

"General, you are looking right well," Hullihen answered. "You will be all right."

Stuart replied, "Well, I don't know how this will turn out; but if it is God's will that I shall die I am ready."

Fontaine could not readily determine the extent of the wound, only that Stuart had a bullet lodged in his lower abdomen, which, if it had pierced the liver, would be fatal. Stuart's immediate danger, however, was going into shock, and the doctor prescribed whisky as a stimulant. Stuart at first declined, citing the pledge of abstinence that he had made to his mother. After some coaxing by Venable, Stuart reluctantly consented.

By this time a large number of men had gathered around their commander. Stuart noticed them and said, "Go back to the front, I will be well taken care of. I want you to do your duty to your country as I always have through my life."

The next order of business would be to transport Stuart to Richmond. Union cavalry held Brook Pike, which compelled the ambulance and escort to make a series of wide detours. Jeb Stuart would endure great pain, apparently caused by peritonitis, on this jostling journey over seven miles of unfamiliar, winding, and bumpy roads before reaching his destination.

Phil Sheridan permitted his men several hours of rest and celebration before resuming his march down Brook Pike toward Richmond. The Rebels had mined the road, and Sheridan ordered twenty-five prisoners to crawl on hands and knees in front of the column to alleviate this threat. But that was not the end of Sheridan's obstacles to taking Richmond. A Rebel spy had managed to appoint himself guide for the march into Richmond and led Wilson's division directly into the city's defenses. Wilson's troops were taking a beating from the home guard and were pinned down. Sheridan wisely called a halt to bivouac for the night and assess his situation in the daylight.

Long after dark, Jeb Stuart arrived at the home of his brother-in-law, Dr. Charles Brewer, on Grace Street in Richmond. Word of his wounding had spread, and the foremost medical men of the city were waiting to attend to the famous cavalry general. After examinations had concluded, however, the consensus of opinion was that nothing could be done but apply ice to the wound. Stuart would remain in intense pain, his disposition in the hands of the Almighty.

Major Heros Von Borcke, who was convalescing in the city, attempted to telegraph Flora, but the wires had been cut by the Union cavalry. The message was finally relayed by a circuitous route and would not reach Flora until about noon on the following day. According to Von Borcke, after he left the telegraph office, the operator heard that Stuart was getting better and changed the wording of his message from "the General is dangerously wounded" to "slightly wounded."

May 12 dawned with rain pouring down, and Phil Sheridan could now fully comprehend the ticklishness of his situation on the outskirts of Richmond. His cavalry was caught between the enemy earthworks and the swollen Chickahominy. The Confederates gave every indication that rather than remain in a defensive posture, they would mount an attack. In addition, Stuart's cavalry under Fitz Lee was engaged with Gregg in the rear. Sheridan remained confident that in spite of his present circumstances, he could take Richmond, but realized that he could not hold it. Therefore, he must fight his way out before becoming trapped by Rebel reinforcements. He ordered Armstrong Custer to secure a crossing for his command five miles above the city on the north side of the Chickahominy River at Meadow Bridge.

Custer reached the swollen river to discover that the planks had been removed from the bridge, which made it impassable. The only other way across was a railroad trestle that was too hazardous for horses to cross. On the north bank, Confederate cavalrymen lay in wait with artillery and rifles at the ready. Custer dismounted Alger's and Kidd's regiments and ordered them to move across the railroad trestle as quickly as possible. The Rebels instantly opened up with artillery in an effort to destroy the trestle. Major Kidd described the precarious crossing: "One man, or at the most two or three, at a time, they tiptoed from tie to tie, watching the chance to make it in the intervals between the shells."

Alger's men were the first across and fanned out toward the left to lay down a base of fire to cover the movement of the 6th. Custer was observing the crossing when a shell exploded in a ditch near him, splattering him with mud. He remarked to Major Charles Deane: "Well, that is pretty hot for us, Major, but we will get them out of that pretty soon." True to his word, before long, Kidd's 6th Michigan had joined Alger on the other side and success-fully kept the Rebels at bay while engineer and pioneer teams laid a floor across the rails utilizing cut timber and lumber from nearby houses.

By midmorning, the trestle was deemed negotiable. Custer led the 7th Michigan and elements of the 5th and 6th across, while the 1st Michigan was dispatched to rout the Rebels. The Wolverines chased their enemy for two miles, capturing several prisoners. General Sheridan was so impressed with Custer's initiative that he remarked to Colonel Alger, "Custer is the ablest man in the Cavalry Corps."

The actions of Brigadier General James H. Wilson, however, were less than acceptable. His blunder the previous evening had nearly cost Sheridan the Cavalry Corps. The 1st Vermont, which had been on detached duty with Custer and now returned to Wilson, sent a message to the Michigan Bri-gade requesting "a pair of Custer's old boots" to lead their division.

While the Union cavalry crossed the Chickahominy, Jeb Stuart's wife, Flora, was receiving the first word of her husband's wounding. The telegram finally arrived in Beaver Dam Station while Flora and the Fontaine fam-ily were at the station assisting wounded troops sent from the fighting at Spotsylvania. Edmund Fontaine had accepted the message but inexplicably neglected to show it to Flora until they had returned home.

Fontaine, president of the Virginia Central Railroad, secured a locomotive and car for Flora and her children. The train took them as far as Ashland before they were compelled to transfer to an ambulance because the tracks between that point and Richmond had been destroyed. The party traveled through a blinding thunderstorm on their difficult journey along treacherous roads. Each time soldiers were encountered, Flora would inquire about her husband's condition. At one point, she was informed that the wound had not been that serious, which raised her hopes of finding him alive when she arrived.

An alert Jeb Stuart was visited by Von Borcke in the morning, and later Henry McClellan, who had delivered messages from Fitz Lee to General Bragg, arrived at his bedside. Between spasms of pain, Stuart dictated his final wishes to his trusted adjutant. Personal effects would go to his wife. Venable was to receive his gray horse; McClellan the bay. "You will find in my hat a small Confederate flag," Stuart related, "which a lady of Columbia, South Carolina, sent me, with the request that I would wear it upon my horse in a battle and return it to her. Send it to her. My spurs, which I have always worn in battle, I promised to give to Mrs. Lilly Lee of Shepardson, Virginia. My sword I leave to my son."

Stuart was interrupted by the sound of distant artillery fire and inquired about its origin. McClellan explained that Fitz Lee was attempting to trap Sheridan down the Chickahominy. "God grant that he be successful," Jeb fervently answered, then, with a sigh, "But I must be prepared for another world." After a moment, Stuart said, "Major, Fitz Lee may need you." McClellan understood that it was time for him to leave. He pressed his commander's hand before heading to the door, where he encountered President Jefferson Davis, who had entered.

"General," Davis asked, taking Stuart's hand, "how do you feel?"

"Easy, but willing to die, if God and my country think I have fulfilled my destiny and done my duty."

The president departed after a brief visit. Stuart's condition worsened throughout the afternoon. He suffered painful seizures and passed in and out of consciousness, occasionally shouting orders, and often asking about Flora.

According to Von Borcke, Jeb Stuart's final connected words were spoken to him. "My dear Von," Stuart said, "I am sinking fast now, but before I die I want you to know that I never loved a man as much as yourself. I pray your life may be long and happy; look after my family after I'm gone and be the same true friend to my wife and children that you have been to me."

He asked Dr. Brewer whether he might survive the night. When told that death was near, Jeb nodded and said, "I am resigned if it be God's will; but I would like to see my wife . . . But God's will be done."

At seven o'clock in the evening, everyone in the house gathered around Jeb's bed. Reverend Joshua Peterkin, an Episcopal minister, led them in prayers and the singing of "Rock of Ages," Stuart's favorite hymn. Jeb made a feeble effort to sing along, then turned to Brewer and said, "I am going fast now. I am resigned; God's will be done." He then drifted into unconsciousness.

At 7:38 p.m., James Ewell Brown Stuart passed into the hands of his God whom he had trusted throughout his life.

Flora and the children arrived at the Brewer home about four hours later to hear the news that they were too late to bid farewell.

The funeral was held the following day at five in the afternoon at St. James' Church, with interment in the Hollywood Cemetery, where his young daughter had been buried the previous fall. The Reverend Mr. Peterkin read the service at the church, and another Episcopal cleric, the Reverend Charles Minnigerode, presided at the cemetery. Eight general officers served as pallbearers, and President Davis, his cabinet, and throngs of mourners stood in the rain to pay their last respects. There was no military display because Stuart's Invincibles remained in pursuit of Sheridan, which, combined with the rumble of distant cannon fire, was a fitting tribute to the man called "the greatest cavalry officer ever foaled in America."

Robert E. Lee's official announcement of Stuart's death read: "The Commanding General announces to the army with heartfelt sorrow the death of Major-General J. E. B. Stuart, late Commander of the cavalry corps of the Army of Northern Virginia. Among the gallant soldiers who have fallen in this war, General Stuart was second to none in valor, in zeal and in unflinching devotion to his country. His achievements form a conspicuous part of the history of this Army, with which his name and services will be forever associated. To military capacity of a high order and all the nobler virtues of the soldier he added the brighter graces of a pure life, guided and sustained by the Christian's faith and hope. The mysterious hand of an all-wise God has removed him from the scene of usefulness and fame. His grateful countrymen will mourn his loss and cherish his memory. To his comrades in arms he left the proud recollection of his deeds, and the inspiring influence of his example."

Privately, Lee was devastated by the loss of his trusted cavalry commander who "never brought me a piece of false information." He mourned, "I can scarcely think of him without weeping."

CHAPTER TWELVE

THE SHENANDOAH

JAMES EWELL BROWN STUART, the heart and soul of the Confederate cavalry, was dead. The question regarding his successor was one that greatly troubled General Lee—Wade Hampton and Fitzhugh Lee were the candidates. Hampton was older than Lee and possessed more prestige within the army than did Fitz. Hampton also had been promoted to brigadier general more than two months before Lee, although both had been made major general on the same date. They were basically equals when it came to field command. Fitz Lee, however, embodied more of Stuart's personality and joy of battle. General Lee's difficulty in choosing between them stemmed from the fact that the two men, who were outwardly cordial to each other, were secret rivals. Virginian Lee represented the domination of the cavalry, and indeed the army, from his home state; Hampton was a South Carolinian who likely resented Virginia's dominion over the army.

Lee judged that appointing one over the other at this critical time might be demoralizing. With the wisdom of Solomon, the Confederate commander decided that each would command a division on equal terms and report directly to and receive separate orders from headquarters.

Custer's Wolverines enjoyed a period of "placid contentment" during the week following the battle at Yellow Tavern. The cavalry had moved to Haxall's Landing on the James River, where they refitted from quartermaster and commissary stores. According to Major Kidd: "The soldiers smoked their pipes, cooked their meals, read the papers, wrote letters to their homes, sang their songs and, around the evening camp fires, recalled incidents, humorous, thrilling or pathetic, of the march and battle-field. There was not a shadow on the scene."

One of those who wrote home was Armstrong Custer. "We have passed through days of carnage and have lost heavily," he told Libbie. "We have been successful ... The Michigan Brigade has covered itself with undying

glory ... Genl. Sheridan sent an aide on the battlefield with his congrat-
ulations. So did Genl. Merritt: 'The Michigan Brigade is at the top of the
ladder.'" But this period of rest and refitting could not last forever. After all,
there was a war to be waged.

On May 21, Sam Grant ordered Meade south with intentions of placing the Federals between Lee's army and Richmond. Lee was aware of this
ploy and hurried his troops to assume a strong defensive position south of
the North Anna River. Grant dispatched three of his four corps across the
waterway to engage his enemy, but the Rebels effectively held their own for
three days to thwart any passage. During this time, Sheridan's cavalry corps
had ridden up the Peninsula to rendezvous with the main force on May 24
near Hanover Court House.

Grant was not about to relinquish his initiative and abort his thrust
toward Richmond on account of this stalemate at the North Anna. He
decided on May 26 to send his reunited army in a southeastly direction with
the objective of skirting Lee's right flank. Wilson's division feinted toward
the Confederate left in hopes of confusing Lee, while the remainder of the
army headed toward the designated crossing point, which would be the
Pamunkey River at Hanoverstown.

Sheridan's two divisions rode through the night in a driving rainstorm
with orders to secure the crossing position. At daylight on May 27, Custer's
brigade was sent to cover the construction by a New York engineer regiment
of a pontoon bridge over the Pamunkey. His men soon came under fire, and
Custer ordered the 1st Michigan across the river to rout the Rebels and clear
the pathway.

Custer, by the way, suffered another dunking when his horse faltered,
and he was compelled to dismount in midstream and swim to shore. He
good-naturedly endured the hoots and cheers of his troops.

By 10 a.m., however, Armstrong was back in the saddle at the front of
the column as Sheridan's men, whose mission it would be to draw Wade
Hampton's cavalry away from the main force, led the way when the Union
army marched safely across the Pamunkey.

It was not long before David Gregg's 2nd Cavalry Division approached
Haw's Shop, a blacksmith establishment located three miles from

Hanoverstown, where he encountered two divisions of Hampton's cavalry. The Rebels were secured in the woods behind a swamp protected by sturdy breastworks and supported by artillery. Gregg ordered a frontal assault. The Union troops determinedly advanced, but in a series of attacks and counter-attacks that would last six hours, they sustained severe casualties and found themselves pinned down. By early afternoon, the Confederate cavalrymen had taken the upper hand and were gradually penetrating the center of Gregg's line.

Custer's troopers had skirmished with a Rebel detachment that morning in a three-mile running battle that had resulted in the capture of forty gray-clad prisoners. The triumphant Union cavalrymen were resting and watering their mounts along Crump's Creek when at two o'clock Sheridan ordered Custer to reinforce Gregg's beleaguered command. The Michigan Brigade immediately mounted and set off on an arduous ride through the thick trees and underbrush west of Haw's Shop. It was not until about 4:00 p.m. that Custer arrived at Gregg's rear to discover that the Union troops were barely managing to hang on to their position at the tree line facing their enemy.

The field was hammered with the impact of bursting artillery shells, and the fire from the Rebel sharpshooters was said to sound "like that of hot flames crackling through dry timber." Custer dismounted his men and formed them into two skirmisher lines—the 1st and 6th Michigan on the right side of the road leading to the enemy entrenchments, the 5th and 7th on the left. At about this time, Wade Hampton learned that the Union army had already crossed the Pamunkey, which had been his original reconnais-sance mission, and commenced a withdrawal. Custer noticed this retreat. True to form, he rode to the front of his men, exposed to enemy fire, waved his hat, called for three cheers, and ordered a charge into what one observer called "that sanguinary hell of fire."

Despite the gradual withdrawal of Confederate forces, several regiments of South Carolinians armed with Enfield rifles had remained at their forti-fications to initiate a cross fire that resulted in the most stubborn foe Mich-igan ever had met in battle. Custer's Wolverines, however, were resolute and eventually convinced their enemy to flee.

The Michigan Brigade lost forty-one killed in what was called by a Union soldier "one of the most gallant charges of the war." Burial and stretcher details combed the battlefield to attend to the "bleeding, mangled multitude [who] covered the surrounding grounds." Custer's aide, Jacob Greene, had been hit in the head by a spent bullet that knocked him from his mount but only stunned him. Lieutenant James Christiancy had ridden to the front in the thickest of the fighting to encourage the troops. He was struck by two bullets, one inflicting a dangerous wound in the thigh, the other clipping off the tip of his thumb, while another round killed his horse. Christiancy was sent to Washington to be nursed by Libbie Custer, and later would be awarded the Medal of Honor for his actions.

One other notable casualty was Private John A. Huff of Company E of the 5th Michigan, the man credited with killing Jeb Stuart at the Yellow Tavern. Huff was reportedly struck in the head by a rifle ball and died three weeks later.

Much praise for the battle at Haw's Shop was reserved for Armstrong Custer, who had a horse shot out from under him during the fray. Typical of the accolades from witnesses was the letter written to his parents by Major Kidd, who described Custer as thus: "So brave a man I never saw and as competent as brave. Under him a man is ashamed to be cowardly. Under *him* our men can achieve wonders."

After dark, Meade's infantry relieved the exhausted cavalry, which then marched five miles southeast to Old Church and camped a mile or so from the mouth of Totopotomy Creek. They would remain at this position until the 30th, when Sheridan ordered them toward Cold Harbor.

Grant had recognized the futility of charging Lee's fortified positions and decided to return his attention to the strategy of attempting to cut off his enemy's main supply routes. Sheridan would lead his two cavalry divisions—Torbert's 1st and Gregg's 2nd, about 6,000 strong—in an attempt to flank Lee to the far west.

On the afternoon of May 30 near Cold Harbor, Torbert's division came under heavy Confederate fire from Fitz Lee's horsemen. Custer's Michigan Brigade had been held in reserve, but on orders from Torbert they dismounted and rushed forward to engage the enemy. The Confederates were quickly pushed back, and as Custer readied a saber charge, the Rebels fled en masse to escape the wrath of the Union cavalrymen.

After dark, with Cold Harbor thought to be relatively secure, Sheridan pulled out, only to be halted in his tracks when ordered by Meade to hold the place at all hazards. The troops spent the night fortifying the breastworks and waiting for an attack.

The efforts of the Union cavalrymen served them well. At dawn on June 1, one division of Confederate infantry supported by artillery burst from the woods and stormed across the field to attack the entrenched Federals. The bravery of the Rebels cannot be understated as they charged, were forced back by barrages of withering fire from Union seven-shot Spencer repeaters, charged again, only to be ripped apart, and then regrouped to assault the position once more.

Custer distinguished himself by riding along the lines—the only Union horseman exposed to the enemy—while exhorting his men to maintain their positions and practice fire discipline. The ferocious battle continued for Custer and his Wolverines until about noon, when they were relieved by the Federal VI Corps commanded by Major General Horatio G. Wright. The cavalry mounted to the sound of the brigade band's rendition of "Hail Columbia," and they rode to White House, where they camped for five restful days while the fighting at Cold Harbor raged on without them.

The outcome of that battle would be disastrous for the Union. At dawn on June 3, General Grant, in a move that he would live to regret, ordered 40,000 soldiers in double lines along a six-mile front to execute a frontal assault against the well-entrenched Confederate positions. When the smoke had cleared and the blood-letting had ended, nearly 7,000 Union soldiers had been killed, while the Rebels lost less than 1,500.

While the two bloodied armies faced each other across the battlefield, Grant formulated an alternate strategy to avoid the folly of assaulting Lee's fortified positions. The plan called for Union forces to once again make an effort to cut off main supply routes from Richmond, this time by crossing the James River. To this end, two divisions of Sheridan's cavalry were dispatched to ride seventy miles to the west with orders to destroy the Virginia Central Railroad and the James River Canal, capture the town of Charlottesville, and, if possible, link up with Major General David Hunter's forces, which were advancing on Lynchburg. The cavalry strike force rendezvoused at New Castle Ferry on June 6, were issued three days' rations and two days' forage, and set out the following morning.

Part of Grant's strategy was to draw the Confederate cavalry away in pursuit, thereby clearing the path for his own movement to Petersburg, the main supply depot twenty-two miles from Richmond. Grant was not disappointed; Wade Hampton's and Fitz Lee's divisions, about 5,000 strong, raced to intercept Sheridan.

By the time Sheridan's cavalry bivouacked at nightfall on June 10 near Clayton's Store, Hampton was in possession of Trevilian Station, three miles to the north on the Virginia Central. Fitz Lee was camped about four miles southeast of Hampton at Louisa Court House, three miles from the position of Custer's brigade.

Both commanders planned to attack without delay. Hampton believed that Sheridan would remain at Clayton's Store and devised a two-prong offensive. His own division would charge into the enemy head-on while Lee's men would hammer them on the flank. It was Sheridan, however, who seized the initiative.

Merritt's and Devin's brigades were in position just after sunrise to greet and surprise two Confederate lead brigades only several hundred yards from Trevilian Station as they moved down the road. The troopers dismounted and engaged in a furious battle from opposite stands of timber.

Custer had been assigned the task of protecting the left flank and, if possible, attacking the enemy from the rear. He led his troops southwestward through growth so thick that his column of fours was reduced to double or single file. At about 8 a.m., Captain Hastings of the advance reported that he had emerged from the woods to observe hundreds of Rebel supply wagons, pack mules, and ambulances moving down the road.

One can only imagine Custer's ecstatic reaction to this news. The caravan that he deduced was Wade Hampton's personal baggage train was a prize that he could not resist attempting to capture. Custer immediately dispatched an aide to order Colonel Alger and the 5th Michigan to charge the wagon train. Major Kidd's 6th Michigan and Pennington's Battery M would support the charge.

Alger dashed from the woods in a hastily formed line and quickly overwhelmed the defenseless string of wagons. The 5th scattered the frightened
teamsters and animals and captured six caissons, forty ambulances, and fifty
wagons. But, instead of being content with his booty, Alger, a man whom
Custer later graciously described as being motivated by "the impulses of a
pardonable zeal," noticed that up ahead waited the horse holders, who were
tending mounts belonging to Hampton's dismounted division, which was
engaged with Merritt and Devin. Alger, contrary to Custer's orders, raced
past Trevilian Station depot and gathered up some 1,500 horses and 800
prisoners.

This bold act was met by a swift response when a wave of dismounted
Confederates disengaged from fighting Merritt to arrive and effectively
cut off Alger from Custer and the trailing 6th Michigan. To make matters
worse, Custer learned that additional Confederate troops were closing in on
him. His rear was under attack by Fitz Lee's brigade, and the brigade commanded by Brigadier General Tom Rosser was routing the 5th Michigan.
The Wolverines would soon find themselves surrounded. Custer, who was
alone except for his staff, orderlies, and Pennington's battery, was determined
to fight his way out. He relayed urgent orders for Kidd's 6th to "take a gallop
and pass the battery."

The 6th Michigan regiment was strung out through the thick woods, and
only four companies were able to respond to the order. Kidd located Custer,
who, with his staff, was returning close-range Rebel fire. Custer, according
to Kidd, "never lost his nerve under any circumstances" but was "unmistak-
ably excited" at that moment and simply shouted, "Charge!" Kidd's troopers
drew sabers and galloped forward into the enemy, which, to their surprise,
permitted the Union horsemen to pass through their ranks. Then, mounting
a pursuit, the Rebels chased the disorganized 6th Michigan directly into the
retreat of the 5th, which was being pressed by Rosser. Kidd's men bore the
brunt of the charge. Many of them were captured by the swarming Confederates, including Major Kidd.

Although Custer was decidedly on the defensive, he counterattacked
with four companies of the 6th Michigan commanded by Captain Manning
D. Birge. Rosser could not withstand the added pressure, and Major Kidd

and many of his men were rescued. In the meantime, the 1st and 7th Michigan had arrived, and Custer barricaded the road and deployed those troops in a field southwest of the station.

The Michigan Brigade, however, remained trapped and outnumbered, "caught on the inside of a living triangle," one participant wrote in his diary. Lee attacked from the east, Rosser from the west, and Hampton advanced from the north. The officer in charge of Custer's baggage train approached and asked if the wagons should be moved to the rear. Custer agreed, then wondered, "Where the hell is the rear?" The answer to that question was obvious—there was no rear. The Rebels were relentless, gleefully taking advantage of their superiority over their beleaguered enemy. Custer formed his men into a circle for a last stand and prayed that Merritt and Devin could fight their way through Hampton and arrive in time to save them.

Rosser blasted into Alger's command to liberate many of the wagons and men that the 5th had recently captured, and rounded up about 150 prisoners. Lee's men crashed through to recover all their lost horses and wagons and also captured Custer's headquarters wagons and records. The Rebels had seized his personal papers, love letters from Libbie, an ambrotype of Libbie, Custer's commission to general, inscribed field glasses, dress uniform, and even his underclothing. In addition to his possessions, Custer's cook, Eliza, was taken but escaped later that day. His chief of staff, Jacob Greene, and orderly Johnny Cisco were not so lucky, and they remained prisoners at Wade Hampton's headquarters.

In Custer's words to his wife: "Would you like to know what they have captured from me? Everything except my toothbrush. I regret the loss of your letters more than all else." The letters were later published in a Richmond newspaper, much to the delight of its readers.

Throughout this ordeal, Custer added to his growing legend as a cool and calculating tactician under the direst of circumstances. "Custer was everywhere present giving instructions to his subordinate commanders," Kidd later wrote. He courageously rode around his lines to deploy and encourage his men, and in the process had three horses shot out from underneath him. When any part of the line was breeched, Custer would quickly dispatch troops to reinforce that position. When one of Pennington's guns was captured, Custer personally led thirty men to retake the piece in a vicious hand-to-hand fight. At one point, Custer ventured alone onto the field and, although struck and stunned by a spent bullet, carried to safety a wounded trooper. When the brigade's color bearer was mortally wounded, it was Custer who grabbed the flag, ripped it from the staff, and draped it over his shoulder for safekeeping.

Custer's prayers were finally answered when Sheridan led an assault of Merritt's and Devin's brigades into Hampton's line north of Trevilian Station to relieve the pressure. Custer formed the 7th Michigan and pursued the retreating Rebels that had captured his headquarters wagon train. He managed to recover a few wagons but none of his personal belongings. Both exhausted armies camped for the night. The Confederates withdrew south and west while the Federals remained in the fields around Trevilian Station. Custer's Wolverines had suffered one of the darkest days in their history with 41 killed, 375 wounded, and 242 captured, including nearly half of the 5th Michigan.

Sheridan was determined to continue the offensive, and at midafternoon the following day Custer was assigned the task of engaging Fitz Lee while Merritt attacked Hampton's flank. The widespread fighting—which featured seven dismounted assaults by the Union cavalry, each repulsed—raged well into the evening and exacted a toll nearly as large as the previous day. At ten o'clock, Sheridan disengaged his troops, bivouacked, then commenced a difficult march to reunite with the main force near Petersburg on June 25.

Sheridan may have failed to severely damage the Virginia Central Railroad or rendezvous with Hunter but had nonetheless succeeded in proving once again superiority over his enemy. In the two-day battle of Trevilian Station, the Federals lost a reported 1,007 killed, wounded, and captured. Although exact figures are not available, Confederate losses likely were slightly higher, which was more devastating to the South than the North due to its dwindling supply of men available as replacements.

Custer was afforded a respite from war when on June 28 he greeted his wife, who had arrived aboard the steamer *River Queen*, at City Point, Virginia. The couple then retired to Washington, where on July 11 Custer requested and was granted a twenty-day furlough. Armstrong and Libbie traveled to Monroe, Michigan, to visit family and friends, and returned to the capital on July 29. Custer reported back to duty the following morning on a day that would change the course of the war.

The Union army on that day detonated four tons of gunpowder that had been stored within a mine chamber situated under Confederate lines at Petersburg. The explosion created a huge crater and killed or maimed about 300 Southerners. The ensuing Union assault resulted in a wholesale slaughter of Yankee troops. At the same time, Confederate cavalry burned the community of Chambersburg, Pennsylvania, to the ground, destroying over 400 buildings. This brazen raid struck fear into the hearts of Northerners, who feared that the Rebels' next stop would be Washington.

These embarrassing events, coupled with Grant's inability to clear the Shenandoah Valley of Confederate troops, threatened Lincoln's reelection chances. The president demanded that Grant find a solution. Sam Grant, whose own reputation had been severely tarnished, decided to consolidate his forces for the purpose of sweeping through the Shenandoah Valley.

To the surprise of most observers who thought he was too young, the leadership of what was called the Middle Military Division of 50,000 troops was bestowed on Little Phil Sheridan. Grant ordered Sheridan's force, which would include the 1st Cavalry Division with Custer's Michigan Brigade, to advance south up the valley and engage in total war—annihilate the enemy, capture stores for army use, and destroy any provisions that could aid the enemy. In other words, demolish the Confederacy.

Sheridan marched from Harpers Ferry on August 10. Torbert had assumed the position of chief of cavalry, and Merritt succeeded him as commander of the division. Holding a position of tremendous influence as Torbert's chief of staff was none other than Brevet Major Marcus Reno, the man who would disobey Custer's orders on June 25, 1876, and contribute greatly to the debacle at the Little Bighorn.

The following month in the Shenandoah could not by any stretch of the imagination be considered a success for the Union cause. Sheridan, perhaps overly cautious due to fears that another defeat would be detrimental to Lincoln's reelection, spent the month maneuvering and skirmishing against Jubal Early's army with little to show for the effort. Confederate opposition became more intense the deeper Sheridan ventured into the valley. Finally, after fifty miles, he began a withdrawal in order to protect supply routes that he feared could be cut off.

Custer was involved in many of these running battles with the elusive enemy. In one early engagement, he was riding along his lines when a bullet grazed his head, clipping off some hair. His most nagging opponent, however, was Lieutenant Colonel John Singleton Mosby, the "Gray Ghost" and legendary leader of an elusive band of guerillas. Mosby, the man who had originated the idea for Jeb Stuart's initial ride around McClellan's army, responded to the Valley invasion by leading his band of bushwhackers on a series of retaliatory acts.

On August 18, a group of Mosby's men, dressed in common farmer clothing or blue uniforms, rode up to Custer's pickets and cold-bloodedly killed and wounded several Wolverines. Soon after that, a number of sentinels were bushwhacked by sharpshooters in the night. A cook and an orderly from the 7th Michigan who had visited a nearby farm to obtain provisions were found hanging from a tree. Three companies of the 5th Michigan were attacked and routed by a superior force of Confederates, many of them dressed in Union blue. Ten Michigan troopers surrendered, only to be murdered by Mosby's guerillas.

Custer vowed revenge and gained some measure of retribution by burning a few houses and barns and managing to capture and hang a number of those deemed spies who had been caught while wearing Union blue. But Mosby, the master of hit-and-run tactics, frustrated Custer at every turn in this escalating blood feud between the two determined warriors.

Sheridan's withdrawal was treated by Northern newspapers as another failure. An element of pressure on Lincoln had been alleviated with Sherman's capture of Atlanta on September 2, but the Shenandoah remained a major problem. On September 16, Grant met with Sheridan, and the two men devised an offensive strategy designed to crush the enemy once and for all.

The initial objective would be the town of Winchester, where Jubal Early's men were entrenched. At 2 a.m. on September 19, Custer and his Wolverines, reinforced by the 25th New York Cavalry, moved out into the darkness. As the tip of Sheridan's right flank, Custer and the dismounted 6th

Michigan came under intense fire at Locke's Ford along Opequon Creek. Custer had his men lay down a base of fire and formed the 25th New York supported by the 7th Michigan for an attempt to cross the waterway.

Rebel riflemen and gunners opened up with a furious barrage, and Custer's men floundered. In a surprise bold move, Custer ordered a charge across the stream by the 1st Michigan. The Confederate soldiers under Custer's West Point friend Gen. Stephen Ramseur were forced into a hasty retreat by Custer's aggressive maneuver.

Custer secured the ford, then began chasing the retreating Rebels in the direction of Winchester. His men engaged in a series of minor skirmishes until midafternoon, before eventually coming upon a Union division under General William Averell, which was engaged with a line of Rebels under Fitz Lee. Custer's appearance and subsequent saber charge drove the gray-coats into the woods, with Yankee horsemen in hot pursuit. Lee managed to form his men behind a stone wall and wide ditch. Custer never paused and ordered a charge over the obstacles, which sent the Confederates reeling once again. Lee, who had his third horse of the day shot out from beneath him, received a wound that would incapacitate him until the following year.

Custer halted to await further orders. Word came that the battle in the center of the town was not going well for the Union. Sheridan, in a bold move, ordered his beleaguered men to charge. Custer, alone except for the sergeant carrying his personal guidon, rode well ahead of his troops as they galloped directly toward an enemy artillery battery. Suddenly, a bullet struck his color bearer, knocking him from his horse. A horde of Rebels raced to close in and finish off the downed man and Custer as well.

Instead of prudently running for his life, Custer leaped from the saddle, grabbed his sergeant by the jacket collar, and pulled him to safety. Custer galloped away with the wounded man, all the while engaged in a saber and bayonet duel with the enemy, until a detachment of the 6th Michigan under Major Charles Deane came to his rescue. Deane later called his commander's actions "as brave a thing as I ever saw Custer do." The Rebel battery had escaped, much to Custer's ire, but the Boy General and his color bearer had been saved.

Custer regrouped his men and moved them to a small crest within 500 yards of the enemy line. The order came from Sheridan: "Tell General Custer that now is the time to strike. Give him my compliments, and order him not to spare one damned ounce of horse-flesh."

Custer was of the opinion that a frontal assault at that time would be suicidal. He requested that his orders be amended to permit him to choose the timing of his charge. Had most commanders made that request, it would have been considered insubordination. Sheridan, however, apparently trusted Custers, assessment of the situation, and agreed.

Finally, Custer determined that the right moment to attack had arrived. He ordered "Yankee Doodle," his song for the charge, be played, and off they went at a trot, then a gallop. Harris Beecher, assistant surgeon of the 114th New York, described the scene. "Away to the right a dull thunder arose. Looking in the direction of the setting sun, our men saw the most impressive and soul-stirring sight it was ever their lot to witness. Custar's [sic] cavalry was making a charge. Ten thousand [actually only about 500] horsemen were pouring down at a keen gallop, upon the already discomfited enemy. Ten thousand sabers glistened and quivered over their heads. Ten thousand chargers threw up a great cloud of dust that obscured the sun . . . Oh! it was glorious to see how terror-stricken the rebels were, at the discovery of this impetuous charge."

The 500 Union horsemen slammed headlong into about 1,700 infantrymen. After the first volley from these entrenched riflemen had been fired, Custer rallied his Wolverines forward before the enemy could reload. The well-timed charge, with sabers decimating the ranks, routed the Confederate boys. "But see the gallant Custer!" one member of the band noted. "He is in the midst of a throng of the enemy, slashing right and left. A Confederate infantryman presents his musket full at Custer's heart and is about to pull the trigger. Quick as lightening the general detects the movement. With a sharp pull he causes his horse to rear upon its haunches, and the ball passes, just grazing the General's leg below the thigh. Then a terrible stroke descends upon the infantryman's head, and he sinks to the ground a lifeless corpse."

The shattered Rebel army fled from Winchester down the road toward Strasburg. Custer's victorious Wolverines had captured more than 700 prisoners, including fifty-two officers, along with seven battle flags. Custer modestly wrote in his official report: "It is confidently believed that, considering the relative numbers engaged and the comparative advantage held on each side, the charge just described, stands unequaled, valued according to its daring and success, in the history of this war."

The Rebels withdrew to Fisher's Hill, where on September 22 the Federals attacked Early's lines and once more routed the Confederates. Custer and his comrades chased the retreating enemy for more than twenty miles without success.

Sheridan blamed the lackadaisical actions of Generals Averell and Torbert for the Union's inability to corral and destroy Early. On September 23, Averell was removed, and then, three days later, Sheridan had the opportunity to rid himself of Torbert when Grant requested either Torbert or James Wilson, commander of the 3rd Division, for assignment in Georgia. Sheridan, however, selected Wilson for this duty and wasted little time naming a successor. Brigadier General George Armstrong Custer was Sheridan's choice.

Custer, who at first had been assigned the 2nd Division, would as of September 30, 1864, be in command of the 3rd Division, which included the 1st Brigade, under Colonel Alexander C. M. Pennington, consisting of the 2nd New York Cavalry, 2nd Ohio Cavalry, 3rd New Jersey Cavalry, 5th New York Cavalry, 18th Pennsylvania; and the 2nd Brigade, under Colonel William Wells, consisting of the 1st Vermont Cavalry, two companies of the 3rd Indiana Cavalry, the 8th New York Cavalry, 22nd New York Cavalry, and one battalion of the 1st New Hampshire Cavalry.

The only downside to this promotion was that Custer would be leaving behind the Michigan Brigade, the unit that he had molded into the most celebrated cavalrymen in the Army of the Potomac. Hundreds of Wolverine troopers signed petitions requesting transfer to the 3rd Division, to no avail. Custer summed up the emotion of the separation in a letter to Libbie. "You would be surprised at the feeling shown," he wrote. "Some of the officers said they would resign if the exchange [an assignment of the Michigan Brigade to the 3rd Division] were not made. Major Drew said some actually cried. Axell, the band leader, wept. Some of the band threatened to break their horns." The Wolverines would continue to wear their red neck ties out of respect and loyalty to their beloved leader.

Meanwhile, six of Mosby's rangers had been hanged on September 23 at Fort Royal. Mosby was infuriated by the act and, believing that Custer was the culprit, requested permission from General Lee to hang an equal number of Custer's men for each that Mosby lost. Permission was granted. After one such lynching party, Mosby pinned a note to one of Custer's dangling troopers: "These men have been hung in retaliation for an equal number of Colonel Mosby's men, hung by order of Gen'l Custer at Fort Royal. Measure for measure." The men hanged at Fort Royal, however, had not been executed by Custer, who had in fact taken a ten-mile detour around that particular city. Regardless, Mosby's brutal actions served to add fuel to the fire of this escalating personal feud between the two adversaries. And it was now Custer's turn to strike back.

Custer's first assignment as commander of the 3rd Division would be a nasty, distasteful bit of business prompted by Mosby's executions. Three guerillas wearing Union uniforms had shot and killed Sheridan's chief engineer not far from headquarters near Dayton, Virginia. Little Phil was outraged and, as punishment for this cowardly act, ordered Custer to burn every house within five miles of the incident.

This policy of Total War (a reign of terror on the civilian populace), also implemented by Sherman in Georgia and the Carolinas, would in later years be taken West and employed with great success against the Plains Indians.

Custer rode out on October 4 and, in what one New Yorker called "the most heart-sickening duty we had ever performed," torched seventeen houses, five barns, and assorted outbuildings. Ironically, the "Burnt District," as it came to be known, was populated for the most part by pacifist Mennonites.

Evidently, Phil Sheridan was pleased with the results of Custer's burning foray and received permission from Grant to continue the destruction. The Federals set out on October 5 to sweep across the countryside from the Alleghenies to the Blue Ridge and commenced a systematic reign of terror. Barns, haystacks, mills, and grain fields were indiscriminately torched, while livestock was either slaughtered or rounded up and taken along to feed the army.

The infuriated Confederates responded to this affront by pursuing and skirmishing with elements of Sheridan's force, which delayed movement and hampered the burning. Much of this harassment was initiated by Tom

Rosser, who was now being called the "Savior of the Valley." Rosser was in charge of all mounted troops attached to Jubal Early, and many of his men were natives of the Valley who sought revenge for the destruction caused by the Northerners. Sheridan vowed to put a stop once and for all to Rosser's aggressive nature. Armstrong Custer was assigned the task of eliminating his West Point friend.

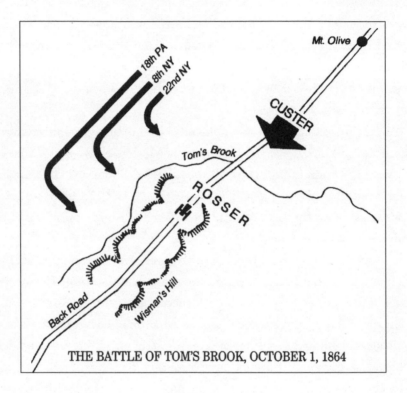

THE BATTLE OF TOM'S BROOK, OCTOBER 1, 1864

Custer led his 2,500-man 3rd Division out of camp on the morning of October 9 and halted on a ridge overlooking Tom's Brook. Rosser's 3,500 men were securely dug into defensive positions behind stone walls on the south side of the brook, which in itself did not present an obstacle for horsemen.

Custer surveyed the scene, then, in an act of bravado of which legends are made, trotted out in front of his command where he could be observed by every man on both sides of the field. In a chivalrous gesture, Custer swept his broad-brimmed hat to his knee in a salute to his old friend, as if to say, "Let's have a fair fight. May the best man win."

Rosser was not particularly amused by Custer's showmanship. "You see that officer down there?" he said to his staff. "That's General Custer, the Yanks are so proud of, and I intend to give him the best whipping today that he ever got!"

Confederate artillery, which was positioned on a higher elevation on the bluffs, opened up to pummel the Union lines. While the artillery dueled, Custer's skirmishers probed Rosser's defenses without success until midmorning.

At that point, Custer decided to take matters into his own hands and try to outflank the entrenched Rebels. Three regiments were dispatched toward the enemy's left, while another brigade was readied for a charge. When the flanking troops hit Rosser's left, Custer led the charge across Tom's Brook into the heart of the enemy line.

Rosser's troops wavered, then broke under the bold attack by the Yankee horsemen and fled to the south. The Rebels engaged in a brief running battle but in the end ran for their lives. Custer chased his fleeing enemy some ten to twelve miles, in the process capturing six cannons and the ambulance train, which included Rosser's headquarters wagon. Confederate Thomas Munford said of the shameful defeat, "[We] lost more in that one fight than we had ever done before, in all our fights together." The Federals, remembering Stuart's "Buckland Races," jib, jokingly referred to the battle as the "Woodstock Races."

An elated Custer wrote to his wife: "Darling little one, Yesterday, the 9th, was a glorious day for your Boy! I attacked Genl. Rosser's Division of 3 Brigades with my Division of 2, and gained the most glorious victory . . . am now arrayed in Gen'l Rosser's coat." Custer also got back the ambrotype of Libbie that had been captured at Trevilian Station and appropriated a pet squirrel that had belonged to Rosser.

That night in camp, he adorned himself in Rosser's baggy, ill-fitting uniform and treated his men to a good laugh. He later added to Rosser's humiliation by writing and asking that his old friend advise his tailor to shorten the coattails for a better fit.

Perhaps more importantly, Custer had without question impressed his new command. One officer wrote in his journal that "with Custer as leader we are all heroes and hankering for a fight."

Sheridan's army, with Custer's division, retired to camp along Cedar Creek in a line stretching a full five miles, with Custer's headquarters at the western end. The men were content to rest, recuperate, and brag about their recent victories. Jubal Early, however, was plotting an assault on the unsuspecting Federal troops.

On the morning of October 19, "Old Jube" launched his surprise attack of five divisions against the eastern tip of the encampment. His audacious action had been perfectly executed, and the Union defenders were being overrun and scattered from their camps, many taken prisoners by the determined Confederates. Custer sprang into action and set out to protect the right flank. His action slowed the attack and forced a stalemate face-off against a superior force of enemy soldiers, commanded by Tom Rosser.

Early's exhausted troops had paused in their attack when an event occurred that would rally Union forces. Phil Sheridan, who had been visiting Washington, was halted up the road in Winchester. He heard about the battle and galloped to Cedar Creek. At the suggestion of a staff officer, Sheridan rode up and down the lines, assuring his men that they would prevail. The nearly whipped Union troops responded to "Sheridan's Ride" with cheers and renewed faith.

Late in the afternoon, Sheridan noticed a gap in the Rebel lines and quickly notified Custer to prepare to charge the right flank. The 2,000-man-strong 3rd Division led by the Boy General advanced from the west to crash into the gap with sabers flashing. The daring charge of Union horsemen split the enemy in half. "Regiment after regiment, brigade after brigade, in rapid succession was crushed," recalled Confederate General John Gordon.

The Rebels began a hasty retreat, with Custer's command nipping at their heels and inflicting heavy casualties while capturing vital Confederate equipment, including forty-five artillery pieces, dozens of wagons, and scores of prisoners, as well as five battle flags.

One severely wounded captive was Custer's West Point friend Stephen Ramseur, whom Custer sent to Sheridan's headquarters for medical attention. Ramseur, the youngest West Pointer to attain the rank of major general in the Confederate army, died the next morning.

That night, a jubilant Custer hugged his diminutive commanding officer, Phil Sheridan, and danced him around the campfire. "By God, Phil," Custer emotionally cried, "we've cleaned them out of their guns and got ours back!" An equally excited Sheridan proclaimed, "There, there, old fellow; don't capture me!"

The following day Custer was dispatched by Sheridan aboard a special train to Washington to present thirteen Rebel battle flags to Secretary of War Stanton. At the same time, Sheridan recommended to Grant that "the brave boys Merritt and Custer" be promoted to brevet major generals.

The ceremony at Stanton's office was postponed until the 25th, which allowed Custer time to fetch Libbie from Newark, New Jersey, where she had been visiting friends. With Libbie at his side, Custer formally presented the battle flags to the secretary of war. Stanton shook Custer's hand and said, "General, a gallant officer always makes gallant soldiers." He then announced that the army had a new major general in its ranks. Custer's promotion would date from October 19.

Typical of the public accolades bestowed upon Custer was the observation of *New York Times* reporter E. A. Paul, who described Custer's actions at Cedar Creek: "Here Gen. Custer, young as he is, displayed judgement worthy of Napoleon."

Once again, Custer had been compared to Napoleon. And, hard as it may be to believe, the Boy General was only getting warmed up for what lay ahead. As the war heated up, Custer's intensity and boldness would rise to match and even exceed the challenge.

CHAPTER THIRTEEN

APPOMATTOX

SHERIDAN'S SHENANDOAH CAMPAIGN had effectively ended the war in the Valley, with much of the credit showered on the cavalry. Battle after battle had been won, which all but guaranteed Lincoln's reelection and made a national hero out of Phil Sheridan.

George Armstrong Custer had proved himself to be an extraordinarily effective commander who had made the transition from a brigade to a division without missing a beat. He had also demonstrated that he was not an impetuous loose cannon but a man with an inherent talent and skill for sizing up the weaknesses of his enemy and exploiting it for his benefit. And, as had been his custom throughout the war, Custer showed that he was not an ambulance officer who viewed his troops in battle from some rear echelon position but rather was a fearless leader who chose to ride at the front of his men as they charged into the enemy's line of fire.

Colonel Henry Capehart, a member of the 3rd Cavalry Division and a future Medal of Honor winner, summed up Custer's actions by later writing: "I have seen him under the most varying and critical circumstances, and never without ample resources of mind and body to meet the most trying contingency. He was counted by some rash; it was because he dared while they dared not . . . If I were to begin giving instances of his daring, brillancy, and skill, I should never stop."

Despite recent successes, the war was not by any means won. Skirmishes with Jubal Early and the torching of the Shenandoah continued for several more weeks, until both armies more or less settled in for the winter. Lincoln defeated peace candidate General George McClellan in the presidential election. One can only imagine the bittersweet taste in Custer's mouth at the realization that his courageous actions had contributed to the defeat of McClellan, the man whom Custer had idolized like a father.

Brevet Major General George Armstrong Custer, 1865.
(Little Bighorn Battlefield National Monument)

Custer sent for Libbie, who arrived on November 6, and the couple took up residence in a mansion called Long Meadow located four miles south of Winchester, the town where Phil Sheridan had moved his headquarters. Shortly after Libbie's arrival, another family member joined them. Tom Custer had received a commission as second lieutenant and managed to secure a position on his older brother's staff.

Thomas Ward Custer, a wild and adventurous youth six years younger than brother Armstrong, had made an attempt to enlist in Monroe, Michigan, at the outbreak of the war. His father had spoiled those plans by alerting the recruiter that Tom was only sixteen years old, too young by two years. Tom was not to be denied. On September 2, 1861, he snuck across the border to New Rumley, Ohio, and was sworn in as a private in the 21st Ohio Infantry.

Tom had fought as a common foot soldier for the next three years in such battles as Shiloh, Stones River, Chickamauga, Missionary Ridge, Chattanooga, and the Atlanta Campaign. He had distinguished himself enough to be promoted to corporal and orderly to Brigadier General James Scott Negley. But Tom recognized where real glory could be attained—the cavalry where his brother had become a general at age twenty-three.

On November 8, 1864, Tom Custer received his commission as a second lieutenant from Colonel James Kidd of the 6th Michigan and, by virtue of Armstrong's influence with Phil Sheridan, was assigned to his brother's staff.

The brothers were extremely close—Armstrong was the protector, and Tom worshiped his brother—and this reunion was cause for elation and celebration. "We could not help spoiling him owing to his charm and our deep affection," Libbie wrote of her and Armstrong's conduct toward Tom. On the other hand, Tom was not treated like a kid brother when on duty, and more than once he complained that Armstrong yelled at him for "every little darned thing just because I happen to be his brother. If anyone thinks that it is a soft thing to be a commanding officer's brother, he misses his guess." Any charges of nepotism or doubt about Tom's worthiness would be replaced with widespread admiration for his actions during the upcoming spring offensive.

The Custer brothers were in the saddle on December 19 when Sheridan ordered a cavalry raid on the Orange & Alexandria Railroad at Gordonsville. At sundown on the 20th, in a miserable sleet, Custer's cavalry bivouacked at Lacy Springs, nine miles north of Harrisonburg and thirty miles north of Staunton.

Custer had been informed by residents when passing through New Market that Confederate cavalry had been observed in the area. He posted pickets and set reveille at 4 a.m. for a 6:30 march. The morning arrived with about five inches of fresh snow—accompanied by "sharp, short, fierce, bark like yells" followed by "a dull thunderous sound." The Rebel cavalry commanded by Tom Rosser had ridden throughout the inclement night to attack the unsuspecting Federals.

Brigadier General George Chapman's brigade was scattered by the action. Custer bolted from his tent into the saddle without his coat, hat, or boots, and encouraged his men to charge. Chapman's brigade regrouped with enough strength to counterattack and forced Rosser to withdraw. Custer set his losses at two dead, twenty-two wounded, and ten to twenty captured. He estimated that Rosser had lost from fifty to eighty killed or wounded and thirty captured. Rosser's daring attack, however, compelled Sheridan to call an end to the raid. The cavalrymen were ordered to return to Winchester and construct permanent winter quarters.

Throughout the winter, Custer and Libbie hosted and attended parties and dinners and entertained and visited relatives. The Michigan Brigade Ball in early February reunited Custer with the officers and ladies of his former unit, who danced to the music of the Michigan Brigade band.

One notable spiritual event in Custer's life occurred on Sunday evening, February 5. The Custers attended a service at the Monroe Presbyterian Church, and Armstrong became a born-again Christian.

He penned a letter dated February 19 to Reverend D. C. Mattoon that read in part: "It was about this very hour two weeks ago tonight that I knealt with you and your family circle in Monroe . . . In your presence I accepted Christ as my Savior . . . I feel somewhat like the pilot of a vessel; who has been steering his ship upon familiar and safe waters but has been called upon to make a voyage fraught with danger. Having in safety and with success completed one voyage, he is imbued with confidence and renewed courage, and the second voyage is robbed of half its terror. So it is with me."

The pleasant winter respite ended on February 27 when Sheridan's rejuvenated 10,000-man cavalry marched. Custer's 3rd Cavalry Division had been dispatched ahead of the column to reconnoiter the area around Waynesboro. Freezing rain pelted the troopers, and the road was transformed into a muddy mire. Horses wallowed almost to their bellies, and wagons became stuck. Regardless, a determined Custer kept his men struggling forward.

At about three o'clock on March 2, Custer spied exactly what he had been seeking. Two thousand Confederates under Jubal Early—two infantry brigades, artillery, and Rosser's cavalry—were entrenched on a bend of the swollen South River.

This position at first glance appeared insurmountable. Custer, however, eventually noticed one chink in Early's armor—a gap between his left flank and the river. He ordered three regiments from Pennington's 1st Brigade to dismount and sneak through the cover of thick timber to flank the Confederates on the left near the waterway. This detachment, armed with Spencer carbines, successfully moved to that position unseen by the enemy. Horse artillery was brought up to soften the lines. Custer then ordered his bugler, Joseph Fought, to sound the charge.

The flankers leaped from the timber to send a murderous volley into the rear of the startled enemy, while the other brigades followed the lead of their commander and tore across the muddy terrain directly toward Early's positions. The Rebel line wavered and collapsed under the weight of Custer's charge. Early's men broke and ran, with Custer's cavalrymen in hot pursuit. "So sudden was our attack," Custer wrote in his official report, "that but little time was offered for resistance." Many battle-weary Rebels simply threw down their weapons and awaited the inevitable. Generals Early and Rosser narrowly escaped Custer's well-executed attack.

Within three hours' time, the 3rd Cavalry Division had captured, according to Custer's official report, 1,800 prisoners, 14 artillery pieces, nearly 200 supply wagons, and 17 battle flags. Amazingly, only nine Union cavalrymen had been killed or wounded in what Sheridan termed "this brilliant fight."

It was a crushing defeat for the Army of Northern Virginia and another colorful feather in Custer's overflowing headdress. Sheridan's aide, Captain George B. Sanford, was present when Custer reported to his commander. "Up came Custer himself with his following," Sanford later recalled. "And in the hands of his orderlies, one to each, were the seventeen battle flags streaming in the wind. It was a great spectacle and the sort of thing which Custer thoroughly enjoyed."

Sheridan's troops then embarked upon an operation into the heart of Virginia. The men endured rainy weather, muddy roads, swollen waterways, and minor skirmishes with their enemy to tear through the countryside like a swarm of vengeful locusts, leaving behind a landscape of devastation and despair. Every vital piece of the Southern infrastructure or element of economic necessity in their pathway was either confiscated or reduced to smoldering ruins.

Railroad tracks were ripped up and cars demolished. Telegraph lines were cut. Bridges were blown up. Water tanks were drained. Boats and barges were sunk. Locks on the St. James River were wrecked. Cotton mills, foundries, lumber yards, great stores of tobacco, wheat, livestock, and any other source of income or sustenance was seized or burned to ashes. The mayor of Charlottesville turned over that town to Custer while the faculty of the University of Virginia stood nearby on their campus under a white flag.

On March 19, the cavalry bivouacked at White House Landing on the Pamunkey River for a week of rest and recuperation spent mending equipment and readying the horses for the spring campaign. Sheridan took this opportunity to send to Washington the seventeen battle flags captured at Waynesborough.

Libbie Custer attended the flag presentation ceremony held in the office of Secretary of War Stanton and later wrote to her husband, "Oh, what a happy day that was—the proudest of my life. The room was full, but Mr. Stanton perceived me and extended his hand most cordially . . . he introduced me as 'the wife of the gallant general.' As every flag was presented General Townsend read at the end, 'Brevet Major-General Custer commanding . . .' every time from the first to the seventeenth . . . I could hardly keep from crying out my praise of my boy. Before leaving I told the Secretary I had waited a long time for a letter from you, but was more than repaid by having witnessed this. Mr. Stanton replied, 'General Custer is writing lasting letters on the pages of his country's history.'"

Sheridan's command headed south across the St. James River on March 25 and rejoined the army two days later at City Point. Sherman had returned from North Carolina for a brief visit to assist Grant in formulating a strategy designed to once and for all crush Lee's battered and weary army. Now was the ideal time to strike. Battle losses and desertions had compelled the desperate Confederates to conscript boys from age fourteen to eighteen as well as older men up to age sixty. And it was Grant's intention to destroy Lee before he could gather strength or make a move to North Carolina to battle Sherman, which would prolong the war.

Custer's 3rd Division was reorganized into three brigades on March 29. Pennington's 1st Brigade would now consist of the 1st Connecticut, 3rd New Jersey, 2nd New York, and 2nd Ohio; Wells's 2nd Brigade had the 8th New York, 15th New York, and 1st Vermont; and the 3rd Brigade, commanded by Henry Capehart, consisted of the 1st New York, 1st West Virginia, 2nd West Virginia, and 3rd West Virginia.

When Sheridan's cavalry rode out on the morning of March 29, Merritt and not Custer led the column. Merritt, who was often openly jealous of Custer, assigned his nemesis the undesirable and frustrating duty of escorting the wagon train. A torrential downpour the night before had created a quagmire that hindered progress to barely a snail's pace. Mules sank to their haunches in the muck, and it became necessary to unload wagons to free them from the saturated ground. Custer battled this stubborn natural enemy and slogged through along the road for three days.

On March 31, Sheridan's advance near Dinwiddie Court House came under a vicious attack by Confederate infantry commanded by General George E. Pickett of Gettysburg fame. Custer and two brigades were summoned to the front; the other brigade would remain behind to guard the wagon train.

Custer and his aides raced ahead of the column, one of them unfurling Custer's new personal guidon that had been made by Libbie and delivered the night before. They arrived at about four in the afternoon to find Dinwiddie Court House in turmoil. The Rebels may have been outnumbered two to one, but nonetheless Pickett had taken the offensive and presently held the upper hand. The Union troops had been driven back by the brutal onslaught but eventually managed to maintain a secure line. Custer received orders from Sheridan to deploy his troops behind hastily constructed barricades along the road to Five Forks. In the ensuing skirmish, one of his orderlies was killed beside him, and his wife's name that she had sewn on the guidon was blasted off in the heavy gunfire.

As the battle intensified, Custer rode along the line exposed to enemy fire in an effort to encourage his men. The resolute Confederate infantry attacked and briefly forced the Yankees back. Custer rallied the troops, imploring them to remain behind rail barricades and hold their position. At sundown, the Rebels were repulsed in one final desperate assault and withdrew toward Five Forks. Custer counterattacked, but darkness impeded progress, and the chase was called off.

Lieutenant Colonel Horace Potter, Grant's aide-de-camp, mentioned to Sheridan that "we at last have drawn the enemy's infantry out of its fortifications, and this is our chance to attack it."

Sheridan had intended to follow Potter's suggestion at dawn on the following morning. Infantry reinforcements, however, did not arrive by daylight, and it was four o'clock in the afternoon before the 12,000-man V Corps commanded by Major General Gouveneur Warren finally made its appearance at Dinwiddie Court House. Sheridan ordered an immediate attack on the Confederate position at Five Forks where Pickett and about 10,000 troops had been positioned and told by Lee to hold "at all hazards."

Custer had been skirmishing with the enemy throughout the day in an effort to determine its size and location. Now, as the Union column proceeded from Dinwiddie Court House, Custer's division led the cavalry. Custer and Devin would act as a diversionary force to distract Pickett while Warren's infantry stormed into the Rebels. The cavalry skirmishers pressed through the timber to probe the enemy lines, but Warren had miscalculated the extent of the Confederate line, charged into a gap, and was caught in a devastating cross fire.

Phil Sheridan was infuriated by Warren's bungled assault and personally rode into the midst of the V Corps to reform and rally the troops. Warren's men responded with renewed fury and crushed into the Confederate left. Sheridan would later that day relieve Warren of his command.

Custer mounted two brigades, signaled the band to play "Hail Columbia," and, accompanied by his staff, led the charge into blazing Rebel fire. The bold thrust was met by stiff resistance as Rooney Lee's cavalry division appeared on the left flank to tear into the Yankees. The opponents fought hand-to-hand until Sheridan and Devin overpowered Pickett's line and

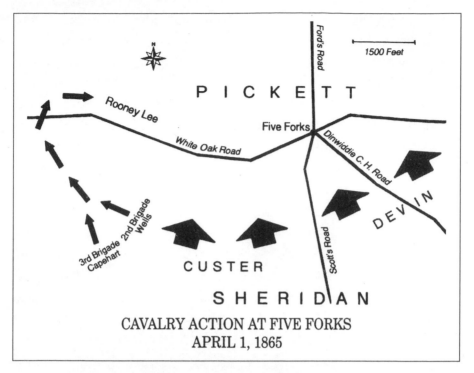

CAVALRY ACTION AT FIVE FORKS
APRIL 1, 1865

began sweeping westward. At that point, Confederate forces executed a hasty withdrawal.

Custer and his red ties chased the Rebels for six miles, rounding up prisoners until darkness descended. Custer reported, "The retreat of over 5,000 of the rebels was then cut off, and this number was secured as prisoners of war. Besides these the loss in killed and wounded was very heavy." Thirteen battle flags and six artillery pieces were also captured.

Sam Grant intended to immediately resume his attack on Petersburg, but reconnaissance revealed that Confederate trenches were empty. Lee's beleaguered army had stolen away in the night and evacuated Petersburg as well as Richmond. Union forces moved in the following day to occupy those strategic locations. Grant feared, however, that Lee was on his way to North Carolina by way of Lynchburg to rendezvous with his forces in that state. If the Federals could intercept the Army of Northern Virginia along the way, there was little doubt that the Confederacy would be doomed.

Sheridan's four cavalry divisions—Devin, Crook, Custer, and MacKensie—were dispatched at 9 a.m. on April 3 with the mission of hunting down and engaging the fleeing Rebels. Custer led the advance, anxious to be the first to locate the enemy and gain additional glory. His 3rd Division followed Lee west along the Appomattox River Valley until reaching Namozine Creek.

The bridge had been destroyed, and Rebel fortifications were observed on the distant bank. Custer was unaware of it at the time, but his men were greatly outnumbered. That small factor likely would not have deterred him had he known. He dispatched one troop to outflank the enemy position while other men with axes were detailed to remove fallen trees from the stream to clear the path for the main force.

An impatient Tom Custer, however, tore a page from his older brother's book and spurred his horse to gallop across the waterway toward the enemy trenches. His act of bravado inspired the troops to follow. The Rebels fired volleys at the onrushing horsemen but soon broke and fled to form a line at Namozine Church. Tom Custer led the charge that overcame that brief stand, and the battle became a running fight as the Rebels endeavored to elude their dogged pursuers. When hostilities had cooled, Tom presented his proud brother with a battle flag along with fourteen prisoners, including three officers. Phil Sheridan recommended that Tom receive the Medal of Honor for his actions.

Robert E. Lee's retreating army was exhausted and in dire need of provisions. Early on April 6, the Confederate commander changed his order of march for the purpose of expediting their movement and staying out of reach of the pursuing Union horsemen. Lee rode ahead of the column with Lieutenant General James Longstreet and the infantry. They were followed by a lengthy line of supply wagons, then Major General John Gordon's II Corps acting as rear guard. Lee was approaching Farmville, where he hoped to procure provisions, when the column inadvertently split into two detachments. Lee continued on as planned, but the wagon train and Gordon veered to the north, where they came under Federal attack at a place called Sayler's Creek.

Custer had been trailing that enemy column, and his opportunistic cavalrymen plunged into the hottest of the engagement. The hastily entrenched Rebels put up an admirable fight, which kept the enemy at bay for some time. During the fray, Custer had his horse shot out from beneath him, and his color bearer was killed. The infantry finally arrived, and Custer led the charge against enemy lines.

The Rebels held their fire until the last moment, then unleashed a vicious barrage. The assaulting cavalrymen were undaunted, and soared over the fortifications with hooves flying, sabers slashing and pistols smoking. Within a matter of minutes, the gray line was sent scattering in the wake of the surging Federals. The Rebels continued to fight as they withdrew to the north. Custer formed his division and gave chase to put the finishing touches on their day's work.

Now that the most serious fighting was over, Tom Custer was intent upon distinguishing himself. He swooped down on a Rebel color bearer, who fired his pistol point-blank at Tom. The bullet struck young Custer in the cheek and exited behind his ear. Blood spurted from the wound, and his face was blackened with powder. The force of the blast had thrown him backward against his horse's rump, but he quickly righted himself in the saddle. He drew his own pistol and coolly shot and killed the standard bearer. Tom then grabbed the coveted battle flag, wheeled his horse, and galloped through the chaotic battlefield to show off the trophy to his brother.

The general ordered Tom to seek medical attention for his wound, but Tom was determined to return to the battle. As a result, Armstrong placed Tom under arrest and had him forcibly escorted to the surgeon. Colonel Capehart had witnessed Tom's heroic action and later said, "For intrepidity I never saw this incident surpassed."

Tom Custer's demonstration of courage was rewarded with a brevet promotion to lieutenant colonel and the awarding of his second Medal of Honor—becoming the first man in history to receive two, and the only double recipient during the Civil War. Armstrong Custer was thrilled about his brother's brave exploits and later wrote to Libbie, saying: "I am as proud of him as I can be, as soldier, brother."

Sayler's Creek had been a smashing victory for the Union. Over 9,000 Confederates—including General Lee's son Custis and six other generals—had been taken prisoner along with thirty-six battle flags. This number of Americans was greater than had ever been captured at any time on this continent, before or after. Nearly one-third of the total force of the once-invincible Army of Virginia had been lost on an afternoon that would forever be remembered by the South as "Black Thursday."

Custer formed his division the following morning for the march just as a long line of Confederate prisoners straggled past on their way to the rear. In a show of respect for his vanquished enemy, Custer ordered the band to play "Dixie" for these brave men, which evoked cheers from the Southern boys.

Custer's division, which had been leading the Union cavalry, had gone into bivouac some two miles from Appomattox Station in the early evening of April 8 when word was received that four trains full of Confederate munitions and supplies were presently unloading at the station. At the same time, a courier from Merritt delivered the order that Custer should rest his troops.

The prospect of capturing these trains naturally took precedence to Custer's way of thinking. He craftily dispatched a courier to inform Merritt about the trains and that he would attack unless receiving orders to the contrary. Custer then quickly roused his brigades and rode out for Appomattox Station before Merritt could respond.

Custer's troops swooped down on the station and easily overpowered the guards to capture the four trains—except for one engine that was uncoupled and steamed away. Within moments of the seizure, a torrent of Rebel artillery shells rained down on the Federals. Confederate Brigadier General R. Lindsay Walker, who commanded a small brigade of cavalry, a wagon train, and around one hundred guns, had opened up from a ridge about a half mile from the station. Custer detailed former engineers and stokers to move the trains to safety, then formed his men for a charge on the enemy cannon.

Without bothering to wait for his trailing brigades Custer sent Pennington's New Yorkers and Ohioans toward the location of the bright flashes of artillery. The Union horsemen charged the cannon's mouth but were shredded by close-range volleys and small arms fire and were forced to fall back. By that time, Walls's and Capehart's regiments had come up.

Custer rode along the line of blue-clad horsemen, and shouted, "Boys, the Third Division must have those guns! I'm going to charge if I go alone!"

Custer then grabbed his guidon, lifted it high, and confidently called out, "I go; who will follow?"

Custer had successfully whipped his weary men into an inspired, battle-hungry group of proud cavalrymen who would accept any challenge that their heroic commander presented. His words were affirmed by a deafening chorus of cheers.

The Boy General, true to custom, personally led the mounted assault on the stubborn Confederate position. The Yankees swiftly closed on the artillery battery in the darkness and braved the initial storm of fire to crush their enemy. The Rebels were forced to abandon their position and left behind twenty-four pieces of artillery, seven battle flags, two hundred wagons, and one thousand prisoners, not to mention the four trainloads of supplies at the station. More importantly, the quick action on Custer's part had cut off Lee's retreat to Lynchburg.

Custer pushed on to Appomattox Court House, where his men encountered enough resistance from Lee's infantry that after an hour or so he ordered them to withdraw to the station. Phil Sheridan had arrived and dispatched a message to Grant requesting that the infantry be brought up in prelude to a morning attack that he was confident would bring Lee to his knees.

Lee was desperate to seek an escape route through the blue line. At daybreak on April 9, Palm Sunday, Rebel cannons commenced firing volleys, and gray-clad cavalry appeared from the dense fog to attack Custer's dismounted troopers. This last-ditch effort by Lee was thwarted when the Yankee infantry roared forward to reinforce the position and push the Rebels back. Custer mounted his men and moved them south with the intention of striking the Confederate flank.

"Custer took the road at a gallop," recalled a member of the 1st New York Cavalry. "It was a glorious sight to see that division as it dashed along, with sabres drawn, the gallant Custer leading, and the Confederate army on a parallel road, only three hundred yards distant, vainly endeavoring to escape." Custer was readying his regiment for a charge when a lone Confederate staff officer rode forward carrying a stick with a towel attached.

Major Robert Sims of General Longstreet's staff was received by Custer, and stated that General Lee requested that hostilities be suspended. Custer admitted that he was not the commander on the field and would attack unless Lee agreed to an unconditional surrender. He then sent word back to Sheridan and dispatched his chief of staff, Lieutenant Colonel Edward W. Whitaker, to accompany Major Sims to obtain an answer to his surrender demand.

The Civil War was about to end on Custer's doorstep—that much can be documented. The exact circumstances surrounding Custer's role in answering this surrender entreaty, however, has become a matter of controversy.

Eyewitness accounts—primarily a questionable remembrance by Longstreet written thirty-one years after the incident—suggest that after dispatching Whitaker, Custer crossed the Confederate line and was presented to Longstreet. Custer demanded that Longstreet surrender the army. Longstreet allegedly was irritated by the brash young general and refused, citing the fact that he was not the commander. In addition, Longstreet was said to have taunted Custer by boldly professing that the Rebs were not beaten and that Custer could attack if he damn well pleased. He then ordered Custer out of his lines. Longstreet claimed that Custer meekly retired, asking for an escort to safely return to friendly lines.

In another account, Major Sims confirmed Longstreet's basic version. Sims entered Union lines carrying a flag that he said was "a new and clean white crash towel, one of a lot for which I had paid $20 or $40 apiece in Richmond a few days before." He had braved Federal pickets that fired upon him and requested to see Sheridan but was told that only Custer was available. Sims relayed his message to Custer, who replied that nothing less than an unconditional surrender would be accepted. Sims departed with Whitaker to report back to Longstreet. When he arrived at Longstreet's headquarters, Sims wrote, "I found General Custer and he [Longstreet] talking together at a short distance from the position occupied by the staff. Custer said he would proceed to attack at once and Longstreet replied: 'As soon as you please,' but he did not attack. Just after I left Custer came in sight of our lines. He halted his troops and, taking a handkerchief from his orderly, displayed it as a flag and rode into our lines. He was surrounded by some of our people and was being handled a little roughly when an old classmate of his recognized him and rescued him."

Although Custer without question would have relished the glory associated with being the officer who accepted the Confederate surrender, he was West Point educated and would have understood protocol in such matters. If he had indeed crossed the lines, it was perhaps out of concern for Whitaker's well-being or his own interest in always being at the center of events. Longstreet's challenge to attack would not have been taken seriously. The Rebels were whipped, and Custer, a man of action, would never have welcomed another fight.

Regardless of Custer's participation in prelude to the actual surrender, that afternoon Lee presented himself to Grant at the home of Wilmer McLean. "General Grant was standing beneath an apple tree when General Lee approached," remembered saddler Charles H. Crocker of the 1st New York Cavalry. "After a hand clasp, Lee removed his side arms and handed them to Grant who, after holding them for a moment, returned them to Lee." The two commanders then retired inside to McLean's parlor and signed the surrender document.

Custer was not present inside the McLean home during the signing; rather, he has been placed on the porch or in the yard renewing acquaintances with Southern friends from their days at West Point.

The small, oval-shaped pine table upon which the surrender document had been signed was purchased for $20 by Phil Sheridan. The next day, the cavalry commander handed the table to Custer as a gift to Libbie Custer. Sheridan enclosed a note, which read: "My dear Madam, I respectfully present to you the small writing table on which the conditions for the surrender of the Army of Northern Virginia were written by Lt. General Grant—and permit me to say, Madam, that there is scarcely an individual in our service who has contributed more to bring about this desirable result than your gallant husband." Libbie Custer treasured the table for the remainder of her life. After her death, the surrender table was added to the collection of the Smithsonian Institution.

Edward W. Whitaker, chief of staff of the 3rd Division, summed up Custer's importance in the closing days of the war: "The country will never know the whole truth, or how much it owes to General Custer for turning the tide of battle to victory in the three last decisive engagements, Waynesboro,

Five Forks and Appomattox Station. Failure in either one of these would have resulted in the prolongation of the war indefinitely."

Custer, never one to ignore or take for granted that his achievements depended on the fidelity of his troops, penned a classic tribute on April 9 to the achievements of the cavalrymen of his 3rd Division: "With profound gratitude toward the God of battles, by whose blessings our enemies have been humbled and our arms rendered triumphant, your commanding general avails himself of this his first opportunity to express to you the admiration of the heroic manner in which you have passed through the series of battles which to-day resulted in the surrender of the enemy's entire army. The record established by your indomitable courage is unparalleled in the annals of war. Your prowess won for you even the respect and admiration of your enemies. During the past six months, although in most instances confronted by superior numbers, you have captured from the enemy in open battle 111 pieces of field artillery, 65 battle-flags, and upward of 10,000 prisoners of war, including 7 general officers. Within the past ten days, and included in the above, you have captured 46 pieces of field artillery and 37 battle-flags. You have never lost a gun, never lost a color, and have never been defeated, and notwithstanding the numerous engagements in which you have borne a prominent part, including those memorable battles of the Shenandoah, you have captured every piece of artillery which the enemy has dared to open upon you. The near approach of peace renders it improbable that you will again be called upon to undergo the fatigues of toilsome march, or the exposure of the battle-field, but should the assistance of keen blades, wielded by your sturdy arms, be required to hasten the coming of that glorious peace for which we have been so long contending, the general commanding is proudly confident that in the future, as in the past, every demand will meet with a hearty and willing response. Let us hope that our work is done, and that, blessed with the comforts of home and friends.

"For our comrades who have fallen, let us ever cherish a grateful remembrance. To the wounded and to those who languish in Southern prisons, let our heartfelt sympathies be tendered.

"And now, speaking for myself alone, when the war is ended and the task of the historian begins; when those deeds of daring which have rendered the name and fame of the Third Cavalry Division imperishable, are inscribed upon the bright pages of our country's history, I only ask that my name be written as that of the commander of the Third Cavalry Division."

The Army of the Potomac was honored by the country on May 23 with a parade in the Nation's capital. Huge crowds of cheering admirers packed the route from the Capitol to the White House, where a reviewing stand had been erected. The cavalry led the procession—first Merritt in place of Sheridan, who was in Louisiana, then Custer's 3rd Division, each man adorned in a bright red necktie.

General Horace Porter later wrote: "Conspicuous among the division leaders was Custer, his long golden curls floating in the wind, his low-cut collar, crimson neck-tie, buckskin breeches—half General, half scout, daredevil in appearance."

Custer proudly led his men down the street seated upon Don Juan, his favorite mount. The reviewing stand was in sight when—by most accounts—a group of young ladies rose to their feet and began to sing while showering Custer with flowers. Don Juan became spooked by this unexpected disturbance and bolted in the direction of the reviewing stand.

General Porter describes the scene: "Within 200 yards of the President's stand his spirited horse took the bit in its teeth, and made a dash past the troops like a tornado. But Custer was more than a match for him. When the Cavalry-man, covered with flowers, afterwards rode by the officials the people screamed with delight." Detractors accused Custer of orchestrating the display simply to show off.

Whatever the circumstances, George Armstrong Custer had made his final charge of the Civil War.

The words of Horace Greeley perhaps best sum up the Civil War legacy of Custer when he wrote: "Future writers of fiction will find in Brig. Gen. Custer most of the qualities which go to make up a first-class hero and stories of his daring will be told around many a hearth stone long after the old flag again kisses the breeze from Maine to the Gulf . . . Gen. Custer is as gallant a cavalier as one would wish to see . . . Always circumspect, never rash, and viewing the circumstances under which he is placed as coolly as a chess player observes his game, Gen. Custer always sees 'the vantage of the ground' at a glance, and, like the eagle watching his prey from some mountain crag, sweeps down upon his adversary, and seldom fails in achieving a signal success. Frank and independent in his demeanor, Gen. C unites the qualities of the true gentleman with that of the accomplished and fearless soldier."

CHAPTER FOURTEEN

THE BOY GENERAL
and
the KNIGHT *of the*
GOLDEN SPURS

HE WAS BORN INTO A LARGE FAMILY with rural roots, and early in life he developed a love of horses. At age twelve, he would leave home to live with relatives in order to further his education. Later, he would enter the US Military Academy at West Point and excel in horsemanship, becoming known as the most skilled rider in his class. His first postgraduate assignment as a second lieutenant would appropriately be duty in the cavalry.

He would neither drink nor smoke—pledging at a young age to abstain from alcohol—and, possessed with great discipline, would honor that promise until the day he died. He was a man of deep spirituality who professed to have experienced a religious conversion that greatly influenced his character and direction in life.

His appreciation of literature can be evidenced by his inclination to express himself by composing poetry inspired by a teenage romantic infatuation, and later by writing official reports that could at times read like a novel.

In his early twenties, he would set his romantic sights on marrying a young lady whose family was on a higher social level. Following a whirlwind courtship that could be likened to a cavalry frontal assault, he would walk down the aisle to the altar with his twenty-one-year-old bride at his side to be united in marriage.

He was a sociable, fun-loving, likable man with a dynamic personality who would choose his companions as if casting a play, and indeed he understood that his world was a stage in which he assumed the starring role. For

that reason, he accepted the responsibilities inherited from such a prestigious status and carried himself with a unique flamboyance and unswerving
confidence that set him apart from his contemporaries.

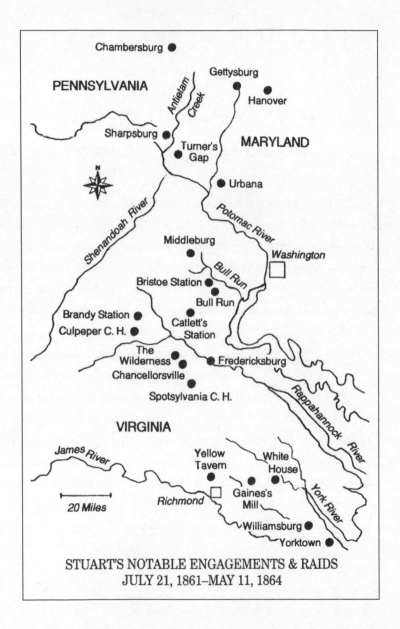

STUART'S NOTABLE ENGAGEMENTS & RAIDS
JULY 21, 1861–MAY 11, 1864

When it came to war, his unique skills under fire would be recognized
by his superiors, and he would rise quickly to the rank of major general. Fear

of injury or death under fire was always inconsequential when there was an objective to attain, and he would often place himself in harm's way to inspire his men.

He was committed to his cause, a tireless, fearless campaigner, ambitious almost to a fault, who pushed himself and his men beyond the limits of endurance. He would lead by example, never asking his troops to do anything that he would not do himself. His daring exploits would capture the fancy of the press, which would gain him the admiration of his countrymen.

His love of ceremony and pageantry and the need to be the center of attention was reflected in his appearance. He would wear an ostentatious uniform of his own design—perhaps called outrageous by some but assuredly one that was distinctive when compared to other officers. The extraordinary characteristic of his uniform would be adopted by his troops as a tribute to their commander's achievements and their loyalty to his leadership.

He would receive orders dated June 22 that would ignite a controversy in his life that would endure beyond his passing. His reputation would be unjustly tarnished due to his inability to defend himself in death, and he would become a scapegoat for a defeat that was not his fault.

He would die honorably at the hands of his enemy, wearing the uniform to which he had pledged allegiance, falling in the thickest of the fighting while rallying his troops. His widow would never remarry and would live for over fifty years embracing the memory of her extraordinary husband.

Remarkably, both Jeb Stuart and Armstrong Custer fit the above description, which demonstrates how closely related these two men were when comparing personal traits and major events in their lives. And the similarities do not necessarily end there, only differing in style to affect the same outcome.

In the game and practice of warfare, both cavalrymen were inherently endowed with the skill and cunning of chess masters. Each viewed the chess board of a battlefield in its totality and possessed the ability to quickly seize upon and exploit any perceived weakness or tactical error by his opponent.

Although Custer would never enjoy the same level of command as Stuart, there is reason to believe that given the same opportunity, he would have been equal to the task. After all, both understood that this chess game called war demanded both knowledge of the opponent and the mental and physical courage to execute brazen and unexpected moves to create confusion designed to break the enemy's will and thereby gain victory.

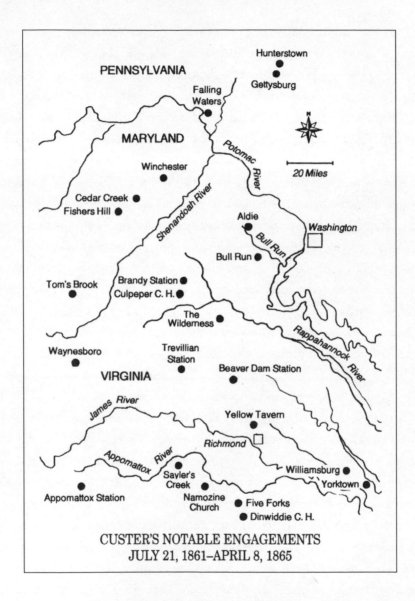

CUSTER'S NOTABLE ENGAGEMENTS
JULY 21, 1861–APRIL 8, 1865

Custer was the more impulsive player, executing his daring moves swiftly but decisively, most of the time choosing the correct tactic. But if mistaken, he was blessed with the uncanny ability to adjust his strategy in the midst of the game and amply compensate for any miscalculation.

Stuart was more deliberate, a thoughtful innovator who was never satisfied simply following tradition when the opportunity for a daring ploy that would challenge the mettle of his enemy, and perhaps himself, presented itself.

To choose which was the best cavalryman between the two would be expected at the close of this book. Arguments for and against each man would not diminish the value that each displayed in their own way to their respective armies.

Stuart benefited from his freedom to roam the countryside unsupervised, and he basked in the glory of adventurous raids that both boosted morale and exposed tactical weaknesses that could be exploited—and he could lead troops into the fight when necessary.

Custer benefited by attaining the confidence of his superiors, which gained him the honor of having his command thrust time and time again against seemingly overwhelming odds where glory awaited the victor.

It would be fair to state that winning battles in a war must certainly count more than reconnaissance or public relations events, like riding around McClellan's army, although knowing the whereabouts of the enemy can be vital. Jeb Stuart had one tragic day at Gettysburg when he did not arrive in time to act as Lee's "eyes and ears," much to the chagrin of his commander. Not only that, but Stuart failed to reach the Union rear and turn the tide of Pickett's charge, and he could certainly be blamed for the battle's failure. The Knight of the Golden Spurs never did recover from that embarrassment or regain the respect of his peers.

Custer, on the other hand, was thrust into the cannon's mouth time and time again, and with only a couple of exceptions had emerged victorious, especially in his encounters with Jeb Stuart. His breathtaking charges and brilliant strategies on the field were the stuff of legend. His heroic actions at Gettysburg deserve much more attention than historians have allotted him. And it was Custer's initiative in leading the charge at Yellow Tavern that ended Jeb Stuart's Civil War career—and his life.

Consequently, between the two men, with no apologies, George Armstrong Custer would be the cavalry general to have leading the charge if only one clash of horsemen wielding sabers remained to be fought, with a war's final victory in the balance.

Bibliography

NEWSPAPERS

Charleston Daily Courier

Grand Rapids Daily Eagle

Harper's Weekly

Memphis Appeal

Mobile Daily Advertiser and Register

Monroe Commercial

New York Herald

New York Times

National Tribune

New York Tribune

Richmond Enquirer

Richmond Examiner

Richmond Dispatch

Southern Illustrated News

COLLECTIONS

Emory University, Atlanta, GA

Duke University, Durham, NC

Gettysburg National Military Park, Gettysburg, PA

Henry E. Huntington Library, San Marino, CA

Private Collection of John Merritt, Colorado Springs, CO

University of Michigan, Ann Arbor, MI

Monroe County Historical Museum Archives, Monroe, MI

Monroe County Library System, Monroe, MI

Museum of the Confederacy, Richmond, VA

Bibliography

Rochester Public Library, Rochester, NY
Stuart-Mosby Historical Society, Centreville, VA
Virginia Historical Society, Richmond, VA
United States Army Military History Institute, Carlisle Barracks, PA
The United States Military Academy Archives, West Point,
University of Virginia

PERIODICALS

Alexander, Ted. "Gettysburg Cavalry Operations, June 27–July 3, 1863." *Blue & Gray Magazine* 6, no. 1 (October 1988).

Beauregard, Erving E. "The General and the Politician: Custer & Bingham." *Blue & Gray Magazine* 6, no. 1 (October 1988).

Brewer, Wilmon. "The Capture of General Custer's Love Letters." *Yankee Magazine*, March 1969.

Brooke-Rawle, William. "The Right Flank at Gettysburg." In *The Annals of the War*, edited by the editors of the *Philadelphia Weekly Times*. Philadelphia: The Times Publishing Company, 1879.

Calkins, Chris. "The Battle of Five Forks: Final Push for the South Side." *Blue & Gray Magazine* 9, no. 4 (April 1992).

Campbell, William. "Stuart's Ride and Death of Latane." *Southern Historical Society Papers* 39 (1911).

Custer, Elizabeth B. "A Beau Sabreur." In *Uncle Sam's Medal of Honor: Some of the Noble Deeds for Which the Medal Has Been Awarded, Described by Those Who Have Won It 1861–1886.* edited by Theodore F. Rodenbough. New York: G. P. Putnam's Sons, 1886.

Devin, Thomas C. "Fierce Resistance at Appomattox." *Civil War Times Illustrated* 17, no. 8 (December 1978).

Dorsey, Frank. "Gen. J. E. B. Stuart's Last Battle." *Confederate Veteran* 17 (1889).

Dunphy, James J. "West Point Class of '61." *Research Review: The Journal of the Little Big Horn Associates* 7, no. 1 (January 1993).

Frayser, Richard E. "A Narrative of Stuart's Raid in the Rear of the Army of the Potomac." *Southern Historical Society Papers* 11 (1883).

Freeman, Douglas Southall. "Cavalry Action of the Third Day at Gettysburg: A Case Study." *Military Collector and Historian: Journal of the Company of Military Historians* 29 (Winter 1977).

Green, Israel. "The Capture of John Brown," *North American Review* (December 1885).

278

Hatch, Thom. "Custer vs. Stuart: The Clash at Gettysburg." *Columbiad: A Quarterly Review of the War Between the States* (Winter 1998).

Imboden, John D. "The Confederate Retreat from Gettysburg." In Robert Underwood Johnson and Clarence Clough Buel, eds. *Battles and Leaders of the Civil War*. 4 vols. Reprint. New York: Thomas Yoseloff, 1956.

Kidd, James H. "The Michigan Cavalry Brigade in the Wilderness." In *War Papers Read before the Commandery of the State of Michigan Military Order of the Loyal Legion of the United States*. vol. 1: *From October 6, 1886 to April 6, 1893*. Detroit: Winn & Hammond Printers, 1893.

Krolick, Marshall D. "Forgotten Fields: The Cavalry Battle East of Gettysburg on July 3, 1863." In *Gettysburg: Historical Articles of Lasting Interest*. Dayton, OH: Morningside House, January 1991.

Longacre, Edward G. "The Long Run for Trevilian Station." *Civil War Times Illustrated* 18 (November 1979).

_____. "Cavalry Clash at Todd's Tavern." *Civil War Times Illustrated* 16 (October 1977).

_____. "'A Perfect Ishmaelite': General Baldy Smith." *Civil War Times Illustrated* 16 (December 1976).

Mackey, T. J. "Duel of General Wade Hampton on the Battle-Field at Gettysburg with a Federal Soldier." *Southern Historical Society Papers* 22 (1894).

McCann, Donald C. "Anna E. Jones: The Spy Who Never Was." *Incidents of the War* 2, no. 1 (Spring 1987).

McIntosh, David Gregg. "Review of the Gettysburg Campaign." *Southern Historical Society Papers*, 37, Richmond, VA: Southern Historical Society, 1909.

McKim, Randolph Harrison. "General J. E. B. Stuart in the Gettysburg Campaign." *Southern Historical Society Papers*. vol. 37. Richmond, VA: Southern Historical Society, 1909.

Miller, Samuel. "Yellow Tavern." *Civil War History* 2 (1956).

Miller, William E. "The Cavalry Battle Near Gettysburg." *Battles and Leaders of the Civil War* 3 (1887–88).

Monaghan, Jay. "Custer's 'Last Stand'—Trevilian Station, 1864." *Civil War History* 8 (September 1962).

Moore, James O. "Custer's Raid in Albemarle County: The Skirmish at Rio Hill, February 29, 1864." *Virginia Magazine of History and Biography* 79, no. 3 (July 1971).

Mosby, John S. "The Ride Around McClellan." *Southern Historical Society Papers* 26 (1898).

Nye, Wilbur. "The Affair at Hunterstown." *Civil War Times Illustrated* 9 (February 1971).

Oliver, J. R. "J. E. B. Stuart's Fate at Yellow Tavern," *Confederate Veteran* 19 (1901).

O'Neil, Thomas E. "Two Men of Ohio: Custer & Bingham." *Research Review: The Journal of the Little Big Horn Associates* 8, no. 1 (January 1994).

_____. "Custer's First Romance Revealed." *Newsletter, Little Big Horn Associates* 28, no. 2 (March 1994).

Robins, W. T. "Stuart's Ride Around McClellan." Robert Underwood Johnson and Clarence Clough Buel, eds. *Battles and Leaders of the Civil War,* 4 vols. Reprint. New York: Thomas Yoseloff, 1956.

Russell, Don. "Jeb Stuart's Other Indian Fight." *Civil War Times Illustrated* 12 (January 1974).

Schultz, Fred L. "A Cavalry Fight Was On." *Civil War Times Illustrated* 23, no. 10 (February 1985).

Shevchuk, Paul M. "The Battle of Hunterstown, Pennsylvania, July 2, 1863." *Gettysburg: Historical Articles of Lasting Interest.* Dayton, OH: Morningside House, January 1991.

_____. "Cut to Pieces: The Cavalry Fight at Fairfield, Pennsylvania, July 3rd, 1863." *Gettysburg: Historical Articles of Lasting Interest.* Dayton, OH: Morningside House, January 1991.

_____. "The Lost Hours of 'JEB' Stuart." *Gettysburg: Historical Articles of Lasting Interest.* Dayton, OH: Morningside House, January 1991.

Shriver, William H. "My Father Led J. E. B. Stuart to Gettysburg," Gettysburg National Military Park Library.

Thomas, Emory M. "The Kilpatrick-Dahlgren Raid." *Civil War Times Illustrated* 16 (February 1978).

Williams, Robert A. "Haw's Shop: A 'Storm of Shot and Shell.'" *Civil War Times Illustrated* 9, no. 9 (January 1971).

BOOKS

Agassiz, George R., ed. *Meade's Headquarters, 1863–1865: Letters of Colonel Theodore Lyman from the Wilderness to Appomattox.* Boston: Atlantic Monthly Press, 1922.

Ambrose, Stephen A. *Crazy Horse and Custer: The Parallel Lives of Two American Warriors.* Reprint. New York: New American Library, 1985.

Baltz, Louis J. III. *The Battle of Cold Harbor May 27–June 13, 1864.* Lynchburg, VA: H. E. Howard, 1994.

Beach, William H. *The First New York (Lincoln) Cavalry from April 19, 1861 to July 7, 1865.* Annandale, VA: Bacon Race Books, 1988.

Bearss, Ed, and Chris Calkins. *Battle of Five Forks.* Lynchburg, VA: H. E. Howard, 1985.

Beecher, Harris H. *Record of the 114th Regiment N. Y. S. V.* New York: J. F. Hubbard, Jr., 1866.

Blackford, Charles Minor, III, ed. *Letters from Lee's Army.* New York: Charles Scribner's Sons, 1947.

Blackford, William W. *War Years with Jeb Stuart.* New York: Charles Scribner's Sons, 1945.

Botkin, B. A., ed. *A Civil War Treasury of Tales, Legends and Folklore.* New York: Promontory Press, 1981.

Bushong, Millard Kessler, and Dean McKain. *Fightin' Tom Rosser, C. S. A.* Shippensburg, PA: Beidel Printing House, 1983.

Calkins, Chris. *The Battles of Appomattox Station and Appomattox Court House April 8-9, 1865.* Lynchburg, VA: H. E. Howard, 1987.

Carroll, John M. *Four on Custer by Carroll.* New Brunswick, NJ: Guidon Press, 1976.

_____. *General Custer and New Rumley, Ohio.* Bryan, TX: privately printed, 1978.

_____. *They Rode With Custer: A Biographical Directory of the Men That Rode With General George A. Custer.* Mattituck, NY: J. M. Carroll & Co., 1993.

_____, ed. *Custer in the Civil War: His Unfinished Memoirs.* San Rafael, CA: Presidio Press, 1977.

_____, ed. *Custer and His Times: Book Two.* Fort Worth: Little Big Horn Associates, 1984.

Carroll, John M., and W. Donald Horn, eds. *Custer Genealogies.* Bryan, TX: Guidon Press, n.d.

Carter III, Samuel. *The Last Cavaliers: Confederate and Union Cavalry in the Civil War.* New York: St. Martin's Press, 1979.

Cauble, Frank P. *The Surrender Proceedings: Aprils 9, 1865 Appomattox Court House.* Lynchburg, VA: H. E. Howard, 1987.

Cheney, Norval. *History of the Ninth Regiment, New York Volunteer Cavalry, War of 1861 to 1865.* Poland Center, NY: Martin Merz & Son, 1901.

Coddington, Edwin B. *The Gettysburg Campaign: A Study in Command.* New York: Charles Scribner's Sons, 1968.

Connell, Evan S. *Son of the Morning Star.* San Francisco: North Point Press, 1984.

Cooke, John Esten. *Wearing of the Gray.* Bloomington: Indiana University Press, 1959.

Custer, Elizabeth B. *"Boots and Saddles": or, Life in Dakota with General Custer.* New York: Harper and Brothers, 1885.

Davis, Burke. *To Appomattox: Nine April Days.* New York: Rinehart & Company, 1959.

_____. *Jeb Stuart: The Last Cavalier.* New York: Holt, Rinehart & Winston, 1957.

Davis, William C. *Battle at Bull Run: A History of the First Major Campaign of the Civil War.* Garden City, NY: Doubleday & Company, Inc., 1977.

Denison, Frederic. *Sabers and Spurs: The First Regiment Rhode Island Cavalry in the Civil War, 1861–1865.* Central Falls, RI: Press of E. L. Freeman & Co., 1876.

Dowdey, Clifford, ed. *The Wartime Papers of R. E. Lee.* New York: Bramhall House, 1961.

Downey, Fairfax. *Clash of Cavalry: The Battle of Brandy Station, June 9, 1863.* New York: David McKay Company, Inc., 1959.

Driver, Robert J., Jr. *1st Virginia Cavalry.* Lynchburg, VA: H. E. Howard, 1991.

Early, Jubal Anderson. *War Memoirs.* Bloomington: University of Indiana Press, 1960.

Faust, Patricia L., ed. *Historical Times Illustrated Encyclopedia of the Civil War.* New York: Harper & Row Publishers, 1986.

Freeman, Douglas Southall. *Lee's Lieutenants: A Study in Command,* 3 vols. New York: Charles Scribner's Sons, 1942–44.

————. *R. E. Lee: A Biography.* New York: Charles Scribner's Sons, 1962.

Frost, Lawrence A. *General Custer's Libbie.* Seattle: Superior Publishing Co., 1976.

————. *Custer Legends.* Bowling Green, OH: Bowling Green University Popular Press, 1981.

Furgurson, Ernest B. *Chancellorsville 1863: The Souls of the Brave.* New York: Alfred A. Knopf, 1992.

Gallagher, Gary W., ed. *The First Day at Gettysburg: Essays on Confederate and Union Leadership.* Kent, OH: The Kent State University Press, 1992.

Grant, Ulysses S. *Personal Memoirs of U. S. Grant.* Edited by E. B. Long. Cleveland: The World Publishing Company, 1952.

Harris, Samuel. *The Michigan Brigade of Cavalry at the Battle of Gettysburg and Why I Was Not Hung.* Reprint. Rochester, MI: Rochester Historical Commission, 1992.

————. *Personal Reminiscences of Samuel Harris.* Chicago: Rogerson Press, 1897.

Hatch, Thom. *Custer and the Battle of the Little Bighorn.* Jefferson, NC: McFarland & Company, 1997.

Henderson, William D. *The Road to Bristoe Station: Campaigning with Lee and Meade, August 1–October 20, 1863.* Lynchburg, VA: H. E. Howard, 1987.

Heth, Henry. *The Memoirs of Henry Heth.* James L. Morrison, ed. Westport, CT: Greenwood Press, 1974.

Hoke, Jacob. *The Great Invasion of 1863 or General Lee in Pennsylvania.* Gettysburg, PA: Stan Clark Military Books, 1992.

Horn, W. Donald. *"Skinned": The Delinquency Record of Cadet George Armstrong Custer U. S. M. A. Class of June 1861.* Short Hills, NJ: W. Donald Horn, 1980.

Hutton, Paul A., ed. *The Custer Reader.* Lincoln: The University of Nebraska Press, 1992.

Johnson, Robert Underwood and Clarence Clough Buel, eds. *Battles and Leaders of the Civil War.* 4 vols. Reprint. New York: Thomas Yoseloff, 1956.

Kidd, James H. *Personal Recollections of a Cavalryman with Custer's Michigan Brigade in the Civil War.* Reprint. Alexandria, VA: Time-Life Books, 1983.

King, W. C., and W. R. Derby, eds. *Camp-Fire Sketches and Battlefield Echoes of the Rebellion.* Cleveland, OH: N. G. Hamilton & Co., 1887.

Krick, Robert K. *Ninth Virginia Cavalry.* Lynchburg, VA: H. E. Howard, Inc., 1982.

Leckie, Shirley A. *Elizabeth Bacon Custer and the Making of a Myth.* Norman: University of Oklahoma Press, 1993.

Lee, Fitzhugh. *General Lee.* Greenwich, CT: Fawcett Publications, Inc., 1961.

Lee, William O. *Personal and Historical Sketches and Facial History of and by Members of the Seventh Regiment Michigan Cavalry, 1862–1865.* Detroit: Ralston-Stroup Printing Co., 1901.

Long, E. B. *The Civil War Day by Day: An Almanac 1861–1865.* Garden City, NY: Doubleday & Company, 1971.

Longacre, Edward G. *Custer and His Wolverines: The Michigan Cavalry Brigade, 1861–1865.* Conshohocken, PA: Combined Publishing, 1997.

————. *The Cavalry at Gettysburg: A Tactical Study of Mounted Operations during the Civil War's Pivotal Campaign, 9 June–14 July 1863.* Lincoln: University of Nebraska Press, 1993.

Longstreet, James. *From Manassas to Appomattox: Memoirs of the Civil War in America.* Bloomington: Indiana University Press, 1960.

McClellan, George B. *McClellan's Own Story: The War for the Union.* London: Sampson, Low, Marston, Searle & Rivington, 1887.

McClellan, Henry B. *I Rode with Jeb Stuart: The Life and Campaigns of Major-General J. E. B. Stuart.* Boston and New York: Houghton Mifflin, 1885.

Merington, Marguerite, ed. *The Custer Story: The Life and Letters of General George A. Custer and His Wife Elizabeth.* New York: Devin-Adair, 1950.

Meyer, Henry C. *Civil War Experiences Under Bayard, Gregg, Kilpatrick, Custer, Raulston, and Newberry 1862, 1863, 1864.* New York: Knickerbocker Press, 1911.

Mitchell, Adele H., ed. *The Letters of Major General James E. B. Stuart.* Stuart-Mosby Historical Society, 1990.

Monaghan, Jay. *Custer: The Life of General George Armstrong Custer.* Reprint. Lincoln, University of Nebraska Press, 1971.

Morris, Roy Jr. *Sheridan: The Life and Wars of General Phil Sheridan.* New York: Crown Publishers, 1992.

Mosby, John S. *Mosby's War Reminiscences, Stuart's Cavalry Campaigns*. New York: Dodd, Mead and Company, 1898.

_____. *Stuart's Cavalry in the Gettysburg Campaign*. New York: Moffat, Yard & Company, 1908. Reprint. Falls Church, VA: Confederate Printers, 1984.

Murfin, James V. *The Gleam of Bayonets: The Battle of Antietam and the Maryland Campaign of 1862*. New York: Bonanza Books, 1965.

Nanzig, Thomas P. *3rd Virginia Cavalry*. Lynchburg, VA: H. E. Howard, Inc., 1989.

Nesbitt, Mark. *Saber and Scapegoat: J. E. B. Stuart and the Gettysburg Controversy*. Mechanicsville, PA: Stackpole Books, 1994.

_____. *35 Days to Gettysburg: The Campaign Diaries of Two American Enemies*. Harrisburg, PA: Stackpole Books, 1992.

Norton, Chauncey S. *"The Red Neck Ties"; or, History of the Fifteenth New York Volunteer Cavalry*. Ithaca, NY: Journal Book & Job Printing House, 1891.

Nye, Wilbur Sturtevant. *Here Comes the Rebels!* Baton Rouge: Louisiana State University Press, 1965.

Official Register of the Officers and Cadets of the U. S. Military Academy, West Point, NY, 1851–70. United States Military Academy Archives, West Point, NY.

O'Neil, Alice. *My Dear Sister: An Analysis of Some Civil War Letters of George Armstrong Custer*. Brooklyn, NY: Arrow & Trooper, 1994.

O'Neil, Thomas E. *Custer Chronicles*, I, Brooklyn, NY: Arrow & Trooper, 1994.

O'Neill, Robert F. *The Cavalry Battles of Aldie, Middleburg, and Upperville: Small but Important Riots June 10–27, 1863*. Lynchburg, VA: H. E. Howard, 1993.

Pyne, Henry R. *The History of the First New Jersey Cavalry*. Trenton: J. A. Beecher, 1871.

Rawle, William Brooke, ed. *History of the Third Pennsylvania Cavalry, Sixtieth Regiment Pennsylvania Volunteers in the American Civil War 1861–1865*. Philadelphia: Franklin Printing Co., 1905.

Register of Delinquencies, 1856-61. United States Military Academy Archives, West Point, NY.

Reynolds, Arlene. *The Civil War Memories of Elizabeth Bacon Custer*. Austin: University of Texas Press, 1994.

Riggs, David F. *East of Gettysburg: Stuart vs. Custer*. Bellevue, NE: Old Army Press, 1970.

Robertson, Jno. *Michigan in the War*. Lansing: W. S. George & Co., 1880.

Ronsheim, Milton. *The Life of General Custer*. Reprint. Monroe, MI: Monroe County Library System, 1991.

Sanford, George B. *Fighting Rebels and Redskins: Experiences in the Army Life of Colonel George B. Sanford, 1861–1892*, edited by E. R. Hagemann. Norman: University of Oklahoma Press, 1969.

Schaff, Morris. *The Spirit of Old West Point, 1858–1862.* Boston and New York: Houghton Mifflin Co., 1907.

Sears, Stephen W. *To the Gates of Richmond: The Peninsula Campaign.* New York: Ticknor & Fields, 1992.

_____. ed. *The Civil War Papers of George B. McClellan: Selected Correspondence, 1860–1865.* New York: Ticknor & Fields, 1989.

Sheridan, Philip H. *Personal Memoirs of P. H. Sheridan.* 2 vols. New York: Charles L. Webster & Company, 1888.

Siepel, Kevin H. *Rebel: The Life and Times of John Singleton Mosby.* New York: St. Martin's Press, 1983.

Stackpole, Edward J. *Chancellorsville: Lee's Greatest Battle.* Harrisburg, PA: The Stackpole Company, 1958.

_____. *From Cedar Mountain to Antietam.* Harrisburg, PA: The Stackpole Company, 1959.

Starr, Stephen Z. *The Union Cavalry in the Civil War.* 2 vols. Baton Rouge: Louisiana State University Press,1979–1985.

Steere, Edward. *The Wilderness Campaign.* Reprint.Gaithersburg, MD: Olde Soldier Books, 1987.

Stevenson, James H. *"Boots and Saddles": A History of the First Volunteer Cavalry Regiment of the War Known as the First New York (Lincoln) Cavalry, and Also as the Sabre Regiment.* Harrisburg, PA: Patriot Publishing Co., 1879.

Swank, Walbrook Davis. *Battle of Trevilian Station: The Civil War's Greatest and Bloodiest All-Cavalry Battle, With Eyewitness Memoirs.* Shippensburg, PA: Burd Street Press, 1994.

Taylor, James E. *The James E. Taylor Sketchbook: With Sheridan up the Shenandoah Valley in 1864.* Dayton: Morningside House, 1989.

Tenney, Luman Harris. *War Diary of Luman Harris Tenney, 1861–1865.* Cleveland: Evangelical Publishing House, 1914.

Thomas, Emory M. *Robert E. Lee: A Biography.* New York: W. W. Norton, 1995.

_____. *Bold Dragoon: The Life of J. E. B. Stuart.* New York: Harper & Row Publishers, 1986.

Thomason, John W., Jr. *Jeb Stuart.* New York: Charles Scribner's Sons, 1930.

Trout, Robert J. *They Followed the Plume: The Story of J. E. B. Stuart and His Staff.* Mechanicsburg, PA: Stackpole Books, 1993.

_____. *With Pen and Saber: The Letters and Diaries of J. E. B. Stuart's Staff Officers.* Mechanicsburg, PA: Stackpole Books, 1995.

Trowbridge, Luther S. *The Operations of the Cavalry in the Gettysburg Campaign.* Detroit, MI: Ostler Printing Company, 1888.

Tucker, Glenn. *High Tide at Gettysburg: The Campaign in Pennsylvania.* Indianapolis, IN: The Bobbs-Merrill Co., Inc., 1958.

_____. *Lee and Longstreet at Gettysburg.* New York: The Bobbs-Merrill, Inc., 1968.

Underwood, Robert, and Clarence Buel, eds. *Battles and Leaders of the Civil War.* 4 vols. New York: The Century Co., 1888.

US War Department. *Atlas to Accompany the Official Records of the Union and Confederate Armies.* Reprint. Gettysburg, PA: National Historical Society, 1978.

_____. *The War of the Rebellion: A Compilation of the Official Records of the Union and Confederate Armies.* 128 volumes. Washington, DC: US Government Printing Office, 1880–1901.

Urwin, Gregory J. W. *Custer Victorious: The Civil War Battles of General George Armstrong Custer.* Lincoln: University of Nebraska Press, 1990.

Utley, Robert M. *Cavalier in Buckskin: George Armstrong Custer and the Western Military Frontier.* Norman: University of Oklahoma Press, 1988.

Von Borcke, Heros. *Memoirs of the Confederate War for Independence.* 2 vols. New York: Peter Smith, 1938.

Wallace, Charles B. *Custer's Ohio Boyhood: A Brief Account of the Early Life of Major General George Armstrong Custer.* Freeport, OH: Freeport Press, 1978.

Warner, Ezra J. *Generals in Gray: Lives of the Confederate Commanders.* Baton Rouge: Louisiana State University Press, 1959.

_____. *Generals in Blue: Lives of the Union Commanders.* Baton Rouge: Louisiana State University Press, 1964.

Wert, Jeffry D. *Custer: The Controversial Life of George Armstrong Custer.* New York: Simon & Schuster, 1996.

____. *Mosby's Rangers.* New York: Simon & Schuster, 1990.

____. *From Winchester to Cedar Creek: The Shenandoah Campaign of 1864.* Carlisle, PA: South Mountain Press, 1987.

Whittaker, Frederick. *A Complete Life of General George Armstrong Custer.* New York: Sheldon & Co., 1876.

Woods, C. J. *Reminiscences of the War.* Privately printed, ca. 1880.

Index